THE INK-STAIN
(*TACHÉ D'ENCRE*)
By RENE BAZIN

Crowned by the French Academy

With a Preface by E. LAVISSE
of the French Academy :: :: ::

WILDSIDE PRESS

RENÉ BAZIN

ENE-FRANÇOIS-NICOLAS-MARIE BAZIN was born at Angers, December 26, 1853. He studied for the bar, became a lawyer and professor of jurisprudence at the Catholic University in his native city, and early contributed to *Le Correspondant*, *L'Illustration*, *Journal des Débats*, *Revue du Deux Mondes*, etc. Although quietly writing fiction for the last fifteen years or so, he was not well known until the dawn of the twentieth century, when his moral studies of provincial life under the form of novels and romances became appreciated. He is a profound psychologist, a force in literature, and his style is very pure and attractive. He advocates resignation and the domestic virtues, yet his books are neither dull, nor tiresome, nor priggish; and as he has advanced in years and experience M. Bazin has shown an increasing ambition to deal with larger problems than are involved for instance, in the innocent love-affairs of *Ma Tante Giron* (1886), a book which enraptured Ludovic Halévy. His novel, *Une Tache d'Encre* (1888), a romance of scholarly life, was crowned by the French Academy, to which he was elected in 1903.

It is safe to say that Bazin will never develop into an

PREFACE

author dangerous to morals. His works may be put
into the hands of cloistered virgins, and there are not, to
my knowledge, many other contemporary French imag-
inative writers who could endure this stringent test.
Some critics, indeed, while praising him, scoff at his
chaste and surprising optimism; but it is refreshing to
recommend to English readers, in these days of Realism
and Naturalism, the works of a recent French writer
which do not require maturity of years in the reader.
Une Tache d'Encre, as I have said, was crowned by
the French Academy; and Bazin received from the
same exalted body the "Prix Vitet" for the ensemble
of his writings in 1896, being finally admitted a member
of the Academy in June, 1903. He occupies the chair
of Ernest Legouvé.

Bazin's first romance, *Stephanette*, was published
under the pseudonym "Bernard Seigny," in 1884; then
followed *Victor Pavie* (1887); *Noellet* (1890); *A l'Aven-
ture* (1891) and *Sicile* (1892), two books on Italy,
of which the last mentioned was likewise crowned
by the French Academy; *La Légende de Sainte-Béga*
(1892); *La Sarcelle Bleue* (1892); *Madame Corentine*
(1893); *Les Italiens d'aujourd'hui* (1894); *Humble
Amour* (1894); *En Province* (1896); *De toute son Ame*
(1897), a realistic but moderate romance of a working-
man's life; *Les Contes de Perrette* (1898); *La Terre qui
Meurt* (1899); *Le Guide de l'Empereur* (1901); *Les Oberlé*
(1902), a tale from Alsace of to-day, sketching the political situation, approximately correct, and lately adapted
for the stage; *Donatienne* (1903).

With Bazin literary life does not become a mirage

PREFACE

obscuring the vision of real life. Before being an author René Bazin is a man, with a family attached to the country, rooted in the soil; a guaranty of the dignity of his work as well as of the writer, and a safeguard against many extravagances. He has remained faithful to his province. He lives in the attractive city of Angers. When he leaves it, it is for a little tour through France, or a rare journey—once to Sicily and once to Spain. He is seldom to be met on the Parisian boulevards. Not that he has any prejudice against Paris, or fails to appreciate the tone of its society, or the quality of its diversions; but he is conscious that he has nothing to gain from a residence in the capital, but, on the contrary, would run a risk of losing his intense originality and the freshness of his genius.

Ernest Lavisse.

de l'Académie Française.

CONTENTS

CONTENTS

CONTENTS

SHORT STORIES

THE INK-STAIN

CHAPTER I

ALL I have to record of the first twenty-three years of my life is the enumeration of them. A simple bead-roll is enough; it represents their family likeness and family monotony.

I lost my parents when I was very young. I can hardly recall their faces; and I should keep no memories of La Châtre, our home, had I not been brought up quite close to it. It was sold, however, and lost to me, like all the rest. Yes, fate is hard, sometimes. I was born at La Châtre; the college of La Châtre absorbed eighteen years of my life. Our head master used to remark that college is a second home; whereby I have always fancied he did some injustice to the first.

My school-days were hardly over when my uncle and guardian, M. Brutus Mouillard, solicitor, of Bourges, packed me off to Paris to go through my law course. I took three years over it. At the end of that time, just eighteen months ago, I became a licentiate, and "in the said capacity"—as my uncle would say—

I   [1]

took an oath that transformed me into a probationary barrister. Every Monday, regularly, I go to sign my name among many others on an attendance list, and thereby, it appears, I am establishing a claim upon the confidence of the widow and the orphan.

In the intervals of my legal studies I have succeeded in taking my Arts Degree. At present I am seeking that of Doctor of Law. My examinations have been passed meritoriously, but without brilliance; my tastes run too much after letters. My professor, M. Flamaran, once told me the truth of the matter: "Law, young man, is a jealous mistress; she allows no divided affection." Are my affections divided? I think not, and I certainly do not confess any such thing to M. Mouillard, who has not yet forgotten what he calls "that freak" of a Degree in Arts. He builds some hopes upon me, and, in return, it is natural that I should build a few upon him.

Really, that sums up all my past: two certificates! A third diploma in prospect and an uncle to leave me his money—that is my future. Can anything more commonplace be imagined?

I may add that I never felt any temptation at all to put these things on record until to-day, the tenth of December, 1884. Nothing had ever happened to me; my history was a blank. I might have died thus. But who can foresee life's sudden transformations? Who can foretell that the skein, hitherto so tranquilly unwound, will not suddenly become tangled? This afternoon a serious adventure befell me. It agitated me at the time, and it agitates me still more upon reflection. A voice within me whispers that this cause will have a series of effects, that I am on the threshold of an epoch, or, as the novelists say, a crisis in my existence. It has struck me that I owe it to myself to write my Memoirs, and that is the reason why I have just purchased this brown memorandum-book in the Odéon Arcade. I intend to make a detailed and particular entry of the event, and, as time goes on, of its consequences, if any should happen to flow from it.

"Flow from it" is just the phrase; for it has to do with a blot of ink.

My blot of ink is hardly dry. It is a large one, too; of abnormal shape, and altogether monstrous, whether one considers it from the physical side or studies it in its moral bearings. It is very much more than an accident; it has something of the nature of an outrage. It was at the National Library that I perpetrated it, and upon—— But I must not anticipate.

I often work in the National Library; not in the main hall, but in that reserved for literary men who have a claim, and are provided with a ticket, to use it. I never enter it without a gentle thrill, in which respect is mingled with satisfied vanity. For not every one who chooses may walk in. I must pass before the office of the porter, who retains my umbrella, before I make my way to the solemn beadle who sits just inside the doorway—a double precaution, attesting to the majesty of the place. The beadle knows me. He no longer demands my ticket. To be sure, I am not yet one of those old acquaintances on whom he smiles; but I am no longer reckoned among those novices whose passport he exacts. An inclination of his head makes me free of the temple, and says, as plainly as words, "You are one of us, albeit a trifle young. Walk in, sir."

And in I walk, and admire on each occasion the vast proportions of the interior, the severe decoration of the walls, traced with broad foliated pattern and wainscoted with books of reference as high as hand can reach; the dread tribunal of librarians and keepers in session down yonder, on a kind of judgment-seat, at the end of the avenue whose carpet deadens all footsteps; and behind again, that holy of holies where work the doubly privileged—the men, I imagine, who are members of two or three academies. To right and left of this avenue are rows of tables and armchairs, where scatters, as caprice has chosen and habit consecrated, the learned population of the library. Men form the large majority. Viewed from the rear, as they bend over their work, they suggest reflections on the ravages wrought by study upon hair-clad cuticles. For every hirsute Southerner whose locks turn gray without dropping off, heavens, what a regiment of bald heads! Visitors who look in through the glass doors see only this aspect of devastation. It gives a wrong impression. Here and there, at haphazard, you may find a few women among these men. George Sand used to come here. I don't know the names of these successors of hers, nor their business; I have merely observed that they dress in sober colors, and that each carries a number of shawls and a thick veil. You feel that love is far from their thoughts. They have left it outside, perhaps —with the porter.

[4]

THE INK-STAIN

Several of these learned folk lift their heads as I pass, and follow me with the dulled eye of the student, an eye still occupied with the written thought and inattentive to what it looks on. Then, suddenly, remorse seizes them for their distraction, they are annoyed with me, a gloomy impatience kindles in their look, and each plunges anew into his open volume. But I have had time to guess their secret ejaculations: "*I* am studying the Origin of Trade Guilds!" "*I*, the Reign of Louis the Twelfth!" "*I*, the Latin Dialects!" "*I*, the Civil Status of Women under Tiberius!" "*I* am elaborating a new translation of Horace!" "*I* am fulminating a seventh article, for the *Gazette of Atheism and Anarchy*, on the Russian Serfs!" And each one seems to add, "But what is *thy* business here, stripling? What canst thou write at thy age? Why troublest thou the peace of these hallowed precincts?" My business, sirs? Alas! it is the thesis for my doctor's degree. My uncle and venerated guardian, M. Brutus Mouillard, solicitor, of Bourges, is urging me to finish it, demands my return to the country, grows impatient over the slow toil of composition. "Have done with theories," he writes, "and get to business! If you *must* strive for this degree, well and good; but what possessed you to choose such a subject?"

I must own that the subject of my thesis in Roman law has been artistically chosen with a view to prolonging my stay in Paris: "On the Latini Juniani." Yes, gentle reader, a new subject, almost incapable of elucidation, having no connection—not the remotest—with the exercise of any profession whatsoever, entirely de-

[5]

void of practical utility. The trouble it gives me is beyond conception.

It is true that I intersperse my researches with some more attractive studies, and one or two visits to the picture-galleries, and more than an occasional evening at the theatre. My uncle knows nothing of this. To keep him soothed I am careful to get my reader's ticket renewed every month, and every month to send him the ticket just out of date, signed by M. Léopold Delisle. He has a box full of them; and in the simplicity of his heart Monsieur Mouillard has a lurking respect for this nephew, this modern young anchorite, who spends his days at the National Library, his nights with Gaius, wholly absorbed in the Junian Latins, and indifferent to whatsoever does not concern the Junian Latins in this Paris which my uncle still calls the Modern Babylon.

I came down this morning in the most industrious mood, when the misfortune befell. Close by the sanctum where the librarians sit are two desks where you write down the list of the books you want. I was doing so at the right-hand desk, on which abuts the first row of tables. Hence all the mischief. Had I written at the left-hand desk, nothing would have happened. But no; I had just set down as legibly as possible the title, author, and size of a certain work on Roman Antiquities, when, in replacing the penholder, which is attached there by a small brass chain, some inattentiveness, some want of care, my ill-luck, in short, led me to set it down in unstable equilibrium on the edge of the desk. It tumbled—I heard the little chain rattle—it tumbled farther—then stopped short. The mischief was done. The sudden jerk, as it pulled up, had detached an enormous drop of ink from the point of the pen, and that drop—— Ah! I can see him yet, as he rose from the shadow of the desk, that small, white-haired man, so thin and so very angry!

"Clumsy idiot! To blot an Early Text!"

I leaned over and looked. Upon the page of folio, close to an illuminated capital, the black drop had flattened itself. Around the original sphere had been shed splashes of all conceivable shapes—rays, rockets, dotted lines, arrowheads, all the freakish impromptu of chaos. Next, the slope lending its aid, the channels had drained into one, and by this time a black rivulet was crawling downward to the margin. One or two readers near had risen, and now eyed me like examining magistrates. I waited for an outbreak, motionless, dazed, muttering words that did not mend the case at all. "What a pity! Oh, I'm so sorry! If I had only known——" The student of the Early Text stood motionless as I. Together we watched the ink trickle. Suddenly, summoning his wits together, he burrowed with feverish haste in his morocco writing-case, pulled out a sheet of blotting-paper, and began to soak up the ink with the carefulness of a Sister of Mercy stanching a wound. I seized the opportunity to withdraw discreetly to the third row of tables, where the attendant had just deposited my books. Fear is so unreasoning. Very likely by saying no more about it, by making off and hiding my head in my hands, like a man crushed by the weight of his remorse, I might disarm this wrath. I tried to

think so. But I knew well enough that there was more
to come. I had hardly taken my seat when, looking up,
I could see between my fingers the little man standing
up and gesticulating beside one of the keepers. At one
moment he rapped the damning page with his forefinger; the next, he turned sidewise and flung out a hand
toward me; and I divined, without hearing a word, all
the bitterness of his invective. The keeper appeared to
take it seriously. I felt myself blushing. "There must
be," thought I, "some law against ink-stains, some de-
cree, some regulation, something drawn up for the pro-
tection of Early Texts. And the penalty is bound to
be terrible, since it has been enacted by the learned;
expulsion, no doubt, besides a fine—an enormous fine.
They are getting ready over there to fleece me. That
book of reference they are consulting is of course the
catalogue of the sale where this treasure was purchased.
I shall have to replace the Early Text! O Uncle
Mouillard!"

I sat there, abandoned to my sad reflections, when one
of the attendants, whom I had not seen approaching,
touched me on the shoulder.

"The keeper wishes to speak to you."

I rose up and went. The terrible reader had gone
back to his seat.

"It was you, sir, I believe, who blotted the folio just
now?"

"It was, sir."

"You did not do so on purpose?"

"Most certainly not, sir! I am indeed sorry for the
accident."

THE INK-STAIN

"You ought to be. The volume is almost unique; and the blot, too, for that matter. I never saw such a blot! Will you, please, leave me your Christian name, surname, profession, and address?"

I wrote down, "Fabien Jean Jacques Mouillard, barrister, 91 Rue de Rennes."

"Is that all?" I asked.

"Yes, sir, that is all for the present. But I warn you that Monsieur Charnot is exceedingly annoyed. It might be as well to offer him some apology."

"Monsieur Charnot?"

"Yes. It is Monsieur Charnot, of the Institute, who was reading the Early Text."

"Merciful Heavens!" I ejaculated, as I went back to my seat; "this must be the man of whom my tutor spoke, the other day! Monsieur Flamaran belongs to the Academy of Moral and Political Science, the other to the Institute of Inscriptions and the Belles-Lettres. Charnot? Yes, I have those two syllables in my ear. The very last time I saw Monsieur Flamaran he let fall 'my very good friend Charnot, of the "*Inscriptions*."' They are friends. And I am in a pretty situation; threatened with I don't know what by the Library— for the keeper told me positively that this was all 'for the present'—but not for the future; threatened to be disgraced in my tutor's eyes; and all because this learned man's temper is upset.

"I must apologize. Let me see, what could I say to Monsieur Charnot? As a matter of fact, it's to the Early Text that I ought to apologize. I have spilled no ink over Monsieur Charnot. He is spotless, collar and cuffs; the blot, the splashes, all fell on the Text. I will say to him, 'Sir, I am exceedingly sorry to have interrupted you so unfortunately in your learned studies.' 'Learned studies' will tickle his vanity, and should go far to appease him."

I was on the point of rising. M. Charnot anticipated me.

Grief is not always keenest when most recent. As he approached I saw he was more irritated and upset than at the moment of the accident. Above his pinched, clean-shaven chin his lips shot out with an angry twitch. The portfolio shook under his arm. He flung me a look full of tragedy and went on his way.

Well, well; go your way, M. Charnot! One doesn't offer apologies to a man in his wrath. You shall have them by-and-bye, when we meet again.

CHAPTER II

December 28, 1884.

THIS afternoon I paid M. Flamaran a visit. I had been thinking about it for the last week, as I wanted him to help my Junian Latins out of a mess. I am acquiring a passion for that interesting class of freedmen. And really it is only natural. These Junian Latins were poor slaves, whose liberation was not recognized by the strict and ancient laws of Rome, because their masters chose to liberate them otherwise than by *vindicta, census,* or *testamentum.* On this account they lost their privileges, poor victims of the legislative intolerance of the haughty city. You see, it begins to be touching, already. Then came on the scene Junius Norbanus, consul by rank, and a true democrat, who brought in a law, carried it, and gave them their freedom. In exchange, they gave him immortality. Henceforward, did a slave obtain a few kind words from his master over his wine? he was a Junian Latin. Was he described as *filius meus* in a public document? Junian Latin. Did he wear the cap of liberty, the *pileus,* at his master's funeral? Junian Latin. Did he disembowel his master's corpse? Junian Latin, once more, for his trouble.

[11]

RENÉ BAZIN

What a fine fellow this Norbanus must have been!
What an eye for everything, down to the details of a
funeral procession, in which he could find an excuse for
emancipation! And that, too, in the midst of the wars
of Marius and Sylla in which he took part. I can picture him seated before his tent, the evening after the
battle. Pensive, he reclines upon his shield as he
watches the slave who is grinding notches out of his
sword. His eyes fill with tears, and he murmurs,
"When peace is made, my faithful Stychus, I shall
have a pleasant surprise for you. You shall hear talk
of the *Lex Junia Norbana*, I promise you!"

Is not this a worthy subject for picture or statue in
a competition for the *Prix de Rome?*

A man so careful of details must have assigned a
special dress to these special freedmen of his creation;
for at Rome even freedom had its livery. What was
this dress? Was there one at all? No authority that I
know of throws any light on the subject. Still one hope
remains: M. Flamaran. He knows so many things,
he might even know this.

M. Flamaran comes from the south—Marseilles,
I think. He is not a specialist in Roman law; but
he is encyclopedic, which comes to the same thing.
He became known while still young, and deservedly;
few lawyers are so clear, so safe, so lucid. He is an excellent lecturer, and his opinions are in demand. Yet
he owes much of his fame to the works which he has not
written. Our fathers, in their day, used to whisper to
one another in the passages of the Law School, "Have
you heard the news? Flamaran is going to bring out

the second volume of his great work. He means to publish his lectures. He has in the press a treatise which will revolutionize the law of mortgages; he has been working twenty years at it; a masterpiece, I assure you." Day follows day; no book appears, no treatise is published, and all the while M. Flamaran grows in reputation. Strange phenomenon!— like the aloe in the Botanical Gardens. The blossoming of the aloe is an event. "Only think!" says the gaping public, "a flower which has taken twenty springs, twenty summers, twenty autumns, and twenty winters to make up its mind to open!" And meanwhile the roses bloom unnoticed by the town. But M. Flamaran's case is still more strange. Every year it is whispered that he is about to bloom afresh; he never does bloom; and his reputation flourishes none the less. People make lists of the books he might have written. Lucky author!

M. Flamaran is a professor of the old school, stern, and at examination a terror to the candidates. Clad in cap and gown, he would reject his own son. Nothing will serve. Recommendations defeat their object. An unquestioned Roumanian ancestry, an extraction indisputably Japanese, find no more favor in his eyes than an assumed stammer, a sham deafness, or a convalescent pallor put on for the occasion. East and west are alike in his sight. The retired registrar, the pensioned usher aspiring late in life to some petty magistrature, are powerless to touch his heart. For him in vain does the youthful volunteer allow his uniform to peep out beneath his student's gown: he will not profit by the patriotic indulgence he counted on inspiring. His sayings in the examination-room are famous, and among them are some ghastly pleasantries. Here is one, addressed to a victim: "And you, sir, are a law student, while our farmers are in want of hands!"

For my own part I won his favor under circumstances that I never shall forget. I was in for my first examination. We were discussing, or rather I was allowing him to lecture on, the law of wardship, and nodding my assent to his learned elucidations. Suddenly he broke off and asked, "How many opinions have been formulated upon this subject?"

"Two, sir."

"One is absurd. Which? Beware how you give the wrong answer!"

I considered for three agonizing seconds, and hazarded a guess. "The first, sir." I had guessed right. We were friends. At bottom the professor is a capital fellow; kindly, so long as the dignity of the Code is not in question, or the extent of one's legal knowledge; proverbially upright and honorable in his private life.

At home he may be seen at his window tending his canaries, which, he says, is no change of occupation. To get to his house I have only to go by my favorite road through the Luxembourg. I am soon at his door.

"Is Monsieur Flamaran at home?"

The old servant who opened the door eyed me solemnly. So many young freshmen come and pester her master under the pretext of paying their respects. Their respects, indeed! They would bore him to death if he had to see them all. The old woman inferred, probably from my moustache, that I had taken at least my bachelor's degree.

"I think he is."

He was very much at home in his overheated study, where he sat wrapped up in a dressing-gown and keeping one eye shut to strengthen the other.

After a moment's hesitation he recognized me, and held out his hand.

"Ah! my Junian Latin. How are you getting on?"

"I am all right, sir; it's my Junian Latins who are not getting on."

"You don't say so. We must look into that. But before we begin—I forget where you come from. I like to know where people come from."

"From La Châtre. But I spend my vacations at Bourges with my Uncle Mouillard."

"Yes, yes, Mouillart with a t, isn't it?"

"No, with a d."

"I asked, you know, because I once knew a General Mouillart who had been through the Crimea, a charming man. But he can not have been a relative, for his name ended with a t."

My good tutor spoke with a delightful simplicity, evidently wishing to be pleasant and to show some interest in me.

"Are you married, young man?"

"No, sir; but I have no conscientious objections."

"Marry young. Marriage is the salvation of young men. There must be plenty of pretty heiresses in Bourges."

[15]

"Heiresses, yes. As to their looks, at this distance——"

"Yes, I understand, at this distance of course you can't tell. You should do as I did; make inquiries, go and see. I went all the way to Forez myself to look for my wife."

"Madame Flamaran comes from Forez?"

"Just so; I stayed there a fortnight, fourteen days exactly, in the middle of term-time, and brought back Sidonie. Bourges is a nice town."

"Yes, in summer."

"Plenty of trees. I remember a grand action I won there. One of my learned colleagues was against me. We had both written opinions, diametrically opposed, of course. But I beat him—my word, yes!"

"I dare say."

"My boy, there was nothing left of him. Do you know the case?"

"No."

"A magnificent case! My notes must be somewhere about; I will get them out for you."

The good man beamed. Evidently he had not had a talk all day, and felt he must expand and let himself out to somebody. I appeared in the nick of time, and came in for all his honey. He rose, went to a bookcase, ran his eye along a shelf, took down a volume, and began, in a low tone: "'Coöperation is the mighty lever upon which an effete society relies to extricate itself from its swaddling-clothes and take a loftier flight.' Tut, tut! What stuff is this? I beg your pardon. I was reading from a work on moral philosophy. Where the deuce is my opinion?"

THE INK-STAIN

He found it and, text in hand, began a long account of the action, with names, dates, moments of excitement, and many quotations *in extenso*.

"Yes, my young friend, two hundred and eighteen thousand francs did I win in that action for Monsieur Prébois, of Bourges; you know Prébois, the manufacturer?"

"By name."

At last he put the note-book back on its shelf, and deigned to remember that I had come about the Junian Latins.

"In which of the authorities do you find a difficulty?"

"My difficulty lies in the want of authorities, sir, I wish to find out whether the Junian Latins had not a special dress."

"To be sure." He scratched his head. "Gaius says nothing on the point?"

"No."

"Papinian?"

"No."

"Justinian?"

"No."

"Then I see only one resource."

"What is that?"

"Go to see Charnot."

I felt myself growing pale, and stammered, with a piteous look:

"Monsieur Charnot, of the Acad——"

"The Academy of Inscriptions; an intimate friend of mine, who will welcome you like a son, for he has none himself, poor man!"

"But perhaps the question is hardly important enough for me to trouble him like this——"

"Hey? Not important enough? All new questions are important. Charnot specializes on coins. Coins and costumes are all one. I will write to tell him you are coming."

"I beg, sir——"

"Nonsense; I'll write him this very evening. He will be delighted to see you. I know him well, you understand. He is like me; he likes industrious young men."

M. Flamaran held out his hand.

"Good-by, young man. Marry as soon as you have taken your degree."

I did not recover from the shock till I was halfway across the Luxembourg Gardens, near the Tennis Court, when I sat down, overcome. See what comes of enthusiasm and going to call on your tutor! Ah, young three-and-twenty, when will you learn wisdom?

CHAPTER III

9 p.m.

HAVE made up my mind. I shall go to see M. Charnot. But before that I shall go to his publisher's and find out something about this famous man's works, of which I know nothing whatever.

December 31st.

He lives in the Rue de l'Université.

I have called. I have seen him. I owe this to an accident, to the servant's forgetting her orders.

As I entered, on the stroke of five, he was spinning a spiral twist of paper beneath the lamplight to amuse his daughter—he a member of the Institute, she a girl of eighteen. So that is how these big-wigs employ their leisure moments!

The library where I found them was full of bookcases—open bookcases, bookcases with glass doors, tall bookcases, dwarf bookcases, bookcases standing on legs, bookcases standing on the floor—of statuettes yellow with smoke, of desks crowded with paper-weights, paper-knives, pens, and inkstands of "artistic" patterns. He was seated at the table, with his back to the fire, his arm lifted, and a hairpin between his finger and

[19]

thumb—the pivot round which his paper twist was spinning briskly. Across the table stood his daughter, leaning forward with her chin on her hands and her white teeth showing as she laughed for laughing's sake, to give play to her young spirits and gladden her old father's heart as he gazed on her, delighted.

I must confess it made a pretty picture; and M. Charnot at that moment was extremely unlike the M. Charnot who had confronted me from behind the desk.

I was not left long to contemplate.

The moment I lifted the *portière* the girl jumped up briskly and regarded me with a touch of haughtiness, meant, I think, to hide a slight confusion. To compare small things with great, Diana must have worn something of that look at sight of Actæon. M. Charnot did not rise, but hearing somebody enter, turned half-round in his armchair, while his eyes, still dazzled with the lamplight, sought the intruder in the partial shadow of the room.

I felt myself doubly uneasy in the presence of this reader of the Early Text and of this laughing girl.

"Sir," I began, "I owe you an apology——"

He recognized me. The girl moved a step.

"Stay, Jeanne, stay. We shall not take long. This gentleman has come to offer an apology."

This was a cruel beginning.

She thought so, too, perhaps, and withdrew discreetly into a dim corner, near the bookcase at the end of the room.

"I have felt deep regret, sir, for that accident the

other day—I set down the penholder clumsily, in equilibrium—unstable equilibrium—besides, I had no notion there was a reader behind the desk. Of course, if I had been aware, I should—I should have acted differently."

M. Charnot allowed me to flounder on with the contemplative satisfaction of an angler who has got a fish at the end of his line. He seemed to find me so very stupid, that as a matter of fact I became stupid. And then, there was no answer—not a word. Silence, alas! is not the reproof of kings alone. It does pretty well for everybody. I stumbled on two or three more phrases quite as flatly infelicitous, and he received them with the same faint smile and the same silence.

To escape from my embarrassment:

"Sir," I said, "I came also to ask for a piece of information."

"I am at your service, sir."

"Monsieur Flamaran has probably written to you on the matter?"

"Flamaran?"

"Yes, three days ago."

"I have received no letter; have I, Jeanne?"

"No, father."

"This is not the first time that my excellent colleague has promised to write a letter and has not written it. Never mind, sir; your own introduction is sufficient."

"Sir, I am about to take my doctor's degree."

"In arts?"

"No, in law; but I have a bachelor's degree in arts."

"You will follow it up with a degree in medicine, no doubt?"

"Really, sir——"

"Why not, since you are collecting these things? You have, then, a bent toward literature?"

"So I have been told."

"A pronounced inclination—hey? to scribble verse."

"Ah, yes!"

"The old story; the family driving a lad into law; his heart leaning toward letters; the Digest open on the table, and the drawers stuffed with verses! Isn't that so?"

I bowed. He glanced toward his daughter.

"Well, sir, I confess to you that I don't understand—don't understand at all—this behavior of yours. Why not follow your natural bent? You youngsters nowadays—I mean no offence—you youngsters have no longer any mind of your own. Take my case; I was seventeen when I began to take an interest in numismatics. My family destined me for the Stamp Office; yes, sir, the Stamp Office. I had against me two grandfathers, two grandmothers, my father, my mother, and six uncles—all furious. I held out, and that has led me to the Institute. Hey, Jeanne?"

Mademoiselle Jeanne had returned to the table, where she was standing when I entered, and seemed, after a moment, to busy herself in arranging the books scattered in disarray on the green cloth. But she had a secret object—to regain possession of the paper spiral that lay there neglected, its pin sticking up beside the lamp-stand. Her light hand, hovering hither and thither, had by a series of cunning manœuvres got the offending object behind a pile of duodecimos, and was now withdrawing it stealthily among the inkstands and paper-weights.

M. Charnot interrupted this little stratagem.

She answered very prettily, with a slight toss of the head:

"But, father, not everybody can be in the Institute."

"Far from it, Jeanne. This gentleman, for instance, devotes himself to one method of inking parchment that never will make him my colleague. Doctor of Laws and Master of Arts,—I presume, sir, you are going to be a notary?"

"Excuse me, an advocate."

"I was sure of it. Jeanne, my dear, in country families it is a standing dilemma; if not a notary, then an advocate; if not an advocate, then a notary."

M. Charnot spoke with an exasperating half-smile. I ought to have laughed, to be sure; I ought to have shown sense enough at any rate to hold my tongue and not to answer the gibes of this vindictive man of learning. Instead, I was stupid enough to be nettled and to lose my head.

"Well," I retorted, "I must have a paying profession. That one or another—what does it matter? Not everybody can belong to the Institute, as your daughter remarked; not everybody can afford himself the luxury of publishing, at his own expense, works that sell twenty-seven copies or so."

I expected a thunderbolt, an explosion. Not a bit of

it. M. Charnot smiled outright with an air of extreme geniality.

"I perceive, sir, that you are given to gossiping with the booksellers."

"Why, yes, sir, now and then."

"It's a very pretty trait, at your age, to be already so strong in bibliography. You will permit me, nevertheless, to add something to your present stock of notions. A large sale is one thing to look at, but not the right thing. Twenty-seven copies of a book, when read by twenty-seven men of intelligence, outweigh a popular success. Would you believe that one of my friends had no more than eight copies printed of a mathematical treatise? Three of these he has given away. The other five are still unsold. And that man, sir, is the first mathematician in France!"

Mademoiselle Jeanne had taken it differently. With lifted chin and reddened cheek she shot this sentence at me from the edge of a lip disdainfully puckered:

"There are such things as 'successes of esteem,' sir!"

Alas! I knew that well, and I had no need of this additional lesson to teach me the rudeness of my remark, to make me feel that I was a brute, an idiot, hopelessly lost in the opinion of M. Charnot and his daughter. It was cruel, all the same. Nothing was left for me but to hurry my departure. I got up to go.

"But," said M. Charnot in the smoothest of tones, "I do not think we have yet discussed the question that brought you here."

"I should hesitate, sir, to trespass further on your time."

"Never mind that. Your question concerns——?"

"The costume of the Latini Juniani."

"Difficult to answer, like most questions of dress. Have you read the work, in seventeen volumes, by the German, Friedchenhausen?"

"No."

"You must have read, at any rate, Smith, the Englishman, on ancient costume?"

"Nor that either. I only know Italian."

"Well, then, look through two or three treatises on numismatics, the *Thesaurus Morellianus*, or the *Præstantiora Numismata*, of Valliant, or Banduri, or Pembrock, or Pellerin. You may chance upon a scent."

"Thank you, thank you, sir!"

He saw me to the door.

As I turned to go I noticed that his daughter was standing motionless still, with the face of an angry Diana. She held between her fingers the recovered spiral.

I found myself in the street.

I could not have been more clumsy, more ill-bred, or more unfortunate. I had come to make an apology and had given further offence. Just like my luck! And the daughter, too—I had hurt her feelings. Still, she had stood up for me; she had said to her father, "Not every one can be in the Institute," evidently meaning, "Why are you torturing this poor young man? He is bashful and ill at ease. I feel sorry for him." Sorry —yes; no doubt she felt sorry for me at first. But then I came out with that impertinence about the twenty-seven copies, and by this time she hates me beyond a doubt. Yes, she hates me. It is too painful to think of.

RENÉ BAZIN

Mademoiselle Charnot will probably remain but a stranger to me, a fugitive apparition in my path of life; yet her anger lies heavy upon me, and the thought of those disdainful lips pursues me.

I had rarely been more thoroughly disgusted with myself, and with all about me. I needed something to divert me, to distract me, to make me forget, and so I set off for home by the longest way, going down the Rue de Beaune to the Seine.

I declare, we get some perfect winter days in Paris! Just now, the folks who sit indoors believe that the sun is down and have lighted their lamps; but outside, the sky —a pale, rain-washed blue—is streaked with broad rays of rose-pink. It is freezing, and the frost has sprinkled diamonds everywhere, on the trees, the roofs, the parapets, even on the cabmen's hats, that gather each a sparkling cockade as they pass along through the mist. The river is running in waves, white-capped here and there. On the penny steamers no one but the helmsman is visible. But what a crowd on the Pont de Carrousel! Fur cuffs and collars pass and repass on the pavements; the roadway trembles beneath the endless line of Batignolles-Clichy omnibuses and other vehicles. Every one seems in a hurry. The pedestrians are brisk, the drivers dexterous. Two lines of traffic meet, mingle without jostling, divide again into fresh lines and are gone like a column of smoke. Although slips are common in this crowd, its intelligent agility is all its own. Every face is ruddy, and almost all are young. The number of young men, young maidens, young wives, is beyond belief. Where are the aged? At home, no doubt, by the chimney-corner. All the city's youth is out of doors. Its step is animated; that is the way of it. It is wide-eyed, and in its eyes is the sparkle of life. The looks of the young are always full of the future; they are sure of life. Each has settled his position, his career, his dream of commonplace well-being. They are all alike; and they might all be judges, so serious they appear about it. They walk in pairs, bolt upright, looking neither right nor left, talking little as they hurry along toward the old Louvre, and are soon swallowed out of sight in the gathering mist, out of which the gaslights glimmer faintly.

They are all on their way to dine on the right bank.

I am going to dine on the left bank, at Carré's, where one sees many odd customers. Farewell, river! Good-night, old Charnot! Blessings on you, Mademoiselle Jeanne!

CHAPTER IV

THE STORY OF SYLVESTRE

AM back in my study. It is very cold; Madame Menin, my housekeeper, has let the fire out. Hallo! she has left her duster, too, lying on the manuscript of my essay.

Is it an omen, a presage of that dust which awaits my still unfinished work? Who can fathom Dame Fortune's ironic humor?

Eight o'clock . . . Counsellor Mouillard has finished his pleadings and must be sitting down to a game of whist with Counsellors Horlet and Hublette, of the Court of Bourges. They wait for me to make up the four. Perish the awful prospect!

And M. Charnot? He, I suppose, is still spinning the paper spiral. How easily serious people are amused! Perhaps *I* am a serious person. The least thing amuses me. By the way, is Mademoiselle Jeanne fair or dark? Let me try to recollect. Why, fair, of course. I remember the glint of gold in the little curls about her temples, as she stood by the lamp. A pleasant face, too; not exactly classic, but rosy and frank; and then she has that animation which so many pretty women lack.

[28]

THE INK-STAIN

Madame Menin has forgotten something else. She has forgotten to shut my window. She has designs upon my life!

I have just shut the window. The night is calm, its stars twinkling through a haze. The year ends mournfully.

I remember at school once waking suddenly on such a night as this, to find the moonlight streaming into my eyes. At such a moment it is always a little hard to collect one's scattered senses, and take in the midnight world around, so unhomely, so absolutely still. First I cast my eyes along the two rows of beds that stretched away down the dormitory—two parallel lines in long perspective; my comrades huddled under their blankets in shapeless masses, gray or white according as they lay near or far from the windows; the smoky glimmer of the oil lamp half-way down the room; and at the end, in the deeper shadows, the enclosure of yellow curtains surrounding the usher's bed.

Not a sound about me; all was still. But without, my ear, excited and almost feverishly awake, caught the sound of a strange call, very sweet, again and again repeated—fugitive notes breathing appeal, tender and troubled. Now they grew quite distant, and I heard no more than a phantom of sound; now they came near, passed over my head, and faded again into the distance. The moon's clear rays invited me to clear up the mystery. I sprang from my bed, and ran in my nightshirt to open the window. It was about eleven o'clock. Together the keen night-air and the moonlight wrapped me round, thrilling me with delight. The large courtyard lay deserted with its leafless poplars and spiked railings. Here and there a grain of sand sparkled. I raised my eyes, and from one constellation to another I sought the deep blue of heaven in vain; not a shadow upon it, not one dark wing outlined. Yet all the while the same sad and gentle cry wandered and was lost in air, the chant of an invisible soul which seemed in want of me, and had perhaps awakened me.

The thought came upon me that it was the soul of my mother calling to me—my mother, whose voice was soft and very musical.

"I am caring for thee," said the voice. "I am caring for thee; I can see thee," it said, "I can see thee. I love thee! I love thee!"

"Reveal thyself!" I called back. "Oh, mother, reveal thyself!" And I strove feverishly to catch sight of her, following the voice as it swept around in circles; and seeing nothing, I burst into tears.

Suddenly I was seized roughly by the ear.

"What are you doing here, you young rascal? Are you mad? The wind is blowing right on to my bed. Five hundred lines!"

The usher, in nightdress and slippers, was rolling his angry eyes on me.

"Yes, sir; certainly, sir! But don't **you hear** her?"

"Who is it?"

"My mother."

He looked to see whether I were awake; cocked his head to one side and listened; then shut the window angrily and went off shrugging his shoulders.

THE INK-STAIN

"It's only the plovers flying about the moon," said he. "Five hundred lines!"

I did my five hundred lines. They taught me that dreaming was illegal and dangerous, but they neither convinced nor cured me.

I still believe that there are scattered up and down in nature voices that speak, but which few hear; just as there are millions of flowers that bloom unseen by man. It is sad for those who catch a hint of it. Perforce they come back and seek the hidden springs. They waste their youth and vigor upon empty dreams, and in return for the fleeting glimpses they have enjoyed, for the perfect phrase half caught and lost again, will have given up the intercourse of their kind, and even friendship itself. Yes, it is sad for the schoolboys who open their windows to gaze at the moon, and never drop the habit! They will find themselves, all too soon, solitaries in the midst of life, desolate as I am desolate to-night, beside my dead fire.

No friend will come to knock at my door; not one. I have a few comrades to whom I give that name. We do not loathe one another. At need they would help me. But we seldom meet. What should they do here? Dreamers make no confidences; they shrivel up into themselves and are caught away on the four winds of heaven. Politics drive them mad; gossip fails to interest them; the sorrows they create have no remedy save the joys that they invent; they are natural only when alone, and talk well only to themselves.

The only man who can put up with this moody contrariety of mine is Sylvestre Lampron. He is nearly twenty years older than I. That explains his forbearance. Besides, between an artist like him and a dreamer like myself there is only the difference of handiwork. He translates his dreams. I waste mine; but both dream. Dear old Lampron! Kindly, stalwart heart! He has withstood that hardening of the moral and physical fibre which comes over so many men as they near their fortieth year. He shows a brave front to work and to life. He is cheerful, with the manly cheerfulness of a noble heart resigned to life's disillusions.

When I enter his home, I nearly always find him sitting before a small ground-glass window in the corner of his studio, bent over some engraving. I have leave to enter at all hours. He is free not to stir from his work. "Good-day," he calls out, without raising his head, without knowing for certain who has come in, and goes on with the engraving he has in hand. I settle down at the end of the room, on the sofa with the faded cover, and, until Lampron deigns to grant me audience, I am free to sleep, or smoke, or turn over the wonderful drawings that lean against the walls. Among them are treasures beyond price; for Lampron is a genius whose only mistake is to live and act with modesty, so that as yet people only say that he has "immense talent." No painter or engraver of repute—and he is both—has served a more conscientious apprenticeship, or sets greater store on thoroughness in his art. His drawing is correct beyond reproach—a little stiff, like the early painters. You can guess from his works his partiality for the old masters—Perugino, Fra Angelico, Botticelli, Memling, Holbein—who, though not

the masters in fashion, will always be masters in vigor
of outline, directness, in simple grace, and genuine feeling.   He has copied in oils, water-colors, pen, or pencil,
nearly all the pictures of these masters in the Louvre,
in Germany, in Holland, and especially in Italy, where
he lived for many years.   With tastes such as his came
the habit, or rather the fixed determination, never to
paint or engrave any but sacred subjects.   Puffs and
cliques are his abomination.   His ideal is the archaic
rendered by modern methods.   An artist of this type
can but obtain the half-grudging esteem of his own profession, and of the few critics who really understand
something about art.   Gladly, and with absolute disdain, he leaves to others the applause of the mob, the
gilded patronage of American purchasers, and the right
to wear lace cuffs.   In short, in an age when the artist
is often half a manufacturer and half a charlatan, he
is an artist only.

Now and then he is rich, but never for long.   Half
of his earnings goes in alms; half into the pockets of his
mendicant brethren.   They hear the gold jingle before
it is counted, and run with outstretched palms.   Each
is in the depths of misfortune; on the eve of ascending
the fatal slope; lost, unless the helpful hand of Lampron
will provide, saved if he will lend wherewithal to buy a
block of marble, to pay a model, to dine that evening.
He lends—I should say gives; the words mean the same
in many societies.   Of all that he has gained, fame alone
remains, and even this he tries to do without—modest,
retiring, shunning all entertainments.   I believe he
would often be without the wherewithal to live were it

not for his mother, whom he supports, and who does him the kindness to need something to live on. Madame Lampron does not hoard; she only fills the place of those dams of cut turf which the peasants build in the channels of the Berry in spring; the water passes over them, beneath them, even through them, but still a little is left for the great droughts.

I love my friend Lampron, though fully aware of his superiority. His energy sets me up, his advice strengthens me, he peoples for me the vast solitude of Paris.

Suppose I go to see him? A lonely watch to-night would be gloomier than usual. The death of the year brings gloomy thoughts, the thirty-first of December, St. Sylvester's day—St. Sylvester! Why, that is his birthday! Ungrateful friend, to give no thought to it! Quick! my coat, my stick, my hat, and let me run to see these two early birds before they seek their roost.

When I entered the studio, Lampron was so deep in his work that he did not hear me. The large room, lighted only in one corner, looked weird enough. Around me, and among the medley of pictures and casts and the piles of canvases stacked against the wall, the eye encountered only a series of cinder-gray tints and undetermined outlines casting long amorphous shadows half-way across the ceiling. A draped lay figure leaning against a door seemed to listen to the whistling of the wind outside; a large glass bay opened upon the night. Nothing was alive in this part of the room, nothing alight except a few rare glints upon the gold of the frames, and the blades of two crossed swords. Only

in a corner, at the far end, at a distance exaggerated by
the shadows, sat Lampron engraving, solitary, motionless, beneath the light of a lamp. His back was toward
me. The lamp's rays threw a strong light on his delicate hand, on the workmanlike pose of his head, which
it surrounded with a nimbus, and on a painting—a
woman's head—which he was copying. He looked
superb like that, and I thought how doubly tempted
Rembrandt would have been by the deep significance
as well as by the chiaroscuro of this interior.

I stamped my foot. Lampron started, and turned
half around, narrowing his eyes as he peered into the
darkness.

"Ah, it's you," he said. He rose and came quickly
toward me, as if to prevent me from approaching the
table.

"You don't wish me to look?"

He hesitated a moment.

"After all, why not?" he answered.

The copper plate was hardly marked with a few
touches of the needle. He turned the reflector so as
to throw all its rays upon the painting.

"O Lampron, what a charming head!"

It was indeed a lovely head; an Italian girl, three-
quarter face, painted after the manner of Leonardo,
with firm but delicate touches, and lights and shades
of infinite subtlety, and possessing, like all that master's
portraits of women, a straightforward look that re-
sponds to the gazer's, but which he seeks to interrogate
in vain. The hair, brown with golden lights, was
dressed in smooth plaits above the temples. The neck,

somewhat long, emerged from a dark robe broadly indicated.

"I do not know this, Sylvestre?"

"No, it's an old thing."

"A portrait, of course?"

"My first."

"You never did better; line, color, life, you have got them all."

"You need not tell me that! In one's young days, look you, there are moments of real inspiration, when some one whispers in the ear and guides the hand; a lightness of touch, the happy audacity of the beginner, a wealth of daring never met with again. Would you believe that I have tried ten times to reproduce that in etching without success?"

"Why do you try?"

"Yes, that is the question. Why? It's a bit foolish."

"You never could find such a model again; that is one reason."

"Ah, no, you are right. I never could find her again."

"An Italian of rank? a princess, eh?"

"Something like it."

"What has become of her?"

"Ah, no doubt what becomes of all princesses. Fabien, my young friend, you who still see life through fairy-tales, doubtless you imagine her happy in her lot —wealthy, spoiled, flattered, speaking with disdainful lips at nightfall, on the terrace of her villa among the great pines, of the barbarian from across the Alps who painted her portrait twenty years since; and, in the same sentence, of her last new frock from Paris?"

"Yes, I see her so—still beautiful."

"You are good at guessing, Fabien. She is dead, my friend, and that ideal beauty is now a few white bones at the bottom of a grave."

"Poor girl!"

Sylvestre had used a sarcastic tone which was not usual with him. He was contemplating his work with such genuine sadness that I was awed. I divined that in his past, of which I knew but little, Lampron kept a sorrow buried that I had all unwittingly revived.

"My friend," said I, "let that be; I come to wish you many happy returns."

"Many happy returns? Ah, yes, my poor mother wished me that this morning; then I set to work and forgot all about it. I am glad you came. She would feel hurt, dear soul, if I forgot to pass a bit of this evening with her. Let us go and find her."

"With all my heart, Sylvestre, but I, too, have forgotten something."

"What?"

"I have brought no flowers."

"Never mind, she has plenty; strong-scented flowers of the south, a whole basketful, enough to keep a hive of bees or kill a man in his sleep, which you will. It is a yearly attention from an unhappy creditor."

"Debtor, you mean."

"I mean what I say—a creditor."

He lifted the lamp. The shadows shifted and ran along the walls like huge spiders, the crossed swords flashed, the Venus of Milo threw us a lofty glance, Polyhymnia stood forth pensive and sank back into shadow. At the door I took the draped lay figure in my arms. "Excuse me," I said as I moved it—and we left the studio for Madame Lampron's little sitting-room.

She was seated near a small round table, knitting socks, her feet on a hot-water bottle. Her kind old rough and wrinkled face beamed upon us. She thrust her needles under the black lace cap she always wore, and drew them out again almost immediately.

"It needed your presence, Monsieur Mouillard," said she, "to drag him from his work."

"Saint Sylvester's day, too. It is fearful! Love for his art has changed your son's nature, Madame Lampron."

She gave him a tender look, as on entering the room he bent over the fire and shook out his half-smoked pipe against the bars, a thing he never failed to do the moment he entered his mother's room.

"Dear child!" said she.

Then turning to me:

"You are a good friend, Monsieur Fabien. Never have we celebrated a Saint Sylvester without you since you came to Paris."

"Yet this evening, Madame, I have failed in my traditions, I have no flowers. But Sylvestre tells me that you have just received flowers from the south, from an unfortunate creditor."

My words produced an unusual effect upon her. She, who never stopped knitting to talk or to listen, laid her work upon her knees, and fixed her eyes upon me, filled with anxiety.

"Has he told you?"

Lampron who was poking the fire, his slippered feet stretched out toward the hearth, turned his head.

"No, mother, I merely told him that we had received a basket of flowers. Not much to confide. Yet why should he not know all? Surely he is our friend enough to know all. He should have known it long since were it not cruel to share between three a burden that two can well bear."

She made no answer, and began again to twist the wool between her needles, but nervously and as if her thoughts were sad.

To change the conversation I told them the story of my twofold mishap at the National Library and at M. Charnot's. I tried to be funny, and fancied I succeeded. The old lady smiled faintly. Lampron remained grave, and tossed his head impatiently. I summed my story thus:

"Net gain: two enemies, one of them charming."

"Oh, enemies!" said Sylvestre, "they spring up like weeds. One can not prevent them, and great sorrows do not come from *them*. Still, beware of charming enemies."

"She hates me, I swear. If you could have seen her!"

"And you?"

"Me? She is nothing to me."

"Are you sure?"

He put the question gravely, without looking in my face, as he twisted a paper spill.

I laughed.

"What is the matter with you to-day, misanthrope? I assure you that she is absolutely indifferent to me. But even were it otherwise, Sylvestre, where would be the wrong?"

"Wrong? No wrong at all; but I should be anxious for you; I should be afraid. See here, my friend. I know you well. You are a born man of letters, a dreamer, an artist in your way. You have to help you on entering the redoubtable lists of love neither foresight, nor a cool head, nor determination. You are guided solely by your impressions; by them you rise or fall. You are no more than a child."

"I quite agree. What next?"

"What next?" He had risen, and was speaking with unusual vehemence. "I once knew some one like you, whose first passion, rash, but deep as yours would be, broke his heart forever. The heart, my friend, is liable to break, and can not be mended like china."

Lampron's mother interrupted him afresh, reproachfully.

"He came to wish you a happy birthday, my child."

"One day, mother, is as good as another to listen to good advice. Besides, I am only talking of one of my friends. 'Tis but a short story, Fabien, and instructive. I will give it you in very few words. My friend was very young and enthusiastic. He was on his way through the galleries of Italy, brush in hand, his heart full of the ceaseless song of youth in holiday. The world never had played him false, nor balked him. He made the future bend to the fancy of his dreams. He seldom descended among common men from those loftier realms where the contemplation of endless masterpieces kept his spirit as on wings. He admired, copied, filled his soul with the glowing beauty of Italian landscape and Italian art. But one day, without reflection, without knowledge, without foresight, he was rash enough to fall in love with a girl of noble birth whose portrait he was painting; to speak to her and to win her love. He thought then, in the silly innocence of his youth, that art abridges all distance and that love effaces it. Crueller nonsense never was uttered, my poor Fabien. He soon found this; he tried to struggle against the parent's denial, against himself, against her, powerless in all alike, beaten at every point. . . . The end was— Do you care to learn the end? The girl was carried off, struck down by a brief illness, soon dead; the man, hurled out of heaven, bruised, a fugitive also, is still so weak in presence of his sorrow that even after these long years he can not think of it without weeping."

Lampron actually was weeping, he who was so seldom moved. Down his brown beard, tinged already with gray, a tear was trickling. I noticed that Madame Lampron was stooping lower and lower over her needles. He went on:

"I have kept the portrait, the one you saw, Fabien. They would like to have it over yonder. They are old folk by now. Every year they ask me for this relic of our common sorrow; every year they send me, about this time a basket of white flowers, chiefly lilacs, the dead girl's flower, and their meaning is, 'Give up to us what is left of her, the masterpiece built up of your youth and hers.' But I am selfish, Fabien. I, like them, am jealous of all the sorrows this portrait recalls to me, and I deny them. Come, mother, where are the flowers? I have promised Fabien to show them to him."

But his old mother could not answer. Having no doubt bewept this sorrow too often to find fresh tears, her eyes followed her son with restless compassion. He, beside the window, was hunting among the chairs and lounges crowded in this corner of the little sitting-room.

He brought us a box of white wood. "See," said he, "'tis my wedding bouquet."

And he emptied it on the table. Parma violets, lilacs, white camellias and moss rolled out in slightly faded bunches, spreading a sweet smell in which there breathed already a vague scent of death and corruption. A violet fell on my knees. I picked it up.

He looked for a moment at the heap on the table.

"I keep none," said he: "I have too many reminders without them. Cursed flowers!"

With one motion of his arm he swept them all up and cast them upon the coals in the hearth. They shrivelled, crackled, grew limp and discolored, and vanished in smoke.

"Now I am going back to my etching. Good-by, Fabien. Good-night, mother."

Without turning his head, he left the room and went back to his studio.

I made a movement to follow him and bring him back.

THE INK-STAIN

Madame Lampron stopped me. "I will go myself," said she, "later—much later."

We sat awhile in silence. When she saw me somewhat recovered from the shock of my feelings she went on:

"You never have seen him like this, but I have seen it often. It is so hard! I knew her whom he loved almost as soon as he, for he never hid anything from me. You can judge from her portrait whether hers was not the face to attract an artist like Sylvestre. I saw at once that it was a trial, in which I could do nothing. They were very great people; different from us, you know."

"They refused to let them marry?"

"Oh, no! Sylvestre did not ask; they never had the opportunity of refusing. No, no; it was I. I said to him: 'Sylvestre, this can never be—never!' He was convinced against his will. Then she spoke to her parents on her own account. They carried her off, and there was an end of it."

"He never saw her again."

"Never; he would not have wished it; and then she lived a very little time. I went back there two years later, when they wanted to buy the picture. We were still living in Italy. That was one of the hardest hours of my life. I was afraid of their reproaches, and I did not feel sure of myself. But no, they suffered for their daughter as I for my son, and that brought us together. Still, I did not give up the portrait; Sylvestre set too great store by it. He insists on keeping it, feeding his eyes on it, reopening his wound day by day. Poor child! Forget all this, Monsieur Fabien; you can do

[43]

nothing to help. Be true to your youth, and tell us next time of Monsieur Charnot and Mademoiselle Jeanne."

Dear Madame Lampron! I tried to console her; but as I never knew my mother, I could find but little to say. All the same, she thanked me and assured me I had done her good.

CHAPTER V

January 1, 1885.

T HE first of January! When one is not
yet an uncle and no longer a godson,
if one is in no government employ
and goes out very little, the number
of one's calls on New Year's Day is
limited. I shall make five or six this
afternoon. It will be "Not at home"
in each case; and that will be all my
compliments of the season.

No, I am wrong. I have received the compliments
of the season. My porter's wife came up just now,
wreathed in smiles.

"Monsieur Mouillard, I wish you a Happy New
Year, good health, and Heaven to end your days."
She had just said the same to the tenants on the first,
second, and third floors. My answer was the same as
theirs. I slipped into her palm (with a "Many thanks!"
of which she took no notice) a piece of gold, which
brought another smile, a curtsey, and she is gone.

This smile comes only once a year; it is not repro-
duced at any other period, but is a dividend payable in
one instalment. This, and a tear on All Souls' Day,
when she has been to place a bunch of chrysanthemums

[45]

on her baby's grave, are the only manifestations of sensibility that I have discovered in her. From the second of January to the second of November she is a human creature tied to a bell-rope, with an immovably stolid face and a monosyllabic vocabulary in which politer terms occur but sparsely.

This morning, contrary to her habits, she has brought up by post two letters; one from my Uncle Mouillard (an answer), and the other—I don't recognize the other. Let's open it first: big envelope, ill-written address, Paris postmark. Hallo! a smaller envelope inside, and on it:

ANTOINE AND MARIE PLUMET.

Poor souls! they have no visiting-cards. But kind hearts are more than pasteboard.

Ten months ago little Madame Plumet, then still unmarried, was in a terrible pother. I remember our first meeting, on a March day, at the corner of the Rue du Quatre-Septembre and the Rue Richelieu. I was walking along quickly, with a bundle of papers under my arm, on my way back to the office where I was head clerk. Suddenly a dressmaker's errand-girl set down her great oilcloth-covered box in my way. I nearly went head first over it, and was preparing to walk around it, when the little woman, red with haste and blushes, addressed me. "Excuse me, sir, are you a lawyer?"

"No, Mademoiselle, not yet."

"Perhaps, sir, you know some lawyers?"

"To be sure I do; my master, to begin with, Counsellor Boule. He is quite close, if you care to follow me."

"I am in a terrible hurry, but I can spare a minute or two. Thank you very much, Monsieur."

And thus I found myself escorted by a small dressmaker and a box of fashions. I remember that I walked a little ahead for fear of being seen in such company by a fellow-clerk, which would have damaged my reputation.

We got to the office. Down went the box again. The little dressmaker told me that she was engaged to M. Plumet, frame-maker. She told her tale very clearly; a little money put by, you see, out of ten years' wages; one may be careful and yet be taken in; and, alas! all has been lent to a cousin in the cabinet-making trade, who wanted to set up shop; and now he refuses to pay up. The dowry is in danger, and the marriage in suspense.

"Do not be alarmed, Mademoiselle; we will summons this atrocious cabinet-maker, and get a judgment against him. We shall not let him go until he has disgorged, and you shall be Madame Plumet."

We kept our word. Less than two months later—thanks to my efforts—the dowry was recovered; the banns were put up; and the little dressmaker paid a second visit to the office, this time with M. Plumet, who was even more embarrassed than she.

"See, Antoine! this is Monsieur Mouillard, who undertook our case! Thank you again and again, Monsieur Mouillard, you really have been too kind! What do I owe you for your trouble?"

"You must ask my master what his fees come to, Mademoiselle."

"Yes, but you? What can I do for you?"

The whole office, from the messenger to the clerk who came next to me, had their eyes upon me. I rose to the occasion, and in my uncle's best manner I replied:

"Be happy, Mademoiselle, and remember me."

We laughed over it for a week.

She has done better, she has remembered it after eight months. But she has not given her address. That is a pity. I should have liked to see them both again. These young married folk are like the birds; you hear their song, but that does not tell you the whereabouts of their nest.

Now, uncle, it's your turn.

Here it is again, your unfailing letter anticipated, like the return of the comets, but less difficult to analyze than the weird substance of which comets are composed. Every year I write to you on December 28th, and you answer me on the 31st in time for your letter to reach me on New Year's morning. You are punctual, dear uncle; you are even attentive; there is something affectionate in this precision. But I do not know why your letters leave me unmoved. The eighteen to twenty-five lines of which each is composed are from your head, rather than your heart. Why do you not tell me of my parents, whom you knew; of your daily life; of your old servant Madeleine, who nursed me as a baby; of the Angora cat almost as old as she; of the big garden, so green, so enticing, which you trim with so much care,

and which rewards your attention with such luxuriance.
It would be so nice, dear uncle, to be a shade more intimate.

Ah, well! let us see what he writes:

"BOURGES, December 31, 1884.
"MY DEAR NEPHEW:

"The approach of the New Year does not find me with the same
sentiments with which it leaves you. I make up my yearly accounts from July 31st, so the advent of the 31st of December finds
me as indifferent as that of any other day of the said month. Your
repinings appear to me the expressions of a dreamer.

"It would, however, not be amiss if you made a start in practical
life. You come of a family not addicted to dreaming. Three Mouillards have, if I may say so, adorned the legal profession at Bourges.
You will be the fourth.

"As soon as you have taken your doctor's degree—which I presume should not be long—I shall expect you the very next day, or
the day after that at the furthest; and I shall place you under my
supervision.

"The practice is not falling off, I can assure you. In spite of age,
I still possess good eyes and good teeth, the chief qualifications for
a lawyer. You will find everything ready and in good order here.

"I am obliged to you for your good wishes, which I entirely
reciprocate.

"Your affectionate uncle,
"BRUTUS MOUILLARD.

"P. S.—The Lorinet family have been to see me. Mademoiselle
Berthe is really quite pretty. They have just inherited 751,351
francs.

"I was employed by them in an action relating thereto.'

Yes, my dear uncle, you were employed, according to
the formula, "in virtue of these and subsequent engagements," and among the "subsequent engagements"

4   [49]

you are kind enough to reckon one between Mademoiselle Berthe Lorinet, spinster, of no occupation, and M. Fabien Mouillard, lawyer. "Fabien Mouillard, lawyer"—that I may perhaps endure, but "Fabien Mouillard, son-in-law of Lorinet," never! One pays too dear for these rich wives. Mademoiselle Berthe is half a foot taller than I, who am moderately tall, and she has breadth in proportion. Moreover, I have heard that her wit is not in proportion. I saw her when she was seventeen, in a short frock of staring blue; she was very thin then, and was escorted by a brother, squeezed inside a schoolboy's suit; they were out for their first walk alone, both red-faced, flurried, shuffling along the sidewalks of Bourges. That was enough. For me she will always wear that look, that frock, that clumsy gait. Recollections, my good uncle, are not unlike instantaneous photographs; and this one is a distinct negative to your designs.

March 3d.

The year is getting on. My essay is growing. The Junian Latin emerges from the fogs of Tiber.

I have had to return to the National Library. My first visits were not made without trepidation. I fancied that the beadle was colder, and that the keepers were shadowing me like a political suspect. I thought it wise to change my side, so now I make out my list of books at the left-hand desk and occupy a seat on the left side of the room.

M. Charnot remains faithful to his post beneath the right-hand inkstand.

I have been watching him. He is usually one of the

first to arrive, with nimble, almost springy, step. His
hair, which he wears rather long, is always carefully
parted in the middle, and he is always freshly shaven.
His habit of filling the pockets of his frock-coat with
bundles of notes has made that garment swell out at the
top into the shape of a basket. He puts on a pair of
spectacles mounted in very thin gold, and reads deter-
minedly, very few books it is true, but they are all bound
in vellum, and that fixes their date. In his way of turning the leaves there is something sacerdotal. He seems
popular with the servants. Some of the keepers worship him. He has very good manners toward every one.
Me he avoids. Still I meet him, sometimes in the
cloakroom, oftener in the Rue Richelieu on his way to
the Seine. He stops, and so do I, near the Fontaine
Molière, to buy chestnuts. We have this taste in common. He buys two sous' worth, I buy one; thus the distinctions of rank are preserved. If he arrives after me,
I allow him the first turn to be served; if he is before
me, I await my turn with a patience which betokens
respect. Yet he never seems to notice it. Once or
twice, certainly, I fancied I caught a smile at the corners
of his mouth, and a sly twinkle in the corners of his
eyes; but these old scholars smile so austerely.

He must have guessed that I wish to meet him. For
I can not deny it. I am looking out for an opportunity
to repair my clumsy mistake and show myself in a less
unfavorable light than I did at that ill-starred visit.
And *she* is the reason why I haunt his path!

Ever since M. Mouillard threatened me with Mademoiselle Berthe Lorinet, the graceful outlines of

Mademoiselle Jeanne have haunted me with a persistence to which I have no objection.

It is not because I love her. It does not go as far as that. I am leaving her and leaving Paris forever in a few months. No; the height of my desire is to see her again—in the street, at the theatre, no matter 'where—to show her by my behavior and, if possible, by my words that I am sorry for the past, and implore her forgiveness. Then there will no longer be a gulf betwixt her and me, I shall be able to meet her without confusion, to invoke her image to put to flight that of Mademoiselle Lorinet without the vision of those disdainful lips to dash me. She will be for me at once the type of Parisian grace and of filial affection. I will carry off her image to the country like the remembered perfume of some rare flower; and if ever I sing *Hymen Hymnæ!* it shall be with one who recalls her face to me.

I do not think my feelings overpass these bounds. Yet I am not quite sure. I watch for her with a keenness and determination which surprise me, and the disappointment which follows a fruitless search is a shade too lively to accord with cool reason.

After all, perhaps my reason is not cool.

Let me see, I will make up the account of my ventures.

One January afternoon I walked up and down the Rue de l'Université eight times in succession, from No. 1 to No. 107, and from No. 107 to No. 1. Jeanne did not come out in spite of the brilliancy of the clear winter day.

On the nineteenth of the same month I went to see

THE INK-STAIN

Andromache, although the classic writers, whom I swear by, are not the writers I most care to hear. I renewed this attempt on the twenty-seventh. Neither on the first nor on the second occasion did I see Mademoiselle Charnot.

And yet if the Institute does not escort its daughters in shoals to applaud *Andromache*, where on earth does it take them?

Perhaps nowhere.

Every time I cross the Tuileries Garden I run my eyes over the groups scattered among the chestnut-trees. I see children playing and falling about; nursemaids who leave them crying; mothers who pick them up again; a vagrant guardsman. No Jeanne.

To wind up, yesterday I spent five hours at the Bon Marché.

The spring show was on, one of the great occasions of the year; and I presumed, not without an apparent foundation of reason, that no young or pretty Parisian could fail to be there. When I arrived, about one o'clock, the crowd already filled the vast bazaar. It was not easy to stand against certain currents that set toward the departments consecrated to spring novelties. Adrift like a floating spar I was swept away and driven ashore amid the baby-linen. There it flung me high and dry among the shop-girls, who laughed at the spectacle of an undergraduate shipwrecked among the necessaries of babyhood. I felt shy, and attaching myself to the fortunes of an Englishwoman, who worked her elbows with the vigor of her nation, I was borne around nearly twenty counters. At last, wearied, mazed, dusty as with a long summer walk, I took refuge in the reading-room.

Poor simpleton! I said to myself, you are too early; you might have known that. She can not come with her father before the National Library closes. Even supposing they take an omnibus, they will not get here before a quarter past four.

I had to find something to fill up the somewhat long interval which separated me from that happy moment. I wrote a letter to my Uncle Mouillard, taking seven minutes over the address alone. I had not shown such penmanship since I was nine years old. When the last flourish was completed I looked for a paper; they were all engaged. The directory was free. I took it, and opened it at *Ch.* I discovered that there were many Charnots in Paris without counting mine: Charnot, grocer; Charnot, upholsterer; Charnot, surgical bandage-maker. I built up a whole family tree for the member of the Institute, choosing, of course, those persons of the name who appeared most worthy to adorn its branches. Of what followed I retain but a vague recollection. I only remember that I felt twice as if some inquisitive individual were looking over my shoulder. The third time I woke up with a start.

"Sir," said a shopwalker, with the utmost politeness, "a gentleman has been waiting three quarters of an hour for the directory. Would you kindly hand it to him if you have quite finished with it?"

It was a quarter to six. I still waited a little while, and then I left, having wasted my day.

O Jeanne! where do you hide yourself? Must I, to

meet you, attend mass at St. Germain des Prés? Are you one of those early birds who, before the world is up, are out in the Champs Elysées catching the first rays of the morning, and the country breeze before it is lost in the smoke of Paris? Are you attending lectures at the Sorbonne? Are you learning to sing? and, if so, who is your teacher?

You sing, Jeanne, of course. You remind me of a bird. You have all the quick and easy graces of the skylark. Why should you not have the skylark's voice?

Fabien, you are dropping into poetry!

CHAPTER VI

April 3d.

FOR a month I have written nothing in this brown note-book. But to-day there is plenty to put down, and worth the trouble too.

Let me begin with the first shock. This morning, my head crammed with passages from Latin authors, I leaned my brow against the pane of my window which looks on the garden. The garden is not mine, of course, since I live on the fourth floor; but I have a view of the big weeping-willow in the centre, the sanded path that runs around it, and the four walls lined with borders, one of which separates it from the huge premises of the Carmelites. It is an almost deserted garden. The first-floor tenant hardly ever walks there. His son, a schoolboy of seventeen, was there this morning. He stood two feet from the street wall, motionless, with head thrown back, whistling a monotonous air, which seemed to me like a signal. Before him, however, was nothing but the moss on the old wall gleaming like golden lights. People do not whistle to amuse stones nor yet moss. Farther off, on the other side of the street, the windows of the opposite houses stretched away in long straight lines, most of them standing open.

[56]

THE INK-STAIN

I thought: "The bird is somewhere there. Some small Abigail with her white cap will look out in a moment."

The suspicion was stupid and ill-natured. How rash are our lightest judgments! Suddenly the school-boy took one step forward, swept his hand quickly along the moss as if he were trying to catch a fly, and ran off to his mother triumphant, delighted, beside himself, with an innocent gray lizard on the tips of his fingers.

"I've got him! I've got him! He was basking in the sun and I charmed him!"

"Basking in the sun!" This was a revelation to me. I flung up the window. Yes, it was true. Warmth and light lay everywhere: on the roofs still glistening with last night's showers; across the sky, whose gay blue proclaimed that winter was done. I looked downward and saw what I had not seen before: the willow bursting into bud; the hepatica in flower at the foot of the camellias, which had ceased to bloom; the pear-trees in the Carmelites' garden flushing red as the sap rose within them; and upon the dead trunk of a fig-tree was a blackbird, escaped from the Luxembourg, who, on tiptoe, with throat outstretched, drunk with delight, answered some far-off call that the wind brought to him, singing, as if in woodland depths, the rapturous 'song of the year's new birth. Then, oh! then, I could contain myself no longer. I ran down the stairs four at a time, cursing Paris and the Junian Latins who had been cheating me of the spring. What! live there cut off from the world which was created for me, tread an artificial earth of stone or asphalt, live with a horizon of chimneys, see only the sky chopped into irregular strips by roofs smirched with smoke, and allow this exquisite spring to fleet by without drinking in her bountiful delight, without renewing in her youthfulness our youth, always a little staled and overcast by winter! No, that can not be; I mean to see the spring.

And I have seen it, in truth, though cut and tied into bouquets, for my aimless steps led me to the Place St. Sulpice, where the flower-sellers were. There were flowers in plenty, but very few people; it was already late. None the less did I enjoy the sight of all the plants arranged by height and kind, from the double hyacinths, dear to hall-porters, to the first carnations, scarcely in bud, whose pink or white tips just peeped from their green sheaths; then the bouquets, bundles of the same kinds and same shades of flowers wrapped up in paper: lilies-of-the-valley, lilacs, forget-me-nots, mignonette, which being grown under glass has guarded its honey from the bees to scent the air here. Everyone had a look of welcome for those exiles. The girls smiled at them without knowing the reason why. The cab-drivers in line along the sidewalk seemed to enjoy their neighborhood. I heard one of them, with a face like a half-ripened strawberry, red, with a white nose, say to a comrade, "Hallo, Francis! that smells good, doesn't it!"

I was walking along slowly, looking into every stall, and when I came to the end I turned right about face.

Great Heavens! Not ten feet off! M. Flamaran, M. Charnot, and Mademoiselle Jeanne!

They had stopped before one of the stalls that I had

just left. M. Flamaran was carrying under his arm a pot of cineraria, which made his stomach a perfect bower. M. Charnot was stooping, examining a superb pink carnation. Jeanne was hovering undecided between twenty bunches of flowers, bending her pretty head in its spring hat over each in turn.

"Which, father?"

"Whichever you like; but make up your mind soon; Flamaran is waiting."

A moment more, and the elective affinities carried the day.

"This bunch of mignonette," she said.

I would have wagered on it. She was sure to choose the mignonette—a fair, well-bred, graceful plant like herself. Others choose their camellias and their hyacinths; Jeanne must have something more refined.

She put down her money, caught up the bunch, looked at it for a moment, and held it close to her breast as a mother might hold her child, while all its golden locks drooped over her arm. Then off she ran after her father, who had only changed one carnation for another. They went on toward St. Sulpice—M. Flamaran on the right, M. Charnot in the middle, Jeanne on the left. She brushed past without seeing me. I followed them at a distance. All three were laughing. At what? I can guess; she because she was eighteen, they for joy to be with her. At the end of the market-place they turned to the left, followed the railings of the church, and bent their steps toward the Rue St. Sulpice, doubtless to take home M. Flamaran, whose cineraria blazed amid the crowd. I was about to turn

in the same direction when an omnibus of the Batignolles-Clichy line stopped my way. In an instant I was
overwhelmed by the flood of passengers which it poured
on the pavements.

"Hallo, you here! How goes it? What are you staring at? My stovepipe? Observe it well, my dear fellow—the latest invention of Léon; the patent ventilat-
ing, anti-sudorific, and evaporating hat!"

It was Larivé who had just climbed down from the
knife-board.

Every one knows Larivé, head clerk in Machin's
office. He is to be seen everywhere—a tall, fair man,
with little close-trimmed beard, and moustache carefully twisted. He is always perfectly dressed, always in
a tall hat and new gloves, full of all the new stories,
which he tells as his own. If you believe him, he is at
home in all the ministries, whatever party is in power;
he has cards for every ball, and tickets for every first
night. With all that he never misses a funeral, is a
good lawyer, and as solemn when in court as a dozen old
mandarins.

"Come, Fabien, will you answer? What are you
staring at?"

He turned his head.

"Oh, I see—pretty Mademoiselle Charnot."

"You know her?"

"Of course I do, and her father, too. A pretty little
thing!"

I blushed with pleasure.

"Yes, a very pretty little thing; but wants style—
dances poorly."

"An admirable defect."

"A little big, too, for her eyes."

"What do you mean by that?"

"Her eyes are a little too small, you understand me?"

"What matters that if they are bright and loving?"

"No matter at all to me; but it seems to have some effect on you. Might you be related?"

"No."

"Or connected by marriage?"

"No."

"So much the better—eh, my boy? And how's uncle? Still going strong?"

"Yes; and longing to snatch me from this Babylon."

"You mean to succeed him?"

"As long hence as possible."

"I had heard you were not enthusiastic. A small practice, isn't it?"

"Not exactly. A matter of a thousand a year!"

"Clear profit?"

"Yes."

"That's good enough. But in the country, my poor fellow, in the country!"

"It would be the death of you, wouldn't it?"

"In forty-eight hours."

"However did you manage to be born there, Larivé? I'm surprised at you."

"So am I. I often think about it. Good-by. I must be off."

I caught him by the hand which he held out to me.

"Larivé, tell me where you have met Mademoiselle Charnot?"

"Oh, come!—I see it's serious. My dear fellow, I am so sorry I did not tell you she was perfection. If I had only known!"

"That's not what I asked you. Where have you seen her?"

"In society, of course. Where do you expect me to see young girls except in society? My *dear* Fabien!"

He went off laughing. When he was about ten yards off he turned, and making a speaking-trumpet of his hands, he shouted through them:

"She's perfection!"

Larivé is decidedly an ass. His jokes strike you as funny at first; but there's nothing in him, he's a mere hawker of stale puns; there's nothing but selfishness under his jesting exterior. I have no belief in him. Yet he is an old school friend; the only one of my twenty-eight classmates whose acquaintance I have kept up. Four are dead, twenty-three others are scattered about in obscure country places; lost for want of news, as they say at the private inquiry offices. Larivé makes up the twenty-eight. I used to admire him, when we were low in the school, because of his long trousers, his lofty contempt of discipline, and his precocious intimacy with tobacco. I preferred him to the good, well-behaved boys. Whenever we had leave out I used to buy gum-arabic at the druggist's in La Châtre, and break it up with a small hammer at the far end of my room, away from prying eyes. I used there to distribute it into three bags ticketed respectively: "large pieces," "middle-sized pieces," "small pieces." When I returned to school with the three bags in my pocket, I would draw out one or the other to offer them to my friends, according to the importance of the occasion, or the degrees of friendship. Larivé always had the big bits, and plenty of them. Yet he was none the more grateful to me, and even did not mind chaffing me about these petty attentions by which he was the gainer. He used to make fun of everything, and I used to look up to him. He still makes fun of everything; but for me the age of gumarabic is past and my faith in Larivé is gone.

If he believes that he will disparage this charming girl in my eyes by telling me that she is a bad dancer, he is wrong. Of great importance it is to have a wife who dances well! She does not dance in her own house, nor with her husband from the wardrobe to the cradle, but at others' houses, and with other men. Besides, a young girl who dances much has a lot of nonsense talked to her. She may acquire a taste for Larivé's buffooneries, for a neat leg, or a sharp tongue. In that case what welcome can she give to simple, timid affection? She will only laugh at it. But you would not laugh, Jeanne, were I to tell you that I loved you. No, I am quite convinced that you would not laugh. And if you loved me, Jeanne, we should not go into society. That would just suit me. I should protect you, yet not hide you. We should have felicity at home instead of running after it to balls and crushes, where it is never to be found. You could not help being aware of the fascination you exert; but you would not squander it on a mob of dancers, and bring home only the last remnants of your good spirits, with the last remnants of your train. Jeanne, I am delighted to hear that you dance badly.

RENÉ BAZIN

Whither away, Fabien, my friend, whither away?
You are letting your imagination run away with you
again. A hint from it, and off you go. Come, do use
your reason a little. You have seen this young lady
again, that is true. You admired her; that was for the
second time. But she, whom you so calmly speak of as
"Jeanne," as if she were something to you, never even
noticed you. You know nothing about her but what
you suspect from her maiden grace and a dozen words
from her lips. You do not know whether she is free,
nor how she would welcome the notions you entertain
if you gave them utterance, yet here you are saying,
"*We* should go here," "*We* should do this and that."
Keep to the singular, my poor fellow. The plural is far
away, very far away, if not entirely beyond your reach.

CHAPTER VII

A WOODLAND SKETCH

April 27th.

T HE end of April. Students, pack and be off! The first warm breezes burst the buds. Meudon is smiling; Clamart breaks into song; the air in the valley of Chevreuse is heavy with violets; the willows shower their catkins on the banks of the Yvette; and farther yet, over yonder beneath the green domes of the forest of Fontainebleau, the deer prick their ears at the sound of the first riding-parties. Off with you! Flowers line the pathways, the moors are pink with bloom, the undergrowth teems with darting wings. All the town troops out to see the country in its gala dress. The very poorest have a favorite nook, a recollection of the bygone year to be revived and renewed; a sheltered corner that invited sleep, a glade where the shade was grateful, a spot beside the river's brink where the fish used to bite. Each one says, "Don't you remember?" Each one seeks his nest like a home-coming swallow. Does it still hold together? What havoc has been made by the winter's winds, and the rain, and the frost? Will it welcome us, as of old?

I, too, said to Lampron, "Don't you remember?" for we, too, have our nest, and summer days that smile

5 [65]

to us in memory. He was in the mood for work, and hesitated. I added in a whisper, "The blackbird's pool!" He smiled, and off we went.

Again, as of old, our destination was St. Germain —not the town, nor the Italian palace, nor yet the terrace whence the view spreads so wide over the Seine, the country dotted with villas, to Montmartre blue in the distance—not these, but the forest. "Our forest," we call it; for we know all its young shoots, all its giant trees, all its paths where poachers and young lovers hide. With my eyes shut I could find the blackbird's pool, the way to which was first shown us by a deer.

Imagine at thirty paces from an avenue, a pool—no, not a pool (the word is incorrect), nor yet a pond—but a fountain hollowed out by the removal of a giant oak. Since the death of this monarch the birches which its branches kept apart have never closed together, and the fountain forms the centre of a little clearing where the moss is thick at all seasons and starred in August with wild pinks. The water, though deep, is deliciously clear. At a depth of more than six feet you can distinguish the dead leaves at the bottom, the grass, the twigs, and here and there a stone's iridescent outline. They all lie asleep there, the waste of seasons gone by, soon to be covered by others in their turn. From time to time out of the depths of these submerged thickets an eft darts up. He comes circling up, quivering his yellow-banded tail, snatches a mouthful of air, and goes down again head first. Save for these alarms the pool is untroubled. It is guarded from the winds by a juniper, which an eglantine has chosen for its guardian and

crowns each year with a wreath of roses. Each year,
too, a blackbird makes his nest here. We keep his secret. He knows we shall not disturb him. And when
I come back to this little nook in the woods, which cus-
tom has endeared to us, merely by looking in the water
I feel my very heart refreshed.

"What a spot to sleep in!" cried Lampron. "Keep
sentry, Fabien; I am going to take a nap."

We had walked fast. It was very hot. He took off
his coat, rolled it into a pillow, and placed it beneath his
head as he lay down on the grass. I stretched myself
prone on a velvety carpet of moss, and gave myself up
to a profound investigation of the one square foot of
ground which lay beneath my eyes. The number of
blades of grass was prodigious. A few, already awned,
stood above their fellows, waving like palms—meadow--
grass, fescue, foxtail, brome-grass—each slender stalk
crowned with a tuft. Others were budding, only half
unfolded, amid the darker mass of spongy moss which
gave them sustenance. Amid the numberless shafts
thus raised toward heaven a thousand paths criss-
crossed, each full of obstacles—chips of bark, juniper-
berries, beech-nuts, tangled roots, hills raised by bur-
rowing insects, ravines formed by the draining off of
the rains. Ants and beetles bustled along them, press-
ing up hill and down to some mysterious goal. Above
them a cunning red spider was tying a blade of grass to
an orchid leaf, the pillars it had chosen for its future
web; and when the wind shook the leaves and the sun
pierced through to this spot, I saw the delicate roof
already mapped out.

[67]

I do not know how long my contemplation lasted.
The woods were still. Save for a swarm of gnats which
hummed in a minor key around the sleeping Lampron,
nothing stirred, not a leaf even. All nature was silent
as it drank in the full sunshine.

A murmur of distant voices stole on my ear. I rose,
and crept through the birches and hazels to the edge of
the glade.

At the top of the slope, on the green margin of the
glade, shaded by the tall trees, two pedestrians were
slowly advancing. At the distance they still were I
could distinguish very little except that the man wore a
frock-coat, and that the girl was dressed in gray, and
was young, to judge by the suppleness of her walk.
Nevertheless I felt at once that it was *she!*

I hid at they came near, and saw her pass on her
father's arm, chatting in low tones, full of joy to have
escaped from the Rue de l'Université. She was looking
before her with wide-open eyes. M. Charnot kept his
eyes on his daughter, more interested in her than in
all the wealth of spring. He kept well to the right of
the path as the sun ate away the edge of the shadows;
and asked, from time to time:

"Are you tired?"

"Oh, no!"

"As soon as you are tired, my dear, we will sit down.
I am not walking too fast?"

She answered "No" again, and laughed, and they
went on.

Soon they left the avenue and were lost in a green
alley. Then a sudden twilight seemed to have closed

down on me, an infinite sadness swelled in my heart. I closed my eyes, and—God forgive my weakness, but the tears came.

"Hallo! What part do you intend me to play in all this?" said Lampron behind me.

"'What part'?"

"Yes. It's an odd notion to invite me to your trysting-place."

"Trysting-place? I haven't one."

"You mean to tell me, perhaps, that you came here by chance?"

"Certainly."

"And chanced upon the very moment and the spot where she was passing?"

"Do you want a proof? That young lady is Mademoiselle Charnot."

"Well?"

"Well, I never have said another word to her since my one visit to her father; I have only seen her once, for a moment, in the street. You see there can be no question of trysting-places in this case. I was wondering at her appearance when you awoke. It is luck, or a friendly providence, that has used the beauty of the sunlight, the breeze, and all the sweets of April to bring her, as it brought us, to the forest."

"And that is what fetched the tears?"

"Well, no."

"What, then?"

"I don't know."

"My full-grown baby, I will tell you. You are in love with her!"

"Indeed, Sylvestre, I believe you're right. I confess it frankly to you as to my best friend. It is an old story already; as old, perhaps, as the day I first met her. At first her figure would rise in my imagination, and I took pleasure in contemplating it. Soon this phantom ceased to satisfy; I longed to see her in person. I sought her in the streets, the shops, the theatre. I still blinded myself, and pretended that I only wanted to ask her pardon, so as to remove, before I left Paris, the unpleasant impression I had made at our first meeting. But now, Sylvestre, all these false reasons have disappeared, and the true one is clear. I love her!"

"Not a doubt of it, my friend, not a doubt of it. I have been through it myself."

He was silent, and his eyes wandered away to the far-off woods, perhaps back to those distant memories of his. A shadow rested on his strong face, but only for an instant. He shook off his depression, and his old smile came back as he said:

"It's serious, then?"

"Yes, very serious."

"I'm not surprised; she is a very pretty girl."

"Isn't she lovely?"

"Better than that, my friend; she is good. What do you know about her?"

"Only that she is a bad dancer."

"That's something, to be sure."

"But it isn't all."

"Well, no. But never mind, find out the rest, speak to her, declare your passion, ask for her hand, and marry her."

THE INK-STAIN

"Good heavens, Sylvestre, you are going ahead!"

"My dear fellow, that is the best and wisest plan; these vague idyls ought to be hurried on, either to a painless separation or an honorable end in wedlock. In your place I should begin to-morrow."

"Why not to-day?"

"How so?"

"Let's catch them up, and see her again at least."

He began to laugh.

"Run after young girls at my age! Well, well, it was my advice. Come along!"

We crossed the avenue, and plunged into the forest.

Lampron had formerly acquired a reputation for tireless agility among the fox-hunters of the Roman Campagna. He still deserves it. In twenty strides he left me behind. I saw him jumping over the heather, knocking off with his cane the young shoots on the oaks, or turning his head to look at me as I struggled after, torn by brambles and pricked by gorse. A startled pheasant brought him to a halt. The bird rose under his feet and soared into the full light.

"Isn't it beautiful?" said he. "Look out, we must be more careful; we are scaring the game. We should come upon the path they took, about sixty yards ahead."

Five minutes later he was signalling to me from behind the trunk of a great beech.

"Here they are."

Jeanne and M. Charnot were seated on a fallen trunk beside the path, which here was almost lost beneath the green boughs. Their backs were toward us. The old man, with his shoulders bent and his gold-knobbed cane stuck into the ground beside him, was reading out of a book which we could not see, while Jeanne, attentive, motionless, her face half turned toward him, was listening. Her profile was outlined against a strip of clear sky. The deep silence of the wood wrapped us round, and we could hear the old scholar's voice; it just reached us.

"Straightway the godlike Odysseus spake these cunning words to the fair Nausicaa: 'Be thou goddess or mortal, O queen, I bow myself before thee! If thou art one of the deities who dwell in boundless heaven, by thy loveliness and grace and height I guess thee to be Artemis, daughter of high Zeus. If thou art a mortal dwelling upon earth, thrice blessed thy father and thy queenly mother, thrice blessed thy dear brothers! Surely their souls ever swell with gladness because of thee, when they see a maiden so lovely step into the circle of the dance. But far the most blessed of all is he who shall prevail on thee with presents and lead thee to his home!' "

I turned to Lampron, who had stopped a few steps in front of me, a little to the right. He had got out his sketch-book, and was drawing hurriedly. Presently he forgot all prudence, and came forth from the shelter of a beech to get nearer to his model. In vain I made sign upon sign, and tried to remind him that we were not there to paint or sketch. It was useless; the artist within him had broken loose. Sitting down at the required distance on a gnarled root, right in the open, he went on with his work with no thought but for his art.

THE INK-STAIN

The inevitable happened. Growing impatient over some difficulty in his sketch, Lampron shuffled his feet; a twig broke, some leaves rustled—Jeanne turned round and saw me looking at her, Lampron sketching her.

What are the feelings of a young girl who in the middle of a forest suddenly discovers that two pairs of eyes are busy with her? A little fright at first; then—when the idea of robbers is dismissed, and a second glance has shown her that it is her beauty, not her life, they want—a touch of satisfied vanity at the compliment, not unmixed with confusion.

This is exactly what we thought we saw. At first she slightly drew back, with brows knitted, on the verge of an exclamation; then her brows unbent, and the pleasure of finding herself admired, confusion at being taken unawares, the desire of appearing at ease, all appeared at once on her rosy cheeks and in her faintly troubled smile.

I bowed. Sylvestre pulled off his cap.

M. Charnot never stirred.

"Another squirrel?" he said.

"Two this time, I think, father," she answered, in a low voice.

He went on reading.

"'My guest,' made answer the fair Nausicaa, 'for I call thee so since thou seemest not base nor foolish, it is Zeus himself that giveth weal to men——'"

Jeanne was no longer listening. She was thinking. Of what? Of several things, perhaps, but certainly of how to beat a retreat. I guessed it by the movement of her sunshade, which was nervously tracing figures in the turf. I signalled to Lampron. We retired backward. Yet it was in vain; the charm was broken, the peace had been disturbed.

She gave two coughs—musical little coughs, produced at will.

M. Charnot broke off his reading.

"You are cold, Jeanne?"

"Why, no, father."

"Yes, yes, you're cold. Why did you not say so before? Lord, Lord, these children! Always the same—think of nothing!"

He rose without delay, put his book in his pocket, buttoned up his coat, and, leaning on his stick, glanced up a moment at the tree-tops. Then, side by side, they disappeared down the path, Jeanne stepping briskly, upright and supple, between the young branches which soon concealed her.

Still Lampron continued to watch the turning in the path down which she had vanished.

"What are you thinking about?" said I.

He stroked his beard, where lurked a few gray hairs.

"I am thinking, my friend, that youth leaves us in this same way, at the time when we love it most, with a faint smile, and without a word to tell us whither. Mine played me this trick."

"What a good idea of yours to sketch them both. Let me see the sketch."

"No!"

"Why not?"

THE INK-STAIN

"It can scarcely be called a sketch; it's a mere scratch."

"Show it, all the same."

"My good Fabien, you ought to know that when I am obstinate I have my reasons, like Balaam's ass. You will not see my sketch-book to-day, nor to-morrow, nor the day after."

I answered with foolish warmth:

"Please yourself; I don't care."

Really I was very much annoyed, and I was rather cool with Lampron when we parted on the platform.

What has come to the fellow? To refuse to show me a sketch he had made before my eyes, and a sketch of Jeanne, too!

April 28th, 9 A.M.

Hide your sketches, Sylvestre; stuff them away in your portfolios, or your pockets; I care little, for I bear Jeanne's image in my heart, and can see it when I will, and I love her, I love her, I love her!

What is to become of her and of me I can not tell. I hope without knowing what or why, or when, and hope alone is comforting.

9 P.M.

This afternoon, at two o'clock, I met Lampron in the Boulevard St. Michel. He was walking fast with a portfolio under his arm. I went up to him. He looked annoyed, and hardly seemed pleased when I offered to accompany him. I grew red and angry.

"Oh, very well," I said; "good-by, then, since you don't care to be seen with me."

He pondered a moment.

[75]

"Oh, come along if you like; I am going to my frame-maker's."

"A picture?"

"Something of the kind."

"And that's all the mystery! Yesterday it was a sketch I mustn't look at; to-day it's a picture. It is not nice of you, Sylvestre; no, decidedly it is not nice."

He gave me a look of friendly compassion.

"Poor little chap!" said he.

Then, in his usual clear, strong voice:

"I am in a great hurry; but come if you like. I would rather it were four days later; but as it is, never mind; it is never too soon to be happy."

When Lampron chooses to hold his tongue it is useless to ask him questions. I gave myself up to meditating on the words, "It is never too soon to be happy."

We went down the boulevard, past the beer-houses. There is distinction in my friend's walk; he is not to be confused with the crowd through which he passes. You can tell, from the simple seriousness of the man, his indifference to the noise and petty incidents of the streets, that he is a stout and noble soul. Among the passers-by he is a somebody. I heard from a group of students seated before a café the following words, which Sylvestre did not seem to notice:

"Look, do you see the taller of those two there? That's Sylvestre Lampron."

"Prix du Salon two years ago?"

"A great gun, you know."

"He looks it."

"To the left," said Lampron.

THE INK-STAIN

We turned to the left, and found ourselves in the Rue Hautefeuille, before a shabby house, within the porch of which hung notices of apartments to let; this was the frame-maker's. The passage was dark, the walls were chipped by the innumerable removals of furniture they had witnessed. We went upstairs. On the fourth floor a smell of glue and sour paste on the landing announced the tenant's profession. To make quite certain there was a card nailed to the door with "*Plumet, Frame-Maker.*"

"Plumet? A newly-married couple?"

But already Madame Plumet is at the door. It is the same little woman who came to Boule's office. She recognizes me in the dim light of the staircase.

"What, Monsieur Lampron, do you know Monsieur Mouillard?"

"As you apparently do, too, Madame Plumet."

"Oh, yes! I know him well; he won my action, you know."

"Ah, to be sure—against the cabinet-maker. Is your husband in?"

"Yes, sir, in the workshop. Plumet!"

Through the half-opened door giving access to an inner room we could see—in the midst of his molders, gilders, burnishers, and framers—a little dark man with a beard, who looked up and hurriedly undid the strings of his working-apron.

"Coming, Marie!"

Little Madame Plumet was a trifle upset at having to receive us in undress, before she had tidied up her rooms. I could see it by her blushes and by the in-

stinctive movement she made to smooth her disordered
curls.

The husband had hardly answered her call before
she left us and went off to the end of the room, into the
obscure recesses of an alcove overcrowded with furniture. There she bent over an oblong object, which I
could not quite see at first, and rocked it with her hand.

"Monsieur Mouillard," said she, looking up to me—
"Monsieur Mouillard, this is my son, Pierre!"

What tender pride in those words, and the smile
which accompanied them! With a finger she drew one
of the curtains aside. Under the blue muslin, between
the pillow and the white coverlet, I discovered two little
black eyes and a tuft of golden hair.

"Isn't he a little rogue!" she went on, and began to
caress the waking baby.

Meanwhile Sylvestre had been talking to Plumet at
the other end of the room.

"Out of the question," said the frame-maker; "we
are up to our knees in arrears; twenty orders waiting."

"I ask you to oblige me as a friend."

"I wish I could oblige you, Monsieur Lampron; but
if I made you a promise, I should not be able to keep
it."

"What a pity! All was so well arranged, too. The
sketch was to have been hung with my two engravings.
Poor Fabien! I was saving up a surprise for you. Come
and look here."

I went across. Sylvestre opened his portfolio.

"Do you recognize it?"

At once I recognized them. M. Charnot's back;

THE INK-STAIN

Jeanne's profile, exactly like her; a forest nook; the
parasol on the ground; the cane stuck into the grass;
a bit of genre, perfect in truth and execution.

"When did you do that?"

"Last night."

"And you want to exhibit it?"

"At the Salon."

"But, Sylvestre, it is too late to send in to the Salon.
The Ides of March are long past."

"Yes, for that very reason I have had the devil of a
time, intriguing all the morning. With a large picture
I never should have succeeded; but with a bit of a
sketch, six inches by nine——"

"Bribery of officials, then?"

"Followed by substitution, which is strictly forbidden. I happened to have hung there between two
engravings a little sketch of underwoods not unlike
this; one comes down, the other is hung instead—a little
bit of jobbery of which I am still ashamed. I risked it
all for you, in the hope that she would come and recognize the subject."

"Of course she will recognize it, and understand;
how on earth could she help it? My dear Sylvestre,
how can I thank you?"

I seized my friend's hand and begged his forgiveness
for my foolish haste of speech.

He, too, was a little touched and overcome by the
pleasure his surprise had given me.

"Look here, Plumet," he said to the frame-maker,
who had taken the sketch over to the light, and was
studying it with a professional eye. "This young man

has even a greater interest than I in the matter. He is a suitor for the lady's hand, and you can be very useful to him. If you do not frame the picture his happiness is blighted."

The frame-maker shook his head.

"Let's see, Antoine," said a coaxing little voice, and Madame Plumet left the cradle to come to our aid.

I considered our cause as won. Plumet repeated in vain, as he pulled his beard, that it was impossible; she declared it was not. He made a move for his workshop; she pulled him back by the sleeve, made him laugh and give his consent.

"Antoine," she insisted, "we owe our marriage to Monsieur Mouillard; you must at least pay what you owe."

I was delighted. Still, a doubt seized me.

"Sylvestre," I said to Lampron, who already had his hand upon the door-handle, "do you really think she will come?"

"I hope so; but I will not answer for it. To make certain, some one must send word to her: 'Mademoiselle Jeanne, your portrait is at the Salon.' If you know any one who would not mind taking this message to the Rue de l'Université——"

"I'm afraid I don't."

"Come on, then, and trust to luck."

"Rue de l'Université, did you say?" broke in little Madame Plumet, who certainly took the liveliest interest in my cause.

"Yes; why?"

THE INK-STAIN

"Because I have a friend in the neighborhood, and perhaps——"

I risked giving her the number and name under the seal of secrecy; and it was a good thing I did so.

In three minutes she had concocted a plan. It was like this: her friend lived near the hotel in the Rue de l'Université, a porter's wife of advanced years, and quite safe; by means of her it might be possible to hint to Mademoiselle Jeanne that her portrait, or something like it, was to be seen at the Salon—discreetly, of course, and as if it were the merest piece of news.

What a plucky, clever little woman it is! Surely I was inspired when I did her that service. I never thought I should be repaid. And here I am repaid both capital and interest.

Yet I hesitated. She snatched my consent.

"No, no," said she, "leave me to act. I promise you, Monsieur Mouillard, that she shall hear of it, and you, Monsieur Lampron, that the picture shall be framed."

She showed us to the top of the stairs, did little Madame Plumet, pleased at having won over her husband, at having shown herself so cunning, and at being employed in a conspiracy of love. In the street Lampron shook me by the hand. "Good-by, my friend," he said; "happy men don't need company. Four days hence, at noon, I shall come to fetch you, and we will pay our first visit to the Salon together."

Yes, I was a happy man! I walked fast, without seeing anything, my eyes lost in day dreams, my ears listening to celestial harmonies. I seemed to wear a halo. It abashed me somewhat; for there is something

6

insolent in proclaiming on the housetops: "Look up at me, my heart is full, Jeanne is going to love me!" Decidedly, my brain was affected.

Near the fountain in the Luxembourg, in front of the old palace where the senate sits, two little girls were playing. One pushed the other, who fell down crying, "Naughty Jeanne, naughty girl!" I rushed to pick her up, and kissed her before the eyes of her astonished nurse, saying, "No, Mademoiselle, she is the most charming girl in the world!"

And M. Legrand! I still blush when I think of my conversation with M. Legrand. He was standing in a dignified attitude at the door of his shop:

"ITALIAN WAREHOUSE; DRESSED PROVISIONS;
SPECIALTY IN COLONIAL PRODUCE."

He and I are upon good terms; I buy oranges, licorice from him, and rum when I want to make punch. But there are distinctions. Well, to-day I called him "Dear Monsieur Legrand;" I addressed him, though I had nothing to buy; I asked after his business; I remarked to him, "What a heavenly day, Monsieur Legrand! We really have got fine weather at last!"

He looked up to the top of the street, and looked down again at me, but refrained from differing, out of respect.

And, as a matter of fact, I noticed afterward that there was a most unpleasant drizzle.

To wind up with, just now as I was coming home after dinner, I passed a workman and his family in the Rue Bonaparte, and the man pointed after me, saying:

"Look! there goes a poet."

THE INK-STAIN

He was right. In me the lawyer's clerk is in abeyance, the lawyer of to-morrow has disappeared, only the poet is left—that is to say, the essence of youth freed from the parasitic growths of everyday life. I feel it roused and stirring. How sweet life is, and what wonderful instruments we are, that Hope can make us thus vibrate by a touch of her little finger!

CHAPTER VIII

JOY AND MADNESS

May 1st.

THESE four days have seemed as if they never would end—especially the last. But now it wants only two minutes of noon. In two minutes, if Lampron is not late——

Rat-a-tat-tat!

"Come in."

"It is twelve o'clock, my friend; are you coming?"

It was Lampron.

For the last hour I had had my hat on my head, my stick between my legs, and had been turning over my essay with gloved hands. He laughed at me. I don't care. We walked, for the day was clear and warm. All the world was out and about. Who can stay indoors on May Day? As we neared the Chamber of Deputies, perambulators full of babies in white capes came pouring from all the neighboring streets, and made their resplendent way toward the Tuileries. Lampron was in a talkative mood. He was pleased with the hanging of his pictures, and his plan of campaign against Mademoiselle Jeanne.

"She is sure to have heard of it, Fabien, and perhaps is there already. Who can tell?"

THE INK-STAIN

"Oh, cease your humbug! Yes, very possibly she is there before us. I have had a feeling that she would be for these last four days."

"You don't say so!"

"I have pictured her a score of times ascending the staircase on her father's arm. We are at the foot, lost in the crowd. Her noble, clear-cut profile stands out against the Gobelin tapestries which frame it with their embroidered flowers; one would say some maiden of bygone days had come to life, and stepped down from her tapestried panel."

"Gentlemen!" said Lampron, with a sweep of his arm which took in the whole of the Place de la Concorde, "allow me to present to you the intending successor of Counsellor Mouillard, lawyer, of Bourges. Every inch of him a man of business!"

We were getting near. Crowds were on their way to the exhibition from all sides, women in spring frocks, many of the men in white waistcoats, one hand in pocket, gayly flourishing their canes with the other, as much as to say, "Look at me—well-to-do, jaunty, and out in fine weather." The turnstiles were crowded, but at last we got through. We made but one step across the gravel court, the realm of sculpture where antique gods in every posture formed a mythological circle round the modern busts in the central walk. There was no loitering here, for my heart was elsewhere. We cast a look at an old wounded Gaul, an ancestor unhonored by the crowd, and started up the staircase—no Jeanne to lead the way. We came to the first room of paintings. Sylvestre beamed like a man who feels at home.

[85]

"Quick, Sylvestre, where is the sketch? Let's hurry to it."

But he dragged me with him around several rooms.

Have you ever experienced the intoxication of color which seizes the uninitiated at the door of a picture-gallery? So many staring hues impinge upon the eyes, so many ideas take confused shape and struggle together in the brain, that the eyes grow weary and the brain harassed. It hovers undecided like an insect in a meadow full of flowers. The buzzing remarks of the crowd add to the feeling of intoxication. They distract one's attention before it can settle anywhere, and carry it off to where some group is gathered before a great name, a costly frame, an enormous canvas, or an outrage on taste; twenty men on a gallows against a yellow sky, with twenty crows hovering over them, or an aged antediluvian, some mighty hunter, completely nude and with no property beyond a loaded club. One turns away, and the struggle begins again between the eye, attracted by a hundred subjects, and the brain, which would prefer to study one.

With Lampron this danger has no existence; he takes in a room at a glance. He has the sportsman's eye which, in a covey of partridges, marks its bird at a glance. He never hesitates. "That is the thing to make for," he says, "come along"—and we make for it. He plants himself right in front of the picture, with both hands in his overcoat pockets, and his chin sunk in his collar; says nothing, but is quite happy developing an idea which has occurred to him on his way to it; comparing the picture before him with some former work by the same artist which he remembers. His whole soul is concentrated on the picture. And when he considers that I have understood and penetrated the meaning of the work, he gives his opinion in few words, but always the right ones, summing up a long sequence of ideas which I must have shared with him, since I see exactly as he does.

In this way we halted before the "Martyrdom of Saint Denis," by Bonnat, the two "Adorations," by Bouguereau, a landscape of Bernier's, some other landscapes, sea pieces, and portraits.

At last we left the oil paintings.

In the open gallery, which runs around the inside of the huge oblong and looks on the court, the water-colors, engravings, and drawings slumbered, neglected. Lampron went straight to his works. I should have awarded them the *médaille d'honneur;* an etching of a man's head, a large engraving of the Virgin and Infant Jesus from the Salon Carré at the Louvre, and the drawing which represents——

"Great Heavens! Sylvestre, she's perfectly lovely; she will make a great mistake if she does not come and see herself!"

"She will come, my dear sir; but I shall not be there to see her."

"Are you going?"

"I leave you to stalk your game; be patient, and do not forget to come and tell me the news this evening."

"I promise."

And Lampron vanished.

The drawing was hung about midway between two

doorways draped with curtains, that opened into the big galleries. I leaned against the woodwork of one of them, and waited. On my left stretched a solitude seldom troubled by the few visitors who risk themselves in the realms of pen and pencil. These, too, only came to get fresh air, or to look down on the many-colored crowd moving among the white statues below.

At my right, on the contrary, the battling currents of the crowd kept passing and repassing, the provincial element easily distinguished by its jaded demeanor. Stout, exhausted matrons, breathless fathers of families, crowded the sofas, raising discouraged glances to the walls, while around them turned and tripped, untiring as at a dance, legions of Parisiennes, at ease, on their high heels, equally attentive to the pictures, their own carriage, and their neighbors' gowns.

O peaceful functionaries, you whose business it is to keep an eye upon this ferment! unless the ceaseless flux of these human phenomena lull you to a trance, what a quantity of silly speeches you must hear! I picked up twenty in as many minutes.

Suddenly there came a sound of little footsteps in the gallery. Two little girls had just come in, two sisters, doubtless, for both had the same black eyes, pink dresses, and white feathers in their hats. Hesitating, with outstretched necks, like fawns on the border of a glade, they seemed disappointed at the unexpected length of the gallery. They looked at each other and whispered. Then both smiled, and turning their backs on each other, they set off, one to the right, the other to the left, to examine the drawings which covered the walls. They made a rapid examination, with which art had obviously little to do; they were looking for something, and I thought it might be for Jeanne's portrait. And so it turned out; the one on my side soon came to a stop, pointed a finger to the wall, and gave a little cry. The other ran up; they clapped their hands.

"Bravo, bravo!"

Then off they went again through the farther door.

I guessed what they were about to do.

I trembled from head to foot, and hid myself farther behind the curtains.

Not a minute elapsed before they were back, not two this time, but three, and the third was Jeanne, whom they were pulling along between them.

They brought her up to Lampron's sketch, and curtsied neatly to her.

Jeanne bent down, smiled, and seemed pleased. Then, a doubt seizing her, she turned her head and saw me. The smile died away; she blushed, a tear seemed ready to start to her eyes. Oh, rapture! Jeanne, you are touched; Jeanne, you understand!

A deep joy surged across my soul, so deep that I never have felt its like.

Alas! at that instant some one called, "Jeanne!"

She stood up, took the two little girls by the hand, and was gone.

Far better had it been had I too fled, carrying with me that dream of delight!

But no, I leaned forward to look after them. In the doorway beyond I saw M. Charnot. A young man

was with him, who spoke to Jeanne. She answered
him. Three words reached me:

"It's nothing, George."

The devil! She loves another!

May 2d.

In what a state of mind did I set out this morning
to face my examiners! Downhearted, worn out by a
night of misery, indifferent to all that might befall me,
whether for good or for evil.

I considered myself, and indeed I was, very wretched,
but I never thought that I should return more wretched
than I went.

It was lovely weather when at half past eleven I
started for the Law School with an annotated copy of
my essay under my arm, thinking more of the regrets for
the past and plans for the future with which I had
wrestled all night, than of the ordeal I was about to
undergo. I met in the Luxembourg the little girl whom
I had kissed the week before. She stopped her hoop
and stood in my way, staring with wide-open eyes and
a coaxing, cunning look, which meant, "I know you, I
do!" I passed by without noticing. She pouted her
lip, and I saw that she was thinking, "What's the matter with him?"

What was the matter? My poor little golden-locks,
when you are grown a fair woman I trust you may know
as little of it as you do to-day.

I went up the Rue Soufflot, and entered the stuffy
courtyard on the stroke of noon.

The morning lectures were over. Beneath the arcades a few scattered students were walking up and

down. I avoided them for fear of meeting a friend and having to talk. Several professors came running from their lunch, rather red in the face, at the summons of the secretary. These were my examiners.

It was time to get into costume, for the candidate, like the criminal, has his costume. The old usher, who has dressed me up I don't know how many times in his hired gowns, saw that I was downcast, and thought I must be suffering from examination fever, a peculiar malady, which is like what a young soldier feels the first time he is under fire.

We were alone in the dark robing-room; he walked round me, brushing and encouraging me; doctors of law have a moral right to this touch of the brush.

"It will be all right, Monsieur Mouillard, never fear. No one has been refused a degree this morning."

"I am not afraid, Michu."

"When I say 'no one,' there was *one* refused—you never heard the like. Just imagine—a little to the right, please, Monsieur Mouillard—imagine, I say, a candidate who knew absolutely nothing. That is nothing extraordinary. But this fellow, after the examination was over, recommended himself to mercy. 'Have compassion on me, gentlemen,' he said, 'I only wish to be a magistrate!' Capital, isn't it?"

"Yes, yes."

"You don't seem to think so. You don't look like laughing this morning."

"No, Michu, every one has his bothers, you know."

"I said to myself as I looked at you just now, Monsieur Mouillard has some bother. Button up all the

[91]

way, if you please, for a doctor's essay; if—you—please.
It's a heartache, then?"

"Something of the kind."

He shrugged his shoulders and went before me,
struggling with an asthmatic chuckle, until we came
to the room set apart for the examination.

It was the smallest and darkest of all, and borrowed
its light from a street which had little enough to spare,
and spared as little as it could. On the left against the
wall is a raised desk for the candidate. At the end, on a
platform before a bookcase, sit the six examiners in red
robes, capes with three bands of ermine, and gold-laced
caps. Between the candidate's desk and the door is a
little enclosure for spectators, of whom there were about
thirty when I entered.

My performance, which had a chance of being brilliant, was only fair.

The three first examiners had read my essay, especially M. Flamaran, who knew it well and had
enjoyed its novel and audacious propositions. He
pursed up his mouth preparatory to putting the first
question, like an epicure sucking a ripe fruit. And
when at length he opened it, amid the general silence,
it was to carry the discussion at once up to such heights
of abstraction that a good number of the audience, not
understanding a word of it, stealthily made for the
door.

Each successive answer put fresh spirit into him.

"Very good," he murmured, "very good; let us carry
it a step farther. Now supposing——"

And, the demon of logic at his heels, we both went

off like inspired lunatics into a world of hypotheses where never man had set foot. He was examining no longer, he was inventing and intoxicating himself with deductions. No one was right or wrong. We were reasoning about chimeras, he radiant, I cool, before his gently tickled colleagues. I never realized till then what imagination a jurist's head could contain.

Perspiring freely, he set down a white mark, having exceeded by ten minutes the recognized time for examination.

The second examiner was less enthusiastic. He made very few suppositions, and devoted all his art to convicting me of a contradiction between page seventeen and page seventy-nine. He kept repeating, "It's a serious matter, sir, very serious." But, nevertheless, he bestowed a second white mark on me. I only got half white from the third. The rest of the examination was taken up in matters extraneous to the subject of my essay, a commonplace trial of strength, in which I replied with threadbare arguments to outworn objections.

And then it ended. Two hours had passed.

I left the room while the examiners made up their minds.

A few friends came up to me.

"Congratulations, old man, I bet on six whites."

"Hallo, Larivé! I never noticed you."

"I quite believe you; you didn't notice anybody, you still look bewildered. Is it the emotion inseparable from——"

"I dare say."

"The candidate is requested to return to the examination-room!" said the usher.

And old Michu added, in a whisper, "You have passed. I told you so. You won't forget old Michu, sir."

M. Flamaran conferred my degree with a paternal smile, and a few kind words for "this conscientious study, full of fresh ideas on a difficult subject."

I bowed to the examiners. Larivé was waiting for me in the courtyard, and seized me by the arm.

"Uncle Mouillard *will* be pleased."

"I suppose so."

"Better pleased than you."

"That's very likely."

"He might easily be that. Upon my word I can't understand you. These two years you have been working like a gang of niggers for your degree, and now you have got it you don't seem to care a bit. You have won a smile from Flamaran and do not consider yourself a spoiled child of Fortune! What more did you want? Did you expect that Mademoiselle Charnot would come in person——"

"Look here, Larivé——"

"To look on at your examination, and applaud your answers with her neatly gloved hands? Surely you know, my dear fellow, that that is no longer possible, and that she is going to be married."

"Going to be married?"

"Don't pretend you didn't know it."

"I have suspected as much since yesterday; I met her at the Salon, and saw a young man with her."

THE INK-STAIN

"Fair?"

"Yes."

"Tall?"

"Rather."

"Good-looking?"

"H'm—well——"

"Dufilleul, old chap, friend Dufilleul. Don't you know Dufilleul?"

"No."

"Oh, yes you do—a bit of a stockjobber, great at écarté, studied law in our year, and is always to be seen at the Opéra with little Tigra of the Bouffes."

"Poor girl!"

"You pity her?"

"It's too awful."

"What is?"

"To see an unhappy child married to a rake who——"

"She will not be the first."

"A gambler!"

"Yes, there *is* that, to be sure."

"A fool, as it seems, who, in exchange for her beauty, grace, and youth, can offer only an assortment of damaged goods! Yes, I do pity girls duped thus, deceived and sacrificed by the very purity that makes them believe in that of others."

"You've some queer notions! It's the way of the world. If the innocent victims were only to marry males of equal innocence, under the guardianship of virtuous parents, the days of this world would be numbered, my boy. I assure you that Dufilleul is a good match, handsome for one thing——"

[95]

"That's worth a deal!"

"Rich."

"The deuce he is!"

"And then a name which can be divided."

"Divided?"

"With all the ease in the world. A very rare quality. At his marriage he describes himself as Monsieur du Filleul. A year later he is Baron du Filleul. At the death of his father, an old cad, he becomes Comte du Filleul. If the young wife is pretty and knows how to cajole her husband, she may even become a marquise."

"Ugh!"

"You are out of spirits, my poor fellow; I will stand you an absinthe, the only beverage that will suit the bitterness of your heart."

"No, I shall go home."

"Good-by, then. You don't take your degree cheerfully."

"Good-by."

He spun round on his heels and went down the Boulevard St. Michel.

So all is over forever between her and me, and, saddest of all, she is even more to be pitied than I. Poor girl! I loved her deeply, but I did it awkwardly, as I do everything, and missed my chance of speaking. The mute declaration which I risked, or rather which a friend risked for me, found her already engaged to this beast who has brought more skill to the task, who has made no blots at the National Library, who has dared all when he had everything to fear——

I have allowed myself to be taken by her maiden

witchery. All the fault, all the folly is mine. She has given me no encouragement, no sign of liking me. If she smiled at St. Germain it was because she was surprised and flattered. If she came near to tears at the Salon it was because she pitied me. I have not the shadow of a reproach to make her.

That is all I shall ever get from her—a tear, a smile. That's all; never mind, I shall contrive to live on it. She has been my first love, and I shall keep her a place in my heart from which no other shall drive her. I shall now set to work to shut this poor heart which did so wrong to open. . . . I thought to be happy to-night, and I am full of sorrow. Henceforward I think I shall understand Sylvestre better. Our sorrows will bring us nearer. I will go to see him at once, and will tell him so.

But first I must write to my uncle to tell him that his nephew is a Doctor of Law. All the rest, my plans, my whole future can be put off till to-morrow, or the day after, unless I get disgusted at the very thought of a future and decide to conjugate my life in the present indicative only. That is what I feel inclined to do.

May 4th.

Lampron has gone to the country to pass a fortnight in an out-of-the-way place with an old relative, where he goes into hiding when he wishes to finish an engraving.

But Madame Lampron was at home. After a little hesitation I told her all, and I am glad I did so. She found in her simple, womanly heart just the counsel

that I needed. One feels that she is used to giving consolation. She possesses the secret of that feminine
deftness which is the great set-off to feminine weakness.
Weak? Yes, women perhaps are weak, yet less weak
than we, the strong sex, for they can raise us to our
feet. She called me, "My dear Monsieur Fabien,"
and there was balm in the very way she said the words.
I used to think she wanted refinement; she does not, she
only lacks reading, and lack of reading may go with the
most delicate and lofty feelings. No one ever taught
her certain turns of expression which she used. "If
your mother was alive," said she, "this is what she
would say." And then she spoke to me of God, who
alone can determinate man's trials, either by the end He
ordains, or the resignation He inspires. I felt myself
carried with her into the regions where our sorrows
shrink into insignificance as the horizon broadens
around them. And I remember she uttered this fine
thought, "See how my son has suffered! It makes one
believe, Monsieur Fabien, that the elect of the earth
are the hardest tried, just as the stones that crown the
building are more deeply cut than their fellows."

I returned from Madame Lampron's, softened,
calmer, wiser.

CHAPTER IX

A VISIT FROM MY UNCLE

May 5th.

A LETTER from M. Mouillard breathing fire and fury. Were I not so low-spirited I could laugh at it.

He would have liked me, after taking my degree at two in the afternoon, to take the train for Bourges the same evening, where my uncle, his practice, and provincial bliss awaited me. M. Mouillard's friends had had due notice, and would have come to meet me at the station. In short, I am an ungrateful wretch. At least I might have fixed the hour of my imminent arrival, for I can not want to stop in Paris with nothing there to detain me. But no, not a sign, not a word of returning; simply the announcement that I have passed. This goes beyond the bounds of mere folly and carelessness. M. Mouillard, his most elementary notions of life shaken to their foundations, concludes in these words:

"Fabien, I have long suspected it; some creature has you in bondage. I am coming to break the bonds!

"BRUTUS MOUILLARD."

I know him well; he will be here to-morrow.

[99]

RENÉ BAZIN

No uncle as yet.

No more uncle than yesterday.

Total eclipse continues. No news of M. Mouillard.
This is very strange.

This evening at seven o'clock, just as I was going out
to dine, I saw, a few yards away, a tall, broad-brimmed
hat surmounting a head of lank white hair, a long neck
throttled in a white neckcloth, a frock-coat flapping
about a pair of attenuated legs. I lifted up my voice:
"Uncle!"
He opened his arms to me and I fell into them. His
first remark was:
"I trust at least that you have not yet dined."
"No, uncle."
"To Foyot's, then!"
When you expect to meet a man in his wrath and get
an invitation to dinner, you feel almost as if you had
been taken in. You are heated, your arguments are
at your fingers' ends, your stock of petulance is ready
for immediate use; and all have to be stored in bond.
When I had recovered from my surprise, I said:
"I expected you sooner, from your letter."
"Your suppositions were correct. I have been two
days here, at the Grand Hôtel. I went there on account
of the dining-room, for my friend Hublette (you remember Hublette at Bourges) told me: 'Mouillard,

you must see that room before you retire from business.' "

"I should have gone to see you there, uncle, if I had known it."

"You would not have found me. Business before pleasure, Fabien. I had to see three barristers and five solicitors. You know that business of that kind can not wait. I saw them. Business over, I can indulge my feelings. Here I am. Does Foyot suit you?"

"Certainly, uncle."

"Come on, then, nephew, quick, march! Paris makes one feel quite young again!"

And really Uncle Mouillard did look quite young, almost as young as he looked provincial. His tall figure, and the countrified cut of his coat, made all who passed him turn to stare, accustomed as Parisians are to curiosities. He tapped the wood pavement with his stick, admired the effects of Wallace's philanthropy, stopped before the enamelled street-signs, and grew enthusiastic over the traffic in the Rue de Vaugirard.

The dinner was capital—just the kind a generous uncle will give to a blameless nephew. M. Mouillard, who has a long standing affection for chambertin, ordered two bottles to begin with. He drank the whole of one and half of the other, eating in proportion, and talked unceasingly and positively at the top of his voice, as his wont was. He told me the story of two of his best actions this year, a judicial separation—my uncle is very strong in judicial separations—and the abduction of a minor. At first I looked out for personal allusions. But no, he told the story from pure love of his art, without omitting an interlocutory judgment, or a judgment reserved, just as he would have told the story of Helen and Paris, if he had been employed in that well-known case. Not a word about myself. I waited, yet nothing came but the successive steps in the action.

After the ice, M. Mouillard called for a cigar.

"Waiter, what cigars have you got?"

"Londres, conchas, regalias, caçadores, partagas, esceptionales. Which would you like, sir?"

"Damn the name! a big one that will take some time to smoke."

Emile displayed at the bottom of a box an object closely resembling a distaff with a straw through the middle, doubtless some relic of the last International Exhibition, abandoned by all, like the *Great Eastern*, on account of its dimensions. My uncle seized it, stuck it in the amber mouthpiece that is so familiar to me, lighted it, and under the pretext that you must always first get the tobacco to burn evenly, went out trailing behind him a cloud of smoke, like a gunboat at full speed.

We "did" the arcades round the Odéon, where my uncle spent an eternity thumbing the books for sale. He took them all up one after another, from the poetry of the *décadents* to the *Veterinary Manual*, gave a glance at the author's name, shrugged his shoulders, and always ended by turning to me with:

"You know that writer?"

"Why, yes, uncle."

THE INK-STAIN

"He must be quite a new author; I can't recall that name."

M. Mouillard forgot that it was forty-five years since he had last visited the bookstalls under the Odéon.

He thought he was a student again, loafing along the arcades after dinner, eager for novelty, careless of draughts. Little by little he lost himself in dim reveries. His cigar never left his lips. The ash grew longer and longer yet, a lovely white ash, slightly swollen at the tip, dotted with little black specks, and connected with the cigar by a thin red band which alternately glowed and faded as he drew his breath.

M. Mouillard was so lost in thought, and the ash was getting so long, that a young student—of the age that knows no mercy—was struck by these twin phenomena. I saw him nudge a friend, hastily roll a cigarette, and, doffing his hat, accost my uncle.

"Might I trouble you for a light, sir!"

M. Mouillard emitted a sigh, turned slowly round, and bent two terrible eyes upon the intruder, knocked off the ash with an angry gesture, and held out the ignited end at arm's length.

"With pleasure, sir!"

Then he replaced the last book he had taken up—a copy of Musset—and called me.

"Come, Fabien."

Arm in arm we strolled up the Rue de Médicis along the railings of the Luxembourg.

I felt the crisis approaching. My uncle has a pet saying: "When a thing is not clear to me, I go straight to the heart of it like a ferret."

[103]

The ferret began to work.

"Now, Fabien, about these bonds I mentioned? Did I guess right?"

"Yes, uncle, I have been in bondage."

"Quite right to make a clean breast of it, my boy; but we must break your bonds."

"They are broken."

"How long ago?"

"Some days ago."

"On your honor?"

"Yes."

"That's quite right. You'd have done better to keep out of bondage. But there, you took your uncle's advice; you saw the abyss, and drew back from it. Quite right of you."

"Uncle, I will not deceive you. Your letter arrived after the event. The cause of the rupture was quite apart from that."

"And the cause was?"

"The sudden shattering of my illusions."

"Men still have illusions about these creatures?"

"She was a perfect creature, and worthy of all respect."

"Come, come!"

"I must ask you to believe me. I thought her affections free."

"And she was——"

"Betrothed."

"Really now, that's very funny!"

"I did not find it funny, uncle. I suffered bitterly, I assure you."

THE INK-STAIN

"I dare say, I dare say. The illusions you spoke
of—— Anyhow, it's all over now?"

"Quite over."

"Well, that being the case, Fabien, I am ready to
help you. Confess frankly to me. How much is required?"

"How much?"

"Yes, you want something, I dare say, to close the
incident. You know what I mean, eh? to purchase
what I might call the veil of oblivion. How much?"

"Why, nothing at all, uncle."

"Don't be afraid, Fabien; I've got the money with
me."

"You have quite mistaken the case, uncle; there is
no question of money. I must tell you again that the
young lady is of the highest respectability."

My uncle stared.

"I assure you, uncle. I am speaking of Mademoiselle Jeanne Charnot."

"I *dare* say."

"The daughter of a member of the Institute."

"What!"

My uncle gave a jump and stood still.

"Yes, of Mademoiselle Charnot, whom I was in love
with and wished to marry. Do you understand?"

He leaned against the railing and folded his arms.

"Marry! Well, I never! A woman you wanted to
marry?"

"Why, yes; what's the matter?"

"To marry! How could I have imagined such a
thing? Here were matters of the utmost importance

[105]

going on, and I knew nothing about them. Marry!
You might be announcing your betrothal to me at this
moment if you'd— Still you are quite sure she is betrothed?"

"Larivé told me so."

"Who's Larivé?"

"A friend of mine."

"Oh, so you have only heard it through a friend?"

"Yes, uncle. Do you really think there may still be
hope, that I still have a chance?"

"No, no; not the slightest. She is sure to be betrothed, very much betrothed. I tell you I am glad she
is. The Mouillards do not come to Paris for their
wives, Fabien—we do not want a Parisienne to carry
on the traditions of the family, and the practice. A
Parisienne! I shudder at the thought of it. Fabien,
you will leave Paris with me to-morrow. That's understood."

"Certainly not, uncle."

"Your reasons?"

"Because I can not leave my friends without saying
good-by, and because I have need to reflect before
definitely binding myself to the legal profession."

"To reflect! You want to reflect before taking over
a family practice, which has been destined for you
since you were an infant, in view of which you have
been working for five years, and which I have
nursed for you, I, your uncle, as if you had been my
son?"

"Yes, uncle."

"Don't be a fool! You can reflect at Bourges quite

as well as here. Your object in staying here is to see her again."

"It is not."

"To wander like a troubled spirit up and down her street. By the way, which is her street?"

"Rue de l'Université."

My uncle took out his pocketbook and made a note, "Charnot, Rue de l'Université." Then all his features expanded. He gave a snort, which I understood, for I had often heard it in court at Bourges, where it meant, "There is no escape now. Old Mouillard has cornered his man."

My uncle replaced his pencil in its case, and his note-book in his pocket, and merely added:

"Fabien, you're not yourself to-night. We'll talk of the matter another time. Five, six, seven, eight, nine, ten." He was counting on his fingers. "These return tickets are very convenient; I need not leave before to-morrow evening. And, what's more, you'll go with me, my boy."

M. Mouillard talked only on indifferent subjects during our brief walk from the Rue Soufflot to catch the omnibus at the Odéon. There he shook me by the hand and sprang nimbly into the first bus. A lady in black, with veil tightly drawn over a little turned-up nose, seeing my uncle burst in like a bomb, and make for the seat beside her, hurriedly drew in the folds of her dress, which were spread over the seat. My uncle noticed her action, and, fearing he had been rude, bent over toward her with an affable expression. "Do not disturb yourself, Madame. I am not going all the way to Batignolles; no farther, indeed, than the Boulevards. I shall inconvenience you for a few moments only, a very few moments, Madame." I had time to remark that the lady, after giving her neighbor a glance of Juno-like disdain, turned her back upon him, and proceeded to study the straps hanging from the roof.

The brake was taken off, the conductor whistled, the three horses, their hoofs hammering the pavement, strained for an instant amid showers of sparks, and the long vehicle vanished down the Rue de Vaugirard, bearing with it Brutus and his fortunes.

CHAPTER X

A FAMILY BREACH

T is an awful fate to be the nephew of M. Mouillard! I always knew he was obstinate, capable alike of guile and daring, but I little imagined what his intentions were when he left me!

My refusal to start, and my prayer for a respite before embarking in his practice, drove him wild. He lost his head, and swore to drag me off, *per fas et nefas*. He has mentally begun a new action—Mouillard *v.* Mouillard, and is already tackling the brief; which is as much as to say that he is fierce, unbridled, heartless, and without remorse.

Some might have bent. I preferred to break.

We are strangers for life. I have just seen him to the landing of my staircase.

He came here about a quarter of an hour ago, proud, and, I may say, swaggering, as he does over his learned friends when he has found a flaw in one of their pleadings.

"Well, nephew?"

"Well, uncle?"

"I've got some news for you."

"Indeed?"

M. Mouillard banged his hat down furiously upon my table.

"Yes, you know my maxim: when anything does not
seem quite clear to me——"

"You ferret it out."

"Quite so; I have always found it answer. Your
business did not seem clear to me. Was Mademoiselle
Charnot betrothed, or was she not? To what extent
had she encouraged your attentions? You never would
have told me the story correctly, and I never should have
known. That being so, I put my maxim into practice,
and went to see her father."

"You did that?"

"Certainly I did."

"You have been to see Monsieur Charnot?"

"In the Rue de l'Université. Wasn't it the simplest
thing to do? Besides, I was not sorry to make the acquaintance of a member of the Institute. And I must
admit that he behaved very nicely to me—not a bit
stuck up."

"And you told him?"

"My name to begin with: Brutus Mouillard. He
reflected a bit, just a moment, and recalled your appearance: a shy youth, a bachelor of arts, wearing an
eyeglass."

"Was that all his description?"

"Yes, he remembered seeing you at the National
Library, and once at his house. I said to him, 'That
is my nephew, Monsieur Charnot.' He replied, 'I con-

gratulate you, sir; he seems a youth of parts.' 'That
he is, but his heart is very inflammable.' 'At his age,
sir, who is not liable to take fire?' That was how we
began. Your friend Monsieur Charnot has a pretty
wit. I did not want to be behindhand with him, so
I answered, 'Well, sir, it caught fire in your house.'
He started with fright and looked all round the room.
I was vastly amused. Then we came to explanations.
I put the case before him, that you were in love with
his daughter, without my consent, but with perfectly
honorable intentions; that I had guessed it from your
letters, from your unpardonable neglect of your duties
to your family, and that I hurried hither from Bourges
to take in the situation. With that I concluded, and
waited for him to develop. There are occasions when
you must let people develop. I could not jump down
his throat with, 'Sir, would you kindly tell me whether
your daughter is betrothed or not?' You follow me?
He thought, no doubt, I had come to ask for his daughter's hand, and passing one hand over his forehead, he
replied, 'Sir, I feel greatly flattered by your proposal,
and I should certainly give it my serious attention, were
it not that my daughter's hand is already sought by the
son of an old schoolfellow of mine, which circumstance,
as you will readily understand, does not permit of my
entertaining an offer which otherwise should have received the most mature consideration.' I had learned
what I came for without risking anything. Well, I
didn't conceal from him that, so far as I was concerned,
I would rather you took your wife from the country than
that you brought home the most charming Parisienne;

and that the Mouillards from father to son had always taken their wives from Bourges. He entered perfectly into my sentiments, and we parted the best of friends. Now, my boy, the facts are ascertained: Mademoiselle Charnot is another's; you must get your mourning over and start with me to-night. To-morrow morning we shall be in Bourges, and you'll soon be laughing over your Parisian delusions, I warrant you!"

I had heard my uncle out without interrupting him, though wrath, astonishment, and my habitual respect for M. Mouillard were struggling for the mastery within me. I needed all my strength of mind to answer, with apparent calm.

"Yesterday, uncle, I had not made up my mind; to-day I have."

"You are coming?"

"I am not. Your action in this matter, uncle—I do not know if you are aware of it—has been perfectly unheard-of. I can not acknowledge your right to act thus. It puts between you and me two hundred miles of rail, and that forever. Do you understand me? You have taken the liberty of disclosing a secret which was not yours to tell; you have revealed a passion which, as it was hopeless, should not have been further mentioned, and certainly not exposed to such humiliation. You went to see Monsieur Charnot without reflecting whether you were not bringing trouble into his household; without reflecting, further, whether such conduct as yours, which may perhaps be usual among your business acquaintances, was likely to succeed with me. Perhaps you thought it would. You have merely completed an experiment, begun long ago, which proves that we do not understand life in the same way, and that it will be better for both of us if I continue to live in Paris, and you continue to live at Bourges."

"Ha! that's how you take it, young man, is it? You refuse to come? you try to bully me?"

"Yes."

"Consider carefully before you let me leave here alone. You know the amount of your fortune—fourteen hundred francs a year, which means poverty in Paris."

"Yes, I do."

"Well, then, attend to what I am about to say. For years past I have been saving my practice for you— that is, an honorable and lucrative position all ready for you to step into. But I am tired at length of your fads and your fancies. If you do not take up your quarters at Bourges within a fortnight from now, the Mouillard practice will change its name within three weeks!" My uncle sniffed with emotion as he looked at me, expecting to see me totter beneath his threats. I made no answer for a moment; but a thought which had been harassing me from the beginning of our interview compelled me to say:

"I have only one thing to ask you, Monsieur Mouillard."

"Further respite, I suppose? Time to reflect and fool me again? No, a hundred times no! I've had enough of you; a fortnight, not a day more!"

"No, sir; I do not ask for respite."

"So much the better, for I should refuse it. What do you want?"

"Monsieur Mouillard, I trust that Jeanne was not present at the interview, that she heard none of it, that she was not forced to blush——"

My uncle sprang to his feet, seized his gloves, which lay spread out on the table, bundled them up, flung them passionately into his hat, clapped the whole on his head, and made for the door with angry strides.

I followed him; he never looked back, never made answer to my "Good-by, uncle." But, at the sixth step, just before turning the corner, he raised his stick, gave the banisters a blow fit to break them, and went on his way downstairs exclaiming:

"Damnation!"

May 20th.

And so we have parted with an oath, my uncle and I! That is how I have broken with the only relative I possess. It is now ten days since then. I now have five left in which to mend the broken thread of the family tradition, and become a lawyer. But nothing points to such conversion. On the contrary, I feel relieved of a heavy weight, pleased to be free, to have no profession. I feel the thrill of pleasure that a fugitive from justice feels on clearing the frontier. Perhaps I was meant for a different course of life than the one I was forced to follow. As a child I was brought up to worship the Mouillard practice, with the fixed idea that this profession alone could suit me; heir apparent to a lawyer's stool —born to it, brought up to it, without any idea, at any rate for a long time, that I could possibly free myself from the traditions of the law's sacred jargon.

I have quite got over that now. The courts, where

THE INK-STAIN

I have been a frequent spectator, seem to me full of talented men who fine down and belittle their talents in the practice of law. Nothing uses up the nobler virtues more quickly than a practice at the bar. Generosity, enthusiasm, sensibility, true and ready sympathy—all are taken, leaving the man, in many instances nothing but a skilful actor, who apes all the emotions while feeling none. And the comedy is none the less repugnant to me because it is played through with a solemn face, and the actors are richly recompensed.

Lampron is not like this. He has given play to all the noble qualities of his nature. I envy him. I admire his disinterestedness, his broad views of life, his faith in good in spite of evil, his belief in poetry in spite of prose, his unspoiled capacity for receiving new impressions and illusions—a capacity which, amid the crowds that grow old in mind before they are old in body, keeps him still young and boyish. I think I might have been devoted to his profession, or to literature, or to anything but law.

We shall see. For the present I have taken a plunge into the unknown. My time is all my own, my freedom is absolute, and I am enjoying it.

I have hidden nothing from Lampron. As my friend he is pleased, I can see, at a resolve which keeps me in Paris; but his prudence cries out upon it.

"It is easy enough to refuse a profession," he said; "harder to find another in its place. What do you intend to do?"

"I don't know."

"My dear fellow, you seem to be trusting to luck

At sixteen that might be permissible, at twenty-four it's a mistake."

"So much the worse, for I shall make the mistake. If I have to live on little—well, you've tried that before now; I shall only be following you."

"That's true; I have known want, and even now it attacks me sometimes; it's like influenza, which does not leave its victims all at once; but it is hard, I can tell you, to do without the necessaries of life; as for its luxuries——"

"Oh, of course, no one can do without its luxuries."

"You are incorrigible," he answered, with a laugh. Then he said no more. Lampron's silence is the only argument which struggles in my heart in favor of the Mouillard practice. Who can guess from what quarter the wind will blow?

CHAPTER XI

IN THE BEATEN PATH

June 5th.

THE die is cast; I will not be a lawyer. The tradition of the Mouillards is broken for good, Sylvestre is defeated for good, and I am free for good—and quite uncertain of my future.

I have written my uncle a calm, polite, and clearly worded letter to confirm my decision. He has not answered it, nor did I expect an answer.

I expected, however, that he would be avenged by some faint regret on my part, by one of those light mists that so often arise and hang about our firmest resolutions. But no such mist has arisen.

Still, Law has had her revenge. Abandoned at Bourges, she has recaptured me at Paris, for a time. I realized that it was impossible for me to live on an income of fourteen hundred francs. The friends whom I discreetly questioned, in behalf of an unnamed acquaintance, as to the means of earning money, gave me various answers. Here is a fairly complete list of their expedients:

"If your friend is at all clever, he should write a novel."

"If he is not, there is the catalogue of the National Library: ten hours of indexing a day."

"If he has ambition, let him become a wine-merchant."

"No; 'Old Clo,' and get his hats gratis."

"If he is very plain, and has no voice, he can sing in the chorus at the opera."

"Shorthand writer in the Senate is a peaceful occupation."

"Teacher of Volapük is the profession of the future."

"Try 'Hallo, are you there?' in the telephones."

"Wants to earn money? Advise him first not to lose any!"

The most sensible one, who guessed the name of the acquaintance I was interested in, said:

"You have been a managing clerk; go back to it."

And as the situation chanced to be vacant, I went back to my old master. I took my old seat and den as managing clerk between the outer office and Counsellor Boule's glass cage. I correct the drafts of the inferior clerks; I see the clients and instruct them how to proceed. They often take me for the counsellor himself. I go to the courts nearly every day, and hang about chief clerks' and judges' chambers; and go to the theatre once a week with the "paper" supplied to the office.

Do I call this a profession? No, merely a stop-gap which allows me to live and wait for something to turn up. I sometimes have forebodings that I shall go on like this forever, waiting for something which will never

turn up; that this temporary occupation may become
only too permanent.

There is an old clerk in the office who has never had
any other occupation, whose appearance is a kind of
warning to me. He has a red face—the effect of the
office stove, I think—straight, white hair, the expression
when spoken to of a startled sheep—gentle, astonished,
slightly flurried. His attenuated back is rounded off
with a stoop between the neck and shoulders. He can
hardly keep his hands from shaking. His signature
is a work of art. He can stick at his desk for six hours
without stirring. While we lunch at a restaurant, he
consumes at the office some nondescript provisions
which he brings in the morning in a paper bag. On
Sundays he fishes, for a change; his rod takes the place
of his pen, and his can of worms serves instead of inkstand.

He and I have already one point of resemblance.
The old clerk was once crossed in love with a flower-
girl, one Mademoiselle Elodie. He has told me this
one tragedy of his life. In days gone by I used to think
this thirty-year-old love-story dull and commonplace;
to-day I understand M. Jupille; I relish him even.
He and I have become sympathetic. I no longer make
him move from his seat by the fire when I want to ask
him a question: I go to him. On Sundays, on the quays
by the Seine, I pick him out from the crowd intent upon
the capture of tittlebats, because he is seated upon his
handkerchief. I go up to him and we have a talk.

"Fish biting, Monsieur Jupille?"

"Hardly at all."

"Sport is not what it used to be?"

"Ah! Monsieur Mouillard, if you could have seen it thirty years ago!"

This date is always cropping up with him. Have we not all our own date, a few months, a few days, perhaps a single hour of full-hearted joy, for which half our life has been a preparation, and of which the other half must be a remembrance?

June 5th.

"Monsieur Mouillard, here is an application for leave to sign judgment in a fresh matter."

"Very well, give it me."

"*To the President of the Civil Court:*

"Monsieur Plumet, of 27 Rue Hauteville, in the city of Paris, by Counsellor Boule, his advocate, craves leave——"

It was a proceeding against a refractory debtor, the commonest thing in the world.

"Monsieur Massinot!"

"Yes, sir."

"Who brought these papers?"

"A very pretty little woman brought them this morning while you were out, sir."

"Monsieur Massinot, whether she was pretty or not, it is no business of yours to criticise the looks of the clients."

"I did not mean to offend you, Monsieur Mouillard."

"You have not offended me, but you have no business to talk of a 'pretty client.' That epithet is not al-

lowed in a pleading, that's all. The lady is coming
back, I suppose?"

"Yes, sir."

Little Madame Plumet soon called again, tricked
out from head to foot in the latest fashion. She was
a little flurried on entering a room full of jocular clerks.
Escorted by Massinot, both of them with their eyes
fixed on the ground, she reached my office. I closed
the door after her. She recognized me.

"Monsieur Mouillard! What a pleasant surprise!"

She held out her hand to me so frankly and grace-
fully that I gave her mine, and felt sure, from the firm,
expressive way in which she clasped it, that Madame
Plumet was really pleased to see me. Her ruddy
cheeks and bright eyes recalled my first impression of
her, the little dressmaker running from the workshop
to the office, full of her love for M. Plumet and her
grievances against the wicked cabinet-maker.

"What, you are back again with Counsellor Boule?
I *am* surprised!"

"So am I, Madame Plumet, very much surprised.
But such is life! How is Master Pierre progressing?"

"Not quite so well, poor darling, since I weaned
him. I had to wean him, Monsieur Mouillard, because
I have gone back to my old trade."

"Dressmaking?"

"Yes, on my own account this time. I have taken
the flat opposite to ours, on the same floor. Plumet
makes frames, while I make gowns. I have already
three workgirls, and enough customers to give me a
start. I do not charge them very dear to begin with.

One of my customers was a very nice young lady—
you know who! I have not talked to her of you, but
I have often wanted to. By the way, Monsieur Mouillard, did I do my errand well?"

"What errand?"

"The important one, about the portrait at the Salon."

"Oh, yes; very well indeed. I must thank you."

"She came?"

"Yes, with her father."

"She must have been pleased! The drawing was
so pretty. Plumet, who is not much of a talker, is
never tired of praising it. I tell you, he and I did not
spare ourselves. He made a bit of a fuss before he
would take the order; he was in a hurry—*such* a hurry;
but when he saw that I was bent on it he gave in. And
it is not the first time he has given in. Plumet is a
good soul, Monsieur Mouillard. When you know him
better you will see what a good soul he is. Well, while
he was cutting out the frame, I went to the porter's
wife. What a business it was! I *am* glad my errand
was successful!"

"It was too good of you, Madame Plumet; but it
was useless, alas! she is to marry another."

"Marry another? Impossible!"

I thought Madame Plumet was about to faint. Had
she heard that her son Pierre had the croup, she could
not have been more upset. Her bosom heaved, she
clasped her hands, and gazed at me with sorrowful
compassion.

"Poor Monsieur Mouillard!"

And two tears, two real tears, coursed down Madame

Plumet's cheeks. I should have liked to catch them.
They were the only tears that had been shed for me
by a living soul since my mother died.

I had to tell her all, every word, down to my rival's
name. When she heard that it was Baron Dufilleul,
her indignation knew no bounds. She exclaimed that
the Baron was an awful man; that she knew all sorts of
things about him! Know him? she should think so!
That such a union was impossible, that it could never
take place, that Plumet, she knew, would agree with
her——

"Madame Plumet," I said, "we have strayed some
distance from the business which brought you here.
Let us return to your affairs; mine are hopeless, and
you can not remedy them."

She got up trembling, her eyes red and her feelings
a little hurt.

"My action? Oh, no! I can't attend to it to-day.
I've no heart to talk about my business. What you've
told me has made me too unhappy. Another day,
Monsieur Mouillard, another day."

She left me with a look of mystery, and a pressure
of the hand which seemed to say: "Rely on me!"

Poor woman!

CHAPTER XII

I GO TO ITALY

June 10th.

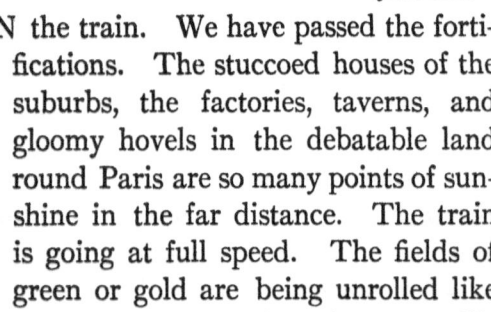N the train. We have passed the forti-
fications. The stuccoed houses of the
suburbs, the factories, taverns, and
gloomy hovels in the debatable land
round Paris are so many points of sunshine in the far distance. The train
is going at full speed. The fields of
green or gold are being unrolled like
ribbons before my eyes. Now and again a metallic
sound and a glimpse of columns and advertisements
show that we are rushing through a station in a whirlwind of dust. A flash of light across our path is a tribu-
tary of the river. I am off, well on my way, and no one
can stop me—not Lampron, nor Counsellor Boule,
nor yet Plumet. The dream of years is about to be
realized. I am going to see Italy—merely a corner of
it; but what a pleasure even that is, and what unlooked-
for luck!

A few days ago, Counsellor Boule called me into his
office.

"Monsieur Mouillard, you speak Italian fluently,
don't you?"

"Yes, sir."

"Would you like a trip at a client's expense?"

THE INK-STAIN

"With pleasure, wherever you like."

"To Italy?"

"With very great pleasure."

"I thought so, and gave your name to the court without asking your consent. It's a commission to examine documents at Milan, to prove some copies of deeds and other papers, put in by a supposititious Italian heir to establish his rights to a rather large property. You remember the case of Zampini against Veldon and others?"

"Quite well."

"It is Zampini's copies of the deeds on which he bases his claim which you will have to compare with the originals, with the help of a clerk from the Record Office and a sworn translator. You can go by Switzerland or by the Corniche route, as you please. You will be allowed six hundred francs and a fortnight's holiday. Does that suit you?"

"I should think so!"

"Then pack up and be off. You must be at Milan by the morning of the eighteenth."

I ran to tell the news to Lampron, who was filled with surprise and not a little emotion at the mention of Italy. And here I am flying along in the Lyons express, without a regret for Paris. All my heart leaps forward toward Switzerland, where I shall be to-morrow. I have chosen this green route to take me to the land of blue skies. Up to the last moment I feared that some obstacle would arise, that the ill-luck which dogs my footsteps would keep me back, and I am quite surprised that it has let me off. True, I nearly lost the train, and

the horse of cab No. 7382 must have been a retired
racer to make up for the loss of time caused by M.
Plumet.

Counsellor Boule sent me on a business errand an
hour before I started. On my way back, just as I was
crossing the Place de l'Opéra in the aforesaid cab, a
voice hailed me:

"Monsieur Mouillard!"

I looked first to the right and then to the left, till,
on a refuge, I caught sight of M. Plumet struggling to
attract my attention. I stopped the cab, and a smile
of satisfaction spread over M. Plumet's countenance.
He stepped off the refuge. I opened the cab-door.
But a brougham passed, and the horse pushed me
back into the cab with his nose. I opened the door a
second time; another brougham came by; then a third;
finally two serried lines of traffic cut me off from M.
Plumet, who kept shouting something to me which the
noise of the wheels and the crowd prevented me from
hearing. I signalled my despair to M. Plumet. He
rose on tiptoe. I could not hear any better.

Five minutes lost! Impossible to wait any longer!
Besides, who could tell that it was not a trap to prevent my departure, though in friendly guise? I shuddered at the thought and shouted:

"Gare de Lyon, cabby, as fast as you can drive!"

My orders were obeyed. We got to the station to
find the train made up and ready to start, and I was the
last to take a ticket.

I suppose M. Plumet managed to escape from his
refuge.

THE INK-STAIN

On my arrival I found, keeping order on the way out-side the station, the drollest policeman that ever stepped out of a comic opera. At home we should have had to protect him against the boys; here he protects others.

Well, it shows that I am really abroad.

I have only two hours to spare in this town. What shall I see? The country; that is always beautiful, whereas many so-called "sights" are not. I will make for the shores of the lake, for the spot where the Rhône leaves it, to flow toward France. The Rhône, which is so muddy at Avignon, is clean here; deep and clear as a creek of the sea. It rushes along in a narrow blue tor-rent compressed between a quay and a line of houses.

The river draws me after it. We leave the town to-gether, and I am soon in the midst of those market-gardens where the infant Töpffer lost himself, and, overtaken by nightfall, fell to making his famous analy-sis of fear. The big pumping wheels still overtop the willows, and cast their shadows over the lettuce-fields. In the distance rise slopes of woodland, on Sundays the haunt of holiday-makers. The Rhône leaps and eddies, singing over its gravel beds. Two trout-fishers are taxing all their strength to pull a boat up stream beneath the shelter of the bank——

Perhaps I was wrong in not waiting to hear what M. Plumet had to tell me. He is not the kind of man to gesticulate wildly without good reason.

The steamer is gaining the open water and Geneva already lies far behind. Not a ripple on the blue water that shades into deep blue behind us. Ahead the scene melts into a milky haze. A little boat, with idle sails embroidered with sunlight, vanishes into it. On the right rise the mountains of Savoy, dotted with forests, veiled in clouds which cast their shadows on the broken slopes. The contrast is happy, and I can not help admiring Léman's lovely smile at the foot of these rugged mountains.

At the bend in the banks near St. Maurice-en-Valais, the wind catches us, quite a squall. The lake becomes a sea. At the first roll an Englishwoman becomes seasick. She casts an expiring glance upon Chillon, the ancient towers of which are being lashed by the foam. Her husband does not think it worth his while to cease reading his guide-book or focusing his field-glass for so trifling a matter.

ON THE DILIGENCE.

I am crossing the Simplon at daybreak, with rose-pink glaciers on every side. We are trotting down the Italian slope. How I have longed for the sight of Italy! Hardly had the diligence put on the brake, and begun bowling down the mountain-side, before I discovered a change on the face of all things. The sky turned to a brighter blue. At the very first glance I seemed to see the dust of long summers on the leaves of the firs, six thousand feet above the sea, in the virgin atmosphere of the mountain-tops: and I was very near taking the creaking of my loosely fixed seat for the southern melody of the first grasshopper.

BAVENO.

No one could be mistaken; this shaven, obsequious,

suavely jovial innkeeper is a Neapolitan. He takes
his stand in his mosaic-paved hall, and is at the service
of all who wish for information about Lago Maggiore,
the list of its sights; in a word, the programme of the
piece.

ISOLA BELLA, ISOLA MADRE.

Yes, they are scraped clean, carefully tended, pretty,
all a-blowing and a-growing; but unreal. The palm-
trees are unhomely, the tropical plants seem to stand
behind footlights. Restore them to their homes, or
give me back Lake Léman, so simply grand.

MENAGGIO.

After the sky-blue of Maggiore and the vivid green
of Lugano, comes the violet-blue of Como, with its
luminous landscape, its banks covered with olives,
Roman ruins, and modern villas. Never have I felt
the air so clear. Here for the first time I said to myself: "This is the spot where I would choose to dwell."
I have even selected my house; it peeps out from a
mass of pomegranates, evergreens, and citrons, on a pen-
insula around which the water swells with gentle
murmur, and whence the view is perfect across lake,
mountain, and sky.

A nightingale is singing, and I can not help reflecting that his fellows here are put to death in thousands.
Yes, the reapers, famed in poems and lithographs, are
desperate bird-catchers. At the season of migration
they capture thousands of these weary travellers with
snares or limed twigs; on Maggiore alone sixty thousand meet their end. We have but those they choose
to leave us to charm our summer nights.

RENÉ BAZIN

Perhaps they will kill my nightingale in the Carmelite garden. The idea fills me with indignation.

Then my thoughts run back to my rooms in the Rue de Rennes, and I see Madame Menin, with a dejected air, dusting my slumbering furniture; Lampron at work, his mother knitting; the old clerk growing sleepy with the heat and lifting his pen as he fancies he has got a bite; Madame Plumet amid her covey of workgirls, and M. Plumet blowing away with impatient breath the gold dust which·the gum has failed to fix on the mouldings of a newly finished frame.

M. Plumet is pensive. He is burdened with a secret. I am convinced I did wrong in not waiting longer on the Place de l'Opéra.

MILAN.

At last I am in Milan, an ancient city, but full of ideas and energy, my destination, and the cradle of the excellent Porfirio Zampini, suspected forger. The examination of documents does not begin till the day after to-morrow, so I am making the best of the time in seeing the sights.

There are four sights to see at Milan if you are a musician, and three if you are not: the Duomo, *vulgo*, cathedral; "The Marriage of the Virgin," by Raphael; "The Last Supper," by Leonardo; and, if it suits your tastes, a performance at La Scala.

I began with the Duomo, and on leaving it I received the news that still worries me.

But first of all I must make a confession. When I ascended through the tropical heat to the marble roof of the cathedral, I expected so much that I was disappointed. Surprise goes for so much in what we admire. Neither this mountain of marble, nor the lacework and pinnacles which adorn the enormous mass, nor the amazing number of statues, nor the sight of men smaller than flies on the Piazza del Duomo, nor the vast stretch of flat country which spreads for miles on every side of the city—none of these sights kindled the spark of enthusiasm within me which has often glowed for much less. No, what pleased me was something quite different, a detail not noticed in the guide-books, I suppose.

I had come down from the roof and was wandering in the vast nave from pillar to pillar, when I found myself beneath the lantern. I raised my eyes, but the flood of golden light compelled me to close them. The sunlight passing through the yellow glass of the windows overhead encircled the mighty vault of the lantern with a fiery crown, and played around the walls of its cage in rays which, growing fainter as they fell, flooded the floor with their expiring flames, a mysterious dayspring, a diffused glory, through which litany and sacred chant winged their way up toward the Infinite.

I left the cathedral tired out, dazed with weariness and sunlight, and fell asleep in a chair as soon as I got back to my room, on the fifth floor of the Albergo dell' Agnello.

I had been asleep for about an hour, perhaps, when I thought I heard a voice near me repeating "*Illustre Signore!*"

I did not wake. The voice continued with a murmur of sibilants:

RENÉ BAZIN

"Illustrissimo Signore!"

This drew me from my sleep, for the human ear is very susceptible to superlatives.

"What is it?"

"A letter for your lordship. As it is marked 'Immediate,' I thought I might take the liberty of disturbing your lordship's slumbers."

"You did quite right, Tomaso."

"You owe me eight sous, signore, which I paid for the postage."

"There's half a franc, keep the change."

He retired calling me Monsieur le Comte; and all for two sous—O fatherland of Brutus! The letter was from Lampron, who had forgotten to put a stamp on it.

"My Dear Friend:

"Madame Plumet, to whom I believe you have given no instructions so to do, is at present busying herself considerably about your affairs. I felt I ought to warn you, because she is all heart and no brains, and I have often seen before the trouble into which an overzealous friend may get one, especially if the friend be a woman.

"I fear some serious indiscretion has been committed, for the following reasons.

"Yesterday evening Monsieur Plumet came to see me, and stood pulling furiously at his beard, which I know from experience is his way of showing that the world is not going around the right way for him. By means of questions, I succeeded, after some difficulty, in dragging from him about half what he had to tell me. The only thing which he made quite clear was his distress on finding that Madame Plumet was a woman whom it was hard to silence or to convince by argument.

"It appears that she has gone back to her old trade of dressmaking, and that one of her first customers—God knows how she got there!—was Mademoiselle Jeanne Charnot.

"Well, last Monday Mademoiselle Jeanne was selecting a hat. She was blithe as dawn, while the dressmaker was gloomy as night.

"'Is your little boy ill, Madame Plumet?'

"'No, Mademoiselle.'

"'You look so sad.'

"Then, according to her husband's words, Madame Plumet took her courage in her two hands, and looking her pretty customer in the face, said:

"'Mademoiselle, why are you marrying?'

"'What a funny question! Why, because I am old enough; because I have had an offer; because all young girls marry, or else they go into convents, or become old maids. Well, Madame Plumet, I never have felt a religious vocation, and I never expected to become an old maid. Why do you ask such a question?'

"'Because, Mademoiselle, married life may be very happy, but it may be quite the reverse!'

"After giving expression to this excellent aphorism, Madame Plumet, unable to contain herself any longer, burst into tears.

"Mademoiselle Jeanne, who had been laughing before, was now amazed and presently grew rather anxious.

"Still, her pride kept her from asking any further questions, and Madame Plumet was too much frightened to add a word to her answer. But they will meet again the day after to-morrow, on account of the hat, as before.

"Here the story grew confused, and I understood no more of it.

"Clearly there is more behind this. Monsieur Plumet never would have gone out of his way merely to inform me that his wife had given him a taste of her tongue, nor would he have looked so upset about it. But you know the fellow's way; whenever it's important for him to make himself clear he loses what little power of speech he has, becomes worse than dumb—unintelligible. He sputtered inconsequent ejaculations at me in this fashion:

"'To think of it, to-morrow, perhaps! And you know what a

business! Oh, damnation! Anyhow, that must not be! Ah! Monsieur Lampron, how women *do* talk!'

"And with this Monsieur Plumet left me.

"I must confess, old fellow, that I am not burning with desire to get mixed up in this mess, or to go and ask Madame Plumet for the explanation which her husband was unable to give me. I shall bide my time. If anything turns up to-morrow, they are sure to tell me, and I will write you word.

"My mother sends you her love, and begs you to wrap up warmly in the evening; she says the twilight is the winter of hot climates.

"The dear woman has been a little out of sorts for the last two days. To-day she is keeping her bed. I trust it is nothing but a cold.

"Your affectionate friend,

"Sylvestre Lampron."

CHAPTER XIII

STARTLING NEWS FROM SYLVESTRE

MILAN, June 18th.

HE examination of documents began this morning. I never thought we should have such a heap to examine, nor papers of such a length. The first sitting passed almost entirely in classifying, in examining signatures, in skirmishes of all kinds around this main body.

My colleagues and I are working in a room in the municipal Palazzo del Marino, a vast deserted building used, I believe, as a storehouse. Our leathern armchairs and the table on which the documents are arranged occupy the middle of the room. Along the walls are several cupboards, nests of registers and rats; a few pictures with their faces to the wall; some carved wood scutcheons, half a dozen flagstaffs and a triumphal arch in cardboard, now taken to pieces and rotting—gloomy apparatus of bygone festivals.

The persons taking part in the examination besides the three Frenchmen, are, in the first place, a little Italian judge, with a mean face, wrinkled like a winter apple, whose eyelids always seem heavy with sleep; secondly, a clerk, shining with fat, his dress, hair, and countenance expressive of restrained jollity, as he dreams voluptuous dreams of the cool drinks he means to absorb through a straw when the hour of deliverance shall sound from the frightful cuckoo clock, a relic of the French occupation, which ticks at the end of the room; thirdly, a creature whose position is difficult to determine—I think he must be employed in some registry; he is here as a mere manual laborer. This third person gives me the idea of being very much interested in the fortunes of Signore Porfirio Zampini, for on each occasion, when his duties required him to bring us documents, he whispered in my ear:

"If you only knew, my lord, what a man Zampini is! what a noble heart, what a paladin!"

Take notice that this "paladin" is a macaroni-seller, strongly suspected of trying to hoodwink the French courts.

Amid the awful heat which penetrated the windows, the doors, even the sun-baked walls, we had to listen to, read, and compare documents. Gnats of a ferocious kind, hatched by thousands in the hangings of this hot-house, flew around our perspiring heads. Their buzzing got the upper hand at intervals when the clerk's voice grew weary and, diminishing in volume, threatened to fade away into snores.

The little judge rapped on the table with his paper-knife and urged the reader afresh upon his wild career. My colleague from the Record Office showed no sign of weariness. Motionless, attentive, classing the smallest papers in his orderly mind, he did not even feel the gnats swooping upon the veins in his hands, stinging

them, sucking them, and flying off red and distended
with his blood.

I sat, both literally and metaphorically, on hot coals.
Just as I came into the room, the man from the Record
Office handed me a letter which had arrived at the hotel
while I was out at lunch. It was a letter from Lampron, in a large, bulky envelope. Clearly something
important must have happened.

My fate, perhaps, was settled, and was in the letter,
while I knew it not. I tried to get it out of my inside
pocket several times, for to me it was a far more interesting document than any that concerned Zampini's
action. I pined to open it furtively, and read at least
the first few lines. A moment would have sufficed for
me to get at the point of this long communication. But
at every attempt the judge's eyes turned slowly upon
me between their half-closed lids, and made me desist.
No—a thousand times no! This smooth-tongued, wily
Italian shall have no excuse for proving that the French,
who have already such a reputation for frivolity, are a
nation without a conscience, incapable of fulfilling the
mission with which they are charged.

And yet . . . there came a moment when he turned
his back and began to sort a fresh bundle with the man
of records. Here was an unlooked-for opportunity. I
cut open the envelope, unfolded the letter, and found
eight pages! Still I began:

"MY DEAR FRIEND:

"In spite of my anxiety about my mother, and the care her illness demands (to-day it is found to be undoubted congestion of the

lungs), I feel bound to tell you the story of what has happened in the Rue Hautefeuille, as it is very important——"

"Excuse me, Monsieur Mou-il-ard," said the little judge, half turning toward me, "does the paper you have there happen to be number twenty-seven, which we are looking for?"

"Oh, dear, no; it's a private letter."

"A private letter? I ask pardon for interrupting you."

He gave a faint smile, closed his eyes to show his pity for such frivolity, and turned away again satisfied, while the other members of the Zampini Commission looked at me with interest.

The letter was important. So much the worse, I must finish it:

"I will try to reconstruct the scene for you, from the details which I have gathered.

"The time is a quarter to ten in the morning. There is a knock at Monsieur Plumet's door. The door opposite is opened half-way and Madame Plumet looks out. She withdraws in a hurry, 'with her heart in her mouth,' as she says; the plot she has formed is about to succeed or fail, the critical moment is at hand; the visitor is her enemy, your rival Dufilleul.

"He is full of self-confidence and comes in plump and flourishing, with light gloves, and a terrier at his heels.

"'My portrait framed, Plumet?'

"'Yes, my lord—yes, to be sure.'

"'Let's see it.'

"I have seen the famous portrait: a miniature of the newly created baron, in fresh butter, I think, done cheap by some poor girl who gains her living by coloring photographs. It is intended

THE INK-STAIN

for Mademoiselle Tigra of the Bouffes. A delicate attention from Dufilleul, isn't it? While Jeanne in her innocence is dreaming of the words of love he has ventured to utter to her, and cherishes but one thought, one image in her heart, he is exerting his ingenuity to perpetuate the recollection of that image's adventures elsewhere.

"He is pleased with the elaborate and costly frame which Plumet has made for him.

"'Very nice. How much?'

"'One hundred and twenty francs.'

"'Six louis? very dear.'

"'That's my price for this kind of work, my lord; I am very busy just now, my lord.'

"'Well, let it be this once. I don't often have a picture framed; to tell the truth, I don't care for pictures.'

"Dufilleul admires and looks at himself in the vile portrait which he holds outstretched in his right hand, while his left hand feels in his purse. Monsieur Plumet looks very stiff, very unhappy, and very nervous. He evidently wants to get his customer off the premises.

"The rustling of skirts is heard on the staircase. Plumet turns pale, and glancing at the half-opened door, through which the terrier is pushing its nose, steps forward to close it. It is too late.

"Some one has noiselessly opened it, and on the threshold stands Mademoiselle Jeanne in walking-dress, looking, with bright eyes and her most charming smile, at Plumet, who steps back in a fright, and Dufilleul, who has not yet seen her.

"'Well, sir, and so I've caught you!'

"Dufilleul starts, and involuntarily clutches the portrait to his waistcoat.

"'Mademoiselle—— No, really, you have come——?'

"'To see Madame Plumet. What wrong is there in that?'

"'None whatever—of course not.'

"'Not the least in the world, eh? Ha, ha! What a trifle flurries you. Come now, collect yourself. There is nothing to be frightened at. As I was coming upstairs, your dog put his muzzle out; I guessed he was not alone, so I left my maid with Madame Plumet, and came in at the right-hand door instead of the left. Do you think it improper?'

"'Oh, no, Mademoiselle.'

"'However, I am inquisitive, and I should like to see what you are hiding there.'

"'It's a portrait.'

"'Hand it to me.'

"'With pleasure; unfortunately it's only a portrait of myself.'

"'Why unfortunately? On the contrary, it flatters you—the nose is not so long as the original; what do you say, Monsieur Plumet?'

"'Do you think it good?'

"'Very.'

"'How do you like the frame?'

"'It's very pretty.'

"'Then I make you a present of it, Mademoiselle.'

"'Why! wasn't it intended for me?'

"'I mean—well! to tell the truth, it wasn't; it's a wedding present, a souvenir—there's nothing extraordinary in that, is there?'

"'Nothing whatever. You can tell me whom it's for, I suppose?'

"'Don't you think that you are pushing your curiosity too far?'

"'Well, really!'

"'Yes, I mean it.'

"'Since you make such a secret of it, I shall ask Monsieur Plumet to tell me. Monsieur Plumet, for whom is this portrait?'

"Plumet, pale as death, fumbled at his workman's cap, like a naughty child.

"'Why, you see, Mademoiselle—I am only a poor frame-maker.'

"'Very well! I shall go to Madame Plumet, who is sure to know, and will not mind telling me.'

"Madame Plumet, who must have been listening at the door, came in at that moment, trembling like a leaf, and prepared to dare all.

THE INK-STAIN

"'I beg you won't, Mademoiselle,' broke in Dufilleul; 'there is no secret. I only wanted to tease you. The portrait is for a friend of mine who lives at Fontainebleau.'

"'His name?'

"'Gonin—he's a solicitor.'

"'It was time you told me. How wretched you both looked. Another time tell me straight out, and frankly, anything you have no reason to conceal. Promise you won't act like this again.'

"'I promise.'

"'Then, let us make peace.'

"She held out her hand to him. Before he could grasp it, Madame Plumet broke in:

"'Excuse me, Mademoiselle, I can not have you deceived like this in my house. Mademoiselle, it is not true!'

"'What is not true, Madame?'

"'That this portrait is for Monsieur Gonin, or anybody else at Fontainebleau.'

"Mademoiselle Charnot drew back in surprise.

"'For whom, then?'

"'An actress.'

"'Take care what you are saying, Madame.'

"'For Mademoiselle Tigra of the Bouffes.'

"'Lies!' cried Dufilleul. 'Prove it, Madame; prove your story, please!'

"'Look at the back,' answered Madame Plumet, quietly.

"Mademoiselle Jeanne, who had not put down the miniature, turned it over, read what was on the back, grew deathly pale, and handed it to her lover.

"'What does it say?' said Dufilleul, stooping over it.

"It said: 'From Monsieur le Baron D—— to Mademoiselle T——, Boulevard Haussmann. To be delivered on Thursday.'

"'You can see at once, Mademoiselle, that this is not my writing. It's an abominable conspiracy. Monsieur Plumet, I call upon you to give your wife the lie. She has written what is false; confess it!'

"The frame-maker hid his face in his hands and made no reply.

"'What, Plumet, have you nothing to say for me?'

"Mademoiselle Charnot was leaving the room.

"'Where are you going, Mademoiselle? Stay, you will soon see that they lie!'

"She was already half-way across the landing when Dufilleul caught her and seized her by the hand.

"'Stay, Jeanne, stay!'

"'Let me go, sir!'

"'No, hear me first; this is some horrible mistake. I swear——'

"At this moment a high-pitched voice was heard on the staircase.

"'Well, George, how much longer are you going to keep me?'

"Dufilleul suddenly lost countenance and dropped Mademoiselle Charnot's hand.

"The young girl bent over the banisters, and saw, at the bottom of the staircase, exactly underneath her, a woman looking up, with head thrown back and mouth still half-opened. Their eyes met. Jeanne at once turned away her gaze.

"Then, turning to Madame Plumet, who leaned motionless against the wall:

"'Come, Madame,' she said, 'we must go and choose a hat.' And she closed the dressmaker's door behind her.

"This, my friend, is the true account of what happened in the Rue Hautefeuille. I learned the details from Madame Plumet in person, who could not contain herself for joy as she described the success of her conspiracy, and how her little hand had guided old Dame Fortune's. For, as you will doubtless have guessed, the meeting between Jeanne and her lover, so dreaded by the framemaker, had been arranged by Madame Plumet unknown to all, and the damning inscription was also in her handwriting.

"I need not add that Mademoiselle Charnot, upset by the scene, had a momentary attack of faintness. However, she soon regained her usual firm and dignified demeanor, which seems to show that she is a woman of energy.

"But the interest of the story does not cease here. I think the betrothal is definitely at an end. A betrothal is always a difficult thing to renew, and after the publicity which attended the rupture of this one, I do not see how they can make it up again. One thing I feel sure of is, that Mademoiselle Jeanne Charnot will never change her name to Madame Dufilleul.

"Do not, however, exaggerate your own chances. They will be less than you think for some time yet. I do not believe that a young girl who has thus been wounded and deceived can forget all at once. There is even the possibility of her never forgetting—of living with her sorrow, preferring certain peace of mind, and the simple joys of filial devotion, to all those dreams of married life by which so many simple-hearted girls have been cruelly taken in.

"In any case do not think of returning yet, for I know you are capable of any imprudence. Stay where you are, examine your documents, and wait.

"My mother and I are passing through a bitter trial. She is ill, I may say seriously ill. I would sooner bear the illness than my present anxiety.

"Your friend,
"SYLVESTRE LAMPRON.

"P. S.—Just as I was about to fasten up this letter, I got a note from Madame Plumet to tell me that Monsieur and Mademoiselle Charnot have left Paris. She does not know where they have gone."

I became completely absorbed over this letter. Some passages I read a second time; and the state of agitation into which it threw me did not at once pass away. I remained for an indefinite time without a notion of what was going on around me, entirely wrapped up in the past or the future.

The Italian attendant brought me back to the present with a jerk of his elbow. He was replacing the last register in the huge drawers of the table. He and I were alone. My colleagues had left, and our first

sitting had come to an end without my assistance,
though before my eyes. They could not have gone far,
so, somewhat ashamed of my want of attention, I put
on my hat, and went to find them and apologize. The
little attendant caught me by the sleeve, and gave a
knowing smile at the letter which I was slipping into
my pocketbook.

"*E d'una donna?*" he asked.

"What's that to you?"

"I am sure of it; a letter from a man would never
take so long to read; and, *per Bacco*, you were a time
about it! Oh, *le donne, illustre signore, le donne!*"

"That's enough, thank you."

I made for the door, but he threw himself nimbly
in my way, grimacing, raising his eyebrows, one finger
on his ribs. "Listen, my lord, I can see you are a true
scholar, a man whom fame alone can tempt. I could
get your lordship such beautiful manuscripts—Italian,
Latin, German manuscripts that never have been
edited, my noble lord!"

"Stolen, too!" I replied, and pushed past him.

I went out, and in the neighboring square, amicably
seated at the same table, under the awning of a café,
I found my French colleagues and the Italian judge.
At a table a little apart the clerk was sucking something
through a straw. And they all laughed as they saw
me making my way toward them through the still
scorching glare of the sun.

MILAN, June 25th.

Our mission was concluded to-day. Zampini is a
mere rogue. Brought face to face with facts he could

not escape from, he confessed that he had intended to "have a lark" with the French heirs by claiming to be the rightful heir himself, though he lacked two degrees of relationship to establish his claim.

We explained to him that this little "lark" was a fraudulent act which exposed him at least to the consequence of having to pay the costs of the action. He accepted our opinion in the politest manner possible. I believe he is hopelessly insolvent. He will pay the usher in macaroni, and the barrister in jests.

My colleagues, the record man and the translator, leave Milan to-morrow. I shall go with them.

CHAPTER XIV

A SURPRISING ENCOUNTER

HAVE just had another letter from Sylvestre. My poor friend is very miserable; his mother is dead—a saint if ever there was one. I was very deeply touched by the news, although I knew this lovable woman very slightly —too slightly, indeed, not having been a son, or related in any way to her, but merely a passing stranger who found his way within the horizon of her heart, that narrow limit within which she spread abroad the treasures of her tenderness and wisdom. How terribly her son must feel her loss!

He described in his letter her last moments, and the calmness with which she met death, and added:

"One thing, which perhaps you will not understand, is the remorse which is mingled with my sorrow. I lived with her forty years, and have some right to be called 'a good son.' But, when I compare the proofs of affection I gave her with those she gave me, the sacrifices I made for her with those she made for me; when I think of the egoism which found its way into our common life, on which I founded my claims to merit, of the wealth of tenderness and sympathy with which she repaid a few walks on my arm, a few kind words, and of her really great forbearance in dwelling beneath the same roof with me—I feel that I was ungrateful, and not worthy of the happiness I enjoyed.

"I am tortured by the thought that it is impossible for me to repair all my neglect, to pay a debt the greatness of which I now recognize for the first time. She is gone. All is over. My prayers alone can reach her, can tell her that I loved her, that I worshipped her, that I might have been capable of doing all that I have left undone for her.

"Oh, my friend, what pleasant duties have I lost! I mean, at least, to fulfil her last wishes, and it is on account of one of them that I am writing to you.

"You know that my mother was never quite pleased at my keeping at home the portrait of her who was my first and only love. She would have preferred that my eyes did not recall so often to my heart the recollection of my long-past sorrows. I withstood her. On her death-bed she begged me to give up the picture to those who should have had it long ago. 'So long as I was here to comfort you in the sorrows which the sight of it revived in you,' she said, 'I did not press this upon you; but soon you will be left alone, with no one to raise you when your spirits fail you. They have often begged you to give up the picture to them. The time is come for you to grant their prayers.'

"I promised.

"And now, dear friend, help me to keep my promise. I do not wish to write to them. My hand would tremble, and they would tremble when they saw my writing. Go and see them.

"They live about nine miles from Milan, on the Monza road, but beyond that town, close to the village of Desio. The villa is called Dannegianti, after its owners. It used to be hidden among poplars, and its groves were famous for their shade. You must send in your card to the old lady of the house together with mine. They will receive you. Then you must break the news to them as you think best, that, in accordance with the dying wish of Sylvestre Lampron's mother, the portrait of Rafaella is to be given in perpetuity to the Villa Dannegianti. Given, you understand.

"You may even tell them that it is on its way. I have just

arranged with Plumet about packing it. He is a good workman, as you know. To-morrow all will be ready, and my home an absolute void.

"I intend to take refuge in hard work, and I count upon you to alleviate to some extent the hardships of such a method of consolation.

"SYLVESTRE LAMPRON."

When I got Lampron's letter, at ten in the morning, I went at once to see the landlord of the Albergo dell' Agnello.

"You can get me a carriage for Desio, can't you?"

"Oh, your lordship thinks of driving to Desio? That is quite right. It is much more picturesque than going by train. A little way beyond Monza. Monza, sir, is one of our richest jewels; you will see there——"

"Yes," said I, repeating my Baedeker as accurately as he, "the Villa Reale, and the Iron Crown of the Emperors of the West."

"Exactly so, sir, and the cathedral built——"

"By Theodolinda, Queen of the Lombards, A.D. 595, restored in the sixteenth century. I know; I only asked whether you could get me a decent carriage."

"A matchless one! At half-past three, when the heat is less intense, your lordship will find the horses harnessed. You will have plenty of time to get to Desio before sunset, and be back in time for supper."

At the appointed time I received notice. My host had more than kept his word, for the horses sped through Milan at a trot which they did not relinquish when we got into the Como road, amid the flat and fertile country which is called the garden of Italy.

THE INK-STAIN

After an hour and a half, including a brief halt at Monza, the coachman drew up his horses before the first house in Desio—an inn.

It was a very poor inn, situated at the corner of the main street and of a road which branched off into the country. In front of it a few plane-trees, trained into an arbor, formed an arch of shade. A few feet of vine clambered about their trunks. The sun was scorching the leaves and the heavy bunches of grapes which hung here and there. The shutters were closed, and the little house seemed to have been lulled to sleep by the heat and light of the atmosphere and the buzzing of the gnats.

"Oh, go in; they'll wake up at once," said the coachman, who had divined my thoughts.

Then, without waiting for my answer, like a man familiar with the customs of the country, he took his horses down the road to the stable.

I went in. A swarm of bees and drones were buzzing like a whirlwind beneath the plane-trees; a frightened white hen ran cackling from her nest in the dust. No one appeared. I opened the door; still nobody was to be seen. Inside I found a passage, with rooms to right and left and a wooden staircase at the end. The house, having been kept well closed, was cool and fresh. As I stood on the threshold striving to accustom my eyes to the darkness of the interior, I heard the sound of voices to my right:

"Picturesque as you please, but the journey has been a failure! These people are no better than savages; introductions, distinctions, and I may say even fame, had no effect upon them!"

"Do you think they have even read your letters?"

"That would be still worse, to refuse to read letters addressed to them! No, I tell you, there's no excuse."

"They have suffered great trouble, I hear, and that is some excuse for them, father."

"No, my dear, there is no possible excuse for their keeping hidden treasures of such scientific interest. I do not consider that even an Italian nobleman, were he orphan from his cradle, and thrice a widower, has any right to keep locked up from the investigation of scholars an unequalled collection of Roman coins, and a very presentable show of medallions and medals properly so-called. Are you aware that this boorish patrician has in his possession the eight types of medal of the gens Attilia?"

"Really?"

"I am certain of it, and he has the thirty-seven of the gens Cassia, one hundred and eighteen to one hundred and twenty-one of the gens Cornelia, the eleven Farsuleia, and dozens of Numitoria, Pompeia, and Scribonia, all in perfect condition, as if fresh from the die. Besides these, he has some large medals of the greatest rarity; the Marcus Aurelius with his son on the reverse side, Theodora bearing the globe, and above all the Annia Faustina with Heliogabalus on the reverse side, an incomparable treasure, of which there is only one other example, and that an imperfect one, in the world —a marvel which I would give a day of my life to see; yes, my dear, a day of my life!"

Such talk as this, in French, in such an inn as this!

THE INK-STAIN

I felt a presentiment, and stepped softly to the right-hand door.

In the darkened room, lighted only by a few rays filtered between the slats of the shutters, sat a young girl. Her hat was hung upon a nail above her head; one arm rested on a wretched white wood table; her head was bent forward in mournful resignation. On the other side of the table, her father was leaning back in his chair against the whitewashed wall, with folded arms, heightened color, and every sign of extreme disgust. Both rose as I entered—Jeanne first, M. Charnot after her. They were astonished at seeing me.

I was no less astounded than they.

We stood and stared at each other for some time, to make sure that we were not dreaming.

M. Charnot was the first to break the silence. He did not seem altogether pleased at my appearance, and turned to his daughter, whose face had grown very red and yet rather chilling:

"Jeanne, put your hat on; it is time to go to the station." Then he addressed me:

"We shall leave you the room to yourself, sir; and since the most extraordinary coincidence"—he emphasized the words—"has brought you to this damnable village, I hope you will enjoy your visit."

"Have you been here long, Monsieur?"

"Two hours, Monsieur, two mortal hours in this inn, fried by the sun, bored to death, murdered piecemeal by flies, and infuriated by the want of hospitality in this out-of-the-way hole in Lombardy."

[151]

"Yes, I noticed that the host was nowhere to be seen, and that is the reason why I came in here; I had no idea that I should have the honor of meeting you."

"Good God! I'm not complaining of *him!* He's asleep in his barn over there. You can wake him up; **he** doesn't mind showing himself; he even makes himself agreeable when he has finished his siesta."

"I only wish to ask him one question, which perhaps you could answer, Monsieur; then I need not waken him. Could you tell me the way to the Villa Dannegianti?"

M. Charnot walked up to me, looked me straight in the eyes, shrugged his shoulders, and burst out laughing.

"The Villa Dannegianti!"

"Yes, Monsieur."

"Are you going to the Villa Dannegianti?"

"Yes, Monsieur."

"Then you may as well turn round and go home again."

"Why?"

"Because there's no admission."

"But I have a letter of introduction."

"I had two, Monsieur, without counting the initials after my name, which are worth something and have opened the doors of more than one foreign collection for me; yet they denied me admission! Think of it! The porter of that insolent family denied me admission! Do *you* expect to succeed after that?"

"I do, Monsieur."

My words seemed to him the height of presumption.

"Come, Jeanne," he said, "let us leave this gentleman to his youthful illusions. They will soon be shattered—very soon."

He gave me an ironical smile and made for the door.

At this moment Jeanne dropped her sunshade. I picked it up for her.

"Thank you, Monsieur," she said.

Of course these words were no more than ordinarily polite. She would have said the same to the first comer. Nothing in her attitude or her look displayed any emotion which might put a value on this common form of speech. But it was her voice, that music I so often dream of. Had it spoken insults, I should have found it sweet. It inspired me with the sudden resolution of detaining this fugitive apparition, of resting, if possible, another hour near her to whose side an unexpected stroke of fortune had brought me.

M. Charnot had already left the room; his rotund shadow rested on the wall of the passage. He held a travelling-bag in his hand.

"Monsieur," said I, "I am sorry that you are obliged to return already to Milan. I am quite certain of admission to the Villa Dannegianti, and it would have given me pleasure to repair a mistake which is clearly due only to the stupidity of the servants."

He stopped; the stroke had told.

"It is certainly quite possible that they never looked at my card or my letters. But allow me to ask, since my card did not reach the host, what secret you possess to enable yours to get to him?"

"No secret at all, still less any merit of my own. I

am the bearer of news of great importance to the owners of the villa, news of a purely private nature. They will be obliged to see me. My first care, when I had fulfilled my mission, would have been to mention your name. You would have been able to go over the house, and inspect a collection of medals which, I have heard, is a very fine one."

"Unique, Monsieur!"

"Unfortunately you are going away, and to-morrow I have to leave Milan myself, for Paris."

"You have been some time in Italy, then?"

"Nearly a fortnight."

M. Charnot gave his daughter a meaning look, and suddenly became more friendly.

"I thought you had just come. We have not been here so long," he added; "my daughter has been a little out of sorts, and the doctor advised us to travel for change of air. Paris is not healthful in this very hot weather."

He looked hard at me to see whether his fib had taken me in. I replied, with an air of the utmost conviction, "That is putting it mildly. Paris, in July, is uninhabitable."

"That's it, Monsieur, uninhabitable; we were forced to leave it. We soon made up our minds, and, in spite of the time of the year, we turned our steps toward the home of the classics, to Italy, the museum of Europe. And you really think, then, that by means of your good offices we should have been admitted to the villa?"

"Yes, Monsieur, but owing only to the missive with which I am entrusted."

THE INK-STAIN

M. Charnot hesitated. He was probably thinking of the blot of ink, and certainly of M. Mouillard's visit. But he doubtless reflected that Jeanne knew nothing of the old lawyer's proceedings, that we were far from Paris, that the opportunity was not to be lost; and in the end his passion for numismatics conquered at once his resentment as a bookworm and his scruples as a father.

"There is a later train at ten minutes to eight, father," said Jeanne.

"Well, dear, do you care to try your luck again, and return to the assault of that Annia Faustina?"

"As you please, father."

We left the inn together by the by-road down the hill. I could not believe my eyes. This old man with refined features who walked on my left, leaning on his malacca cane, was M. Charnot. The same man who received me so discourteously the day after I made my blot was now relying on me to introduce him to an Italian nobleman; on me, a lawyer's clerk. I led him on with confidence, and both of us, carried away by our divers hopes, he dreaming of medals, I of the reopened horizon full of possibilities, conversed on indifferent subjects with a freedom hitherto unknown between us.

And this charming Parisienne, whose presence I divined rather than saw, whom I dared not look in the face, who stepped along by her father's side, light of foot, her eyes seeking the vault of heaven, her ear attentive though her thoughts were elsewhere, catching her Parisian sunshade in the hawthorns of Desio, was

Jeanne, Jeanne of the flower-market, Jeanne whom Lampron had sketched in the woods of St. Germain! It did not seem possible.

Yet it was so, for we arrived together at the gates of the Villa Dannegianti, which is hardly a mile from the inn.

I rang the bell. The fat, idle, insolent Italian porter was beginning to refuse me admission, with the same words and gestures which he had so often used. But I explained, in my purest Tuscan, that I was not of the ordinary kind of importunate tourist. I told him that he ran a serious risk if he did not immediately hand my card and my letter—Lampron's card in an envelope—to the Comtesse Dannegianti.

From his stony glare I could not tell whether I had produced any impression, nor even whether he had understood. He turned on his heel with his keys in one hand and the letter in the other, and went on his way through the shady avenue, rolling his broad back from side to side, attired in a jacket which might have fitted in front, but was all too short behind.

The shady precincts of which Lampron wrote did not seem to have been pruned. The park was cool and green. At the end of the avenue of plane-trees, alternating with secular hawthorns cut into pyramids, we could see the square mass of the villa just peeping over the immense clumps of trees. Beyond it the tops and naked trunks of a group of umbrella pines stood silhouetted against the sky.

The porter returned, solemn and impassive. He opened the gate without a word. We all passed through

THE INK-STAIN

—M. Charnot somewhat uneasy at entering under false pretenses, as I guessed from the way he suddenly drew up his head. Jeanne seemed pleased; she smoothed down a fold which the wind had raised in her frock, spread out a flounce, drew herself up, pushed back a hairpin which her fair tresses had dragged out of its place, all in quick, deft, and graceful movements, like a goldfinch preening its feathers.

We reached the terrace, and arranged that M. and Mademoiselle Charnot should wait in an alley close at hand till I received permission to visit the collections.

I entered the house, and following a lackey, crossed a large mosaic-paved hall, divided by columns of rare marbles into panels filled with mediocre frescoes on a very large scale. At the end of this hall was the Countess's room, which formed a striking contrast, being small, panelled with wood, and filled with devotional knick-knacks that gave it the look of a chapel.

As I entered, an old lady half rose from an arm-chair, which she could have used as a house, the chair was so large and she was so small. At first I could distinguish only two bright, anxious eyes. She looked at me like a prisoner awaiting a verdict. I began by telling her of the death of Lampron's mother. Her only answer was an attentive nod. She guessed something else was coming and stood on guard, so to speak. I went on and told her that the portrait of her daughter was on its way to her. Then she forgot everything—her age, her rank, and the mournful reserve which had hitherto hedged her about. Her motherly heart alone spoke within her; a ray of light had come to brighten the incurable gloom which was killing her; she rushed toward me and fell into my arms, and I felt against my heart her poor aged body shaking with sobs. She thanked me in a flood of words which I did not catch. Then she drew back and gazed at me, seeking to read in my eyes some emotion responsive to her own, and her eyes, red and swollen and feverishly bright, questioned me more clearly than her words.

"How good are you, sir! and how generous is he! What life does he lead? Has he ever lived down the sorrow which blasted his youth here? Men forget more easily, happily for them. I had given up all hope of obtaining the portrait. Every year I sent him flowers which meant, 'Restore to us all that is left of our dead Rafaella.' Perhaps it was unkind. I did reproach myself at times for it. But I was her mother, you know; the mother of that peerless girl! And the portrait is so good, so like! He has never altered it? tell me; never retouched it? Time has not marred the lifelike coloring? I shall now have the mournful consolation I have so long desired; I shall always have before me the counterpart of my lost darling, and can gaze upon that face which none could depict save he who loved her; for, dreadful though it be to think of, the image of the best beloved will change and fade away even in a mother's heart, and at times I doubt whether my old memory is still faithful, and recalls all her grace and beauty as clearly as it used to do when the wound was fresh in my heart and my eyes were still filled with the loveliness of her. Oh, Monsieur, Monsieur! to think that I shall see that face once more!"

THE INK-STAIN

She left me as quickly as she had come, and went to open a door on the left, into an adjoining room, whose red hangings threw a ruddy glow upon the polished floor.

"Cristoforo!" she cried, "Cristoforo! come and see a French gentleman who brings us great news. The portrait of our Rafaella, Cristoforo, the portrait we have so long desired, is at last to be given to us!"

I heard a chair move, and a slow footstep. Cristoforo appeared, with white hair and black moustache, his tall figure buttoned up in an old-fashioned frock-coat, the petrified, mummified remains of a once handsome man. He walked up to me, took both my hands and shook them ceremoniously. His face showed no traces of emotion; his eyes were dry, and he had not a word to say. Did he understand? I really do not know. He seemed to think the affair was an ordinary introduction. As I looked at him his wife's words came back to me, "Men forget sooner." She gazed at him as if she would put blood into his veins, where it had long ceased to flow.

"Cristoforo, I know this will be a great joy to you, and you will join with me in thanking Monsieur Lampron for his generosity. You, sir, will express to him all the Count's gratitude and my own, and also the sympathy we feel for him in his recent loss. Besides, we shall write to him. Is Monsieur Lampron rich?"

"I had forgotten to tell you, Madame, that my friend will accept nothing but thanks."

"Ah, that is truly noble of him, is it not, Cristoforo?"

All the answer the old Count made was to take my hands and shake them again.

I used the opportunity to put forward my request in behalf of M. Charnot. He listened attentively.

"I will give orders. You shall see everything— everything."

Then, considering our interview at an end, he bowed and withdrew to his own apartments.

I looked for the Countess Dannegianti. She had sunk into her great armchair, and was weeping hot tears.

Ten minutes later, M. Charnot and Jeanne entered with me into the jealously guarded museum.

Museum was the only name to give to a collection of such artistic value, occupying, as it did, the whole of the ground floor to the right of the hall. Two rooms ran parallel to each other, filled with pictures, medals, and engravings, and were connected by a narrow gallery devoted to sculpture.

Hardly was the door opened when M. Charnot sought the famous medals with his eye. There they were in the middle of the room in two rows of cases. He was deeply moved. I thought he was about to make a raid upon them, attracted after his kind by the *auri sacra fames*, by the yellow gleam of those ancient coins, the names, family, obverse and reverse of which he knew by heart. But I little understood the enthusiast.

He drew out his handkerchief and spectacles, and while he was wiping the glasses he gave a rapid and impatient glance at the works that adorned the walls. None of them could charm the numismatist's heart. After he had enjoyed the pleasure of proving how feeble in comparison were the charms of a Titian or a Veronese, then only did M. Charnot walk step by step to the first case and bend reverently over it.

Yet the collection of paintings was unworthy of such disdain. The pictures were few, but all were signed with great names, most of them Italian, a few Dutch, Flemish, or German. I began to work systematically through them, pleased at the want of a catalogue and the small number of inscriptions on the frames. To be your own guide doubles your pleasure; you can get your impression of a picture entirely at first hand; you are filled with admiration without any one having told you that you are bound to go into ecstasies. You can work out for yourself from a picture, by induction and comparison, its subject, its school, and its author, unless it proclaims, in every stroke of the brush, "I am a Hobbema," "a Perugino," or "a Giotto."

I was somewhat distracted, however, by the voice of the old numismatist, as he peered into the cases, and constrained his daughter to share in the exuberance of his learned enthusiasm.

"Jeanne, look at this; crowned head of Cleopatra, Mark Antony on the reverse; in perfect condition, isn't it? See, an Italian *as—Iguvium Umbriæ*, which my friend Pousselot has sought these thirty years! Oh, my dear, this *is* important: Annius Verus on the reverse of Commodus, both as children, a rare example—yet not as rare as—Jeanne, you must engrave this gold medal in your heart, it is priceless: head of Augustus with laurel, Diana walking on the reverse. You ought to take an interest in her. Diana the fair huntress.

This collection is heavenly! Wait a minute; we shall soon come to the Annia Faustina."

Jeanne made no objection, but smiled softly upon the Cleopatra, the Umbrian *as*, and the fair huntress.

Little by little her father's enthusiasm expanded over the vast collection of treasures. He took out his pocket-book and began to make notes. Jeanne raised her eyes to the walls, took one glance, then a second, and, not being called back to the medals, stepped softly up to the picture at which I had begun.

She went quickly from one to another having evidently no more than a child's untutored taste for pictures. As I, on the contrary, was getting on very slowly, she was bound to overtake me. You may be sure I took no steps to prevent it, and so in a very short time we were both standing before the same picture, a portrait of Holbein the younger. A subject of conversation was ready to hand.

"Mademoiselle," said I, "do you like this Holbein?"

"You must admit, sir, that the old gentleman is exceedingly plain."

"Yes, but the painting is exquisite. See how powerful is the drawing of the head, how clear and deep the colors remain after more than three hundred years. What a good likeness it must have been! The subject tells his own story: he must have been a nobleman of the court of Henry VIII, a Protestant in favor with the King, wily but illiterate, and wishing from the bottom of his heart that he were back with the companions of his youth at home in his country house, hunting and drinking at his ease. It is really the study of a man's

character. Look at this Rubens beside it, a mere mass
of flesh scarcely held together by a spirit, a style that is
exuberantly material, all color and no expression.
Here you have spirituality on one side and materialism
on the other, unconscious, perhaps, but unmistakable.
Compare, again, with these two pictures this little drawing, doubtless by Perugino, just a sketch of an angel
for an Annunciation; notice the purity of outline, the
ideal atmosphere in which the painter lives and with
which he impregnates his work. You see he comes of
a school of poets and mystics, gifted with a second sight
which enabled them to beautify this world and raise
themselves above it."

I was pleased with my little lecture, and so was
Jeanne. I could tell it by her surprised expression,
and by the looks she cast toward her father, who was
still taking notes, to see whether she might go on with
her first lesson in art.

He smiled in a friendly way, which meant:

"I'm happy here, my dear, thank you; *va piano va
sano.*"

This was as good as permission. We went on our
way, saluting, as we passed, Tintoretto and Titian,
Veronese and Andrea Solari, old Cimabue, and a few
early paintings of angular virgins on golden back-
grounds.

Jeanne was no longer bored.

"And is this," she would say, "another Venetian,
or a Lombard, or a Florentine?"

We soon completed the round of the first room, and
made our way into the gallery beyond, devoted to sculpt-

ure. The marble gods and goddesses, the lovely fragments of frieze or cornice from the excavations at Rome,
Pompeii, or Greece, had but a moderate interest for
Mademoiselle Charnot. She never gave more than one
glance to each statue, to some none at all.

We soon came to the end of the gallery, and the door
which gave access into the second room of paintings.

Suddenly Jeanne gave an exclamation of surprise.

"What is that?" she said.

Beneath the large and lofty window, fanned on the
outside by leafy branches, a wooden panel, bearing an
inscription, stood upright against the wall. The words
were painted in black on a white ground, and arranged
with considerable skill, after the style of the classic epi-
taphs which the Italians still cultivate.

I drew aside the folds of a curtain, and read:

*A te Rafaella Dannegianti—Che—Nata da venti
anni, e poco piu—Avesti esperienza piena—Delle illusi-
oni ei dolori di questo mondo—E il giorno 6 gennaio—
Come angelo che anela al suo cielo—Serena e contenta
te ne volasti a Dio—Il clero di Desio—Gl'impiegati e
gli artisti della Eccma casa Dannegianti—Queste solenni
esequie.*

"It is one of those memorial tablets, Mademoiselle,
such as people hang up in this part of the country upon
the church doors on the day of the funeral. It means:

"To thee, Rafaella Dannegianti—who, aged twenty
years and few months—having fully experienced the
sorrows and illusions of this world—on January 6—
like an angel longing for its heavenly home—didst wing

thy way to God in peace and happiness—the clergy of
Desio—and the laborers and artificers of the noble
house of Dannegianti—tender these last solemn offices."

"This Rafaella, then, was the Count's daughter?"

"His only child, a girl lovely and gracious beyond
rivalry."

"Oh, of course, beyond rivalry. Are not all only
daughters lovely and perfect when once they are dead?"
she replied with a bitter smile. "They have their
legend, their cult, and usually a flattering portrait. I
am surprised that Rafaella's is not here. I imagine
her portrait as representing a tall girl, with long, well-
arched eyebrows, and brown eyes——"

"Greenish-brown."

"Green, if you prefer it; a small nose, cherry lips,
and a mass of light brown hair."

"Golden brown would be more correct."

"Have you seen it, then? Is there one?"

"Yes, Mademoiselle, and it lacks no perfection that
you could imagine, not even that smile of happy youth
which was a falsehood ere the paint had yet dried on
the canvas. Here, before this relic, which recalls it to
my thoughts, I must confess that I am touched."

She looked at me in astonishment.

"Where is the portrait? Not here?"

"No, it is at Paris, in my friend Lampron's studio."

"O—oh!" She blushed slightly.

"Yes, Mademoiselle, it is at once a masterpiece and
a sad reminder. The story is very simple, and I am
sure my friend would not mind my telling it to you—to
you if to no other—before these relics of the past.

When Lampron was a young man travelling in Italy he
fell in love with this young girl, whose portrait he was
painting. He loved her, perhaps without confessing it
to himself, certainly without avowing it to her.   Such is
the way of timid and humble men of heart, men whose
love is nearly always misconstrued when it ceases to be
unnoticed.   My friend risked the happiness of his life,
fearlessly, without calculation—and lost it.   A day came
when Rafaella Dannegianti was carried off by her
parents, who shuddered at the thought of her stooping
to a painter, even though he were a genius."

"So she died?"

"A year later.   He never got over it.   Even while I
speak to you, he in his loneliness is pondering and weeping over these very lines which you have just read without a suspicion of the depth of their bitterness."

"He has known bereavement," said she; "I pity him
with all my heart."

Her eyes filled with tears.   She repeated the words,
whose meaning was now clear to her, "A te Rafaella."
Then she knelt down softly before the mournful inscription.   I saw her bow her head.   Jeanne was praying.

It was touching to see the young girl, whom chance
had placed before this simple testimony of a sorrow
now long past, deeply moved by the sad tale of love,
filled with tender pity for the dead Rafaella, her fellow
in youth and beauty and perhaps in destiny, finding in
her heart the tender impulse to kneel without a word,
as if beside the grave of a friend.   The daylight's last
rays streaming in through the window illumined her
bowed head.

THE INK-STAIN

I drew back, with a touch of awe.

M. Charnot appeared.

He went up to his daughter and tapped her on the shoulder. She rose with a blush.

"What are you doing there?" he said.

Then he adjusted his glasses and read the Italian inscription.

"You really take unnecessary trouble in kneeling down to decipher a thing like that. You can see at once that it's a modern panel, and of no value. Monsieur," he added, turning to me, "I do not know what your plans are, but unless you intend to sleep at Desio, we must be off, for the night is falling."

We left the villa.

Out of doors it was still light, but with the afterglow. The sun was out of sight, but the earth was still enveloped, as it were, in a haze of luminous dust.

M. Charnot pulled out his watch.

"Seven minutes past eight. What time does the last train start, Jeanne?"

"At ten minutes to eight."

"Confusion! we are stranded in Desio! The mere thought of passing the night in that inn gives me the creeps. I see no way out of it unless Monsieur Mouillard can get us one of the Count's state coaches. There isn't a carriage to be got in this infernal village!"

"There is mine, Monsieur, which luckily holds four, and is quite at your service."

"Upon my word, I am very much obliged to you. The drive by moonlight will be quite romantic."

He drew near to Jeanne and whispered in her ear:

"Are you sure you've wraps enough? a shawl, or a cape, or some kind of pelisse?"

She gave a merry nod of assent.

"Don't worry yourself, father; I am prepared for all emergencies."

At half-past eight we left Desio together, and I silently blessed the host of the Albergo dell' Agnello, who had assured me that the carriage road was "so much more picturesque." I found it so, indeed.

M. Charnot and Jeanne faced the horses. I sat opposite to M. Charnot, who was in the best of spirits after all the medals he had seen. Comfortably settled in the cushions, careless of the accidents of the road, with graphic and untiring forefinger, he undertook to describe his travels in Greece, whither he had been sent on some learned enterprise by the Minister of Education, and had carried an imagination already pre-possessed and dazzled with Homeric visions. He told his story well and with detail, combining the recollections of the scholar with the impressions of an artist. The pediment of the Parthenon, the oleanders of the Ilissus, the stream "that runs in rain-time," the naked peak of Parnassus, the green slopes of Helicon, the blue gulf of Argus, the pine forest beside Alpheus, where the ancients worshipped "Death the Gentle"—all of them passed in recount upon his learned lips.

I must acknowledge, to my shame, that I did not listen to all he said, but, in a favorite way I have, reserved some of my own freedom of thought, while I gave him complete freedom of speech. And I am bound to say he did not abuse it, but consented to

THE INK-STAIN

pause at the frontiers of Thessaly. Then followed silence. I gave him room to stretch. Soon, lulled by the motion of the carriage, the stream of reminiscence ran more slowly—then ran dry. M. Charnot slept.

We bowled at a good pace, without jolting, over the white road. A warm mist rose around us laden with the smell of vegetation, ripe corn, and clover from the overheated earth and the neighboring fields, which had drunk their full of sunlight. Now and again a breath of fresh air was blown to us from the mountains. As the darkness deepened the country grew to look like a vast chessboard, with dark and light squares of grass and corn land, melting at no great distance into a colorless and unbroken horizon. But as night blotted out the earth, the heaven lighted up its stars. Never have I seen them so lustrous nor in such number. Jeanne reclined with her eyes upturned toward those limitless fields of prayer and vision; and their radiance, benignly gentle, rested on her face. Was she tired or downcast, or merely dreaming? I knew not. But there was something so singularly poetic in her look and attitude that she seemed to me to epitomize in herself all the beauty of the night.

I was afraid to speak. Her father's sleep, and our consequent isolation, made me ill at ease. She, too, seemed so careless of my presence, so far away in dreamland, that I had to await opportunity, or rather her leave, to recall her from it.

Finally she broke the silence herself. A little beyond Monza she drew closer her shawl, that the night wind had ruffled, and bent over toward me.

[169]

"You must excuse my father; he is rather tired this evening, for he has been on his feet since five o'clock."

"The day has been so hot, too, Mademoiselle, and the medals 'came not in single spies, but in battalions'; he has a right to sleep after the battle."

"Dear old father! You gave him a real treat, for which he will always be obliged to you."

"I trust the recollection of to-day will efface that of the blot of ink, for which I am still filled with remorse."

"Remorse is rather a serious word."

"No, Mademoiselle, I really mean remorse, for I wounded the feelings of a gentleman who has every claim on my respect. I never have dared to speak of this before. But if you would be kind enough to tell Monsieur Charnot how sorry I have been for it, you would relieve me of a burden."

I saw her eyes fixed upon me for a moment with a look of attention not previously granted to me. She seemed pleased.

"With all my heart," she said.

There was a moment's silence.

"Was this Rafaella, whose story you have told me, worthy of your friend's long regret?"

"I must believe so."

"It is a very touching story. Are you fond of Monsieur Lampron?"

"Beyond expression, Mademoiselle; he is so openhearted, so true a friend, he has the soul of the artist and the seer. I am sure you would rate him very highly if you knew him."

"But I do know him, at least by his works. Where

am I to be seen now, by the way? What has become of my portrait?"

"It's at Lampron's house, in his mother's room, where Monsieur Charnot can go and see it if he likes."

"My father does not know of its existence," she said, with a glance at the slumbering man of learning.

"Has he not seen it?"

"No, he would have made so much ado about nothing. So Monsieur Lampron has kept the sketch? I thought it had been sold long ago."

"Sold! you did not think he would sell it!"

"Why not? Every artist has the right to sell his works."

"Not work of that kind."

"Just as much as any other kind."

"No, he could not have done that. He would no more sell it than he would sell the portrait of Rafaella Dannegianti. They are two similar relics, two precious reminiscences."

Mademoiselle Charnot turned, without a reply, to look at the country which was flying past us in the darkness.

I could just see her profile, and the nervous movement of her eyelids.

As she made no attempt to speak, her silence emboldened me.

"Yes, Mademoiselle, two similar relics, yet sometimes in my hours of madness—as to-day, for instance, here, with you near me—I dare to think that I might be less unfortunate than my friend—that his dream is gone forever—but that mine might return to me—if you were willing."

She quickly turned toward me, and in the darkness I saw her eyes fixed on mine.

Did the darkness deceive me as to the meaning of this mute response? Was I the victim of a fresh delusion? I fancied that Jeanne looked sad, that perhaps she was thinking of the oaths sworn only to be broken by her former lover, but that she was not quite displeased.

However, it lasted only for a second. When she spoke, it was in a higher key:

"Don't you think the breeze is very fresh this evening?"

A long-drawn sigh came from the back part of the carriage. M. Charnot was waking up.

He wished to prove that he had only been meditating.

"Yes, my dear, it's a charming evening," he replied; "these Italian nights certainly keep up their reputation."

Ten minutes later the carriage drew up, and M. Charnot shook hands with me before the door of his hotel.

"Many thanks, my dear young sir, for this delightful drive home! I hope we shall meet again. We are off to Florence to-morrow; is there anything I can do for you there?"

"No, thank you."

Mademoiselle Charnot gave me a slight bow. I watched her mount the first few steps of the staircase, with one hand shading her eyes from the glare of the gaslights, and the other holding up her wraps, which had come unfolded and were falling around her.

CHAPTER XV

BACK TO PARIS

MILAN, June 27th.   Before daybreak.

E asked me whether there was anything he could do for me at Florence. There is something, but he would refuse to do it; for I wish him to inform his charming daughter that my thoughts are all of her; that I have spent the night recalling yesterday's trip—now the roads of Desio and the galleries of the villa, now the drive back to Milan.   M. Charnot only figured in my dreams as sleeping.   I seemed to have found my tongue, and to be pouring forth a string of well-turned speeches which I never should have ready at real need.   If I could only see her again now that all my plans are weighed and thought out and combined!   Really, it is hard that one can not live one's life over twice—at least certain passages in it—this episode, for instance. . . .

What is her opinion of me?   When her eyes fixed themselves on mine I thought I could read in their depths a look of inquiry, a touch of surprise, a grain of disquiet.   But her answer?   She is going to Florence bearing with her the answer on which my life depends. They are leaving by the early express.   Shall I take

[173]

it, too? Florènce, Rome, Naples—why not? Italy is free to all, and particularly to lovers. I will toss my cap over the mill for the second time. I will get money from somewhere. If I am not allowed to show myself, I will look on from a distance, hidden in the crowd. At a pinch I will disguise myself—as a guide at Pompeii, a lazzarone at Naples. She shall find a sonnet in the bunch of fresh flowers offered her by a peasant at the door of her hotel. And at least I shall bask in her smile, the sound of her voice, the glints of gold about her temples, and the pleasure of knowing that she is near even when I do not see her.

On second thoughts, no; I will not go to Florence. As I always distrust first impulses, which so often run reason to a standstill, I had recourse to a favorite device of mine. I asked myself: What would Lampron advise? And at once I conjured up his melancholy, noble face, and heard his answer: "Come back, my dear boy."

Paris, July 2d.

When you arrive by night, and from the windows of the flying train, as it whirls past the streets at full speed, you see Paris enveloped in red steam, pierced by starry lines of gas-lamps crisscrossing in every direction, the sight is weird, and almost beautiful. You might fancy it the closing scene of some gigantic gala, where strings upon strings of colored lanterns brighten the night above a moving throng, passing, repassing, and raising a cloud of dust that reddens in the glow of expiring Bengal lights.

Moreover, the illusion is in part a reality, for the

great city is in truth lighted for its nightly revel. Till one o'clock in the morning it is alight and riotous with the stir and swing of life.

But the dawn is bleak enough.

That delicious hour which puts a spirit of joy into green field and hedgerow is awful to look upon in Paris. You leave the train half-frozen, to find the porters red-eyed from their watch. The customs officials, in a kind of stupor, scrawl cabalistic signs upon your trunk. You get outside the station, to find a few scattered cabs, their drivers asleep inside, their lamps blinking in the mist.

"Cabby, are you disengaged?"

"Depends where you want to go."

"No. 91 Rue de Rennes."

"Jump in!"

The blank streets stretch out interminably, gray and silent; the shops on either hand are shuttered; in the squares you will find only a dog or a scavenger; theatre bills hang in rags around the kiosks, the wind sweeps their tattered fragments along the asphalt in yesterday's dust, with here and there a bunch of faded flowers. The Seine washes around its motionless boats; two greatcoated policemen patrol the bank and wake the echoes with their tramp. The fountains have ceased to play, and their basins are dry. The air is chilly, and sick with evil odors. The whole drive is like a bad dream. Such was my drive from the Gare de Lyon to my rooms. When I was once at home, installed in my own domains, this unpleasant impression gradually wore off. There was friendliness in my sticks of furniture. I examined those silent witnesses, my chair, my table, and my books. What had happened while I was away? Apparently nothing important. The furniture had a light coating of dust, which showed that no one had touched it, not even Madame Menin. It was funny, but I wished to see Madame Menin. A sound, and I heard my opposite neighbor getting to work. He is a hydrographer, and engraves maps for a neighboring publisher. I never could get up as early as he. The willow seemed to have made great progress during the summer. I flung up the window and said "Good-morning!" to the wallflowers, to the old wall of the Carmelites, and the old black tower. Then the sparrows began. What o'clock could it be? They came all together with a rush, chirping, the hungry thieves, wheeling about, skirting the walls in their flight, quick as lightning, borne on their pointed wings. They had seen the sun—day had broken!

And almost immediately I heard a cart pass, and a hawker crying:

"Ground-SEL! Groundsel for your dickey-birds!"

To think that there are people who get up at that unearthly hour to buy groundsel for their canaries! I looked to see whether any one had called in my absence; their cards should be on my table. Two were there: "Monsieur Lorinet, retired solicitor, town councillor, of Bourbonnoux-lez-Bourges, deputy-magistrate"; "Madame Lorinet, née Poupard."

I was surprised not to find a third card: "Berthe Lorinet, of no occupation, anxious to change her name." Berthe will be difficult to get rid of. I presume she didn't dare to leave a card on a young man, it wouldn't

have been proper. But I have no doubt she was here.
I scent a trick of my uncle's, one of those Atlantic cables
he takes for spider's threads and makes his snares of.
The Lorinet family have been here, with the twofold
intention of taking news of me to my "dear good
uncle," and discreetly recalling to my forgetful heart
the charms of Berthe of the big feet.

"Good-morning, Monsieur Mouillard!"

"Hallo! Madame Menin! Good-morning, Madame Menin!"

"So you are back at last, sir! How brown you have
got—quite sunburnt. You are quite well, I hope, sir?"

"Very well, thank you; has any one been here in my
absence?"

"I was going to tell you, sir; the plumber has been
here, because the tap of your cistern came off in my
hand. It wasn't my fault; there had been a heavy rain
that morning. So——"

"Never mind, it's only a tap to pay for. We won't
say any more about it. But did any one come to see
me?"

"Ah, let me see—yes. A big gentleman, rather red-
faced, with his wife, a fat lady, with a small voice; a
fine woman, rather in my style, and their daughter—
but perhaps you know her, sir?"

"Yes, Madame Menin, you need not describe her.
You told them that I was away, and they said they were
very sorry."

"Especially the lady. She puffed and panted and
sighed: 'Dear Monsieur Mouillard! How unlucky we
are, Madame Menin; we have just come to Paris as

he has gone to Italy. My husband and I would have liked *so* much to see him! You may think it fanciful, but I should like above all things to look round his rooms. A student's rooms must be *so* interesting. Stay there, Berthe, my child.' I told them there was nothing very interesting, and that their daughter might just as well come in too, and then I showed them everything."

"They didn't stay long, I suppose?"

"Quite long enough. They were an age looking at your photograph album. I suppose they haven't got such things where they come from. Madame Lorinet couldn't tear herself away from it. 'Nothing but men,' she said, 'have you noticed that, Jules?' 'Well, Madame,' I said, 'that's just how it is here; except for me, and I don't count, only gentlemen come here. I've kept house for bachelors where—well, there are not many——'"

"That will do, Madame Menin; that will do. I know you always think too highly of me. Hasn't Lampron been here?"

"Yes, sir; the day before yesterday. He was going off for a fortnight or three weeks into the country to paint a portrait of some priest—a bishop, I think."

July 15th.

"*Midi, roi des étés.*" I know by heart that poem by "Monsieur le Comte de l'Isle," as my Uncle Mouillard calls him. Its lines chime in my ears every day when I return from luncheon to the office I have left an hour before. Merciful heaven, how hot it is! I am just back from a hot climate, but it was nothing compared to Paris in July. The asphalt melts underfoot; the wood pavement is simmering in a viscous mess of tar; the ideal is forced to descend again and again to iced lager beer; the walls beat back the heat in your face; the dust in the public gardens, ground to atoms beneath the tread of many feet, rises in clouds from under the water-cart to fall, a little farther on, in white showers upon the passers-by. I wonder that, as a finishing stroke, the cannon in the Palais Royal does not detonate all day long.

To complete my misery, all my acquaintances are out of town: the Boule family is bathing at Trouville; the second clerk has not returned from his holiday; the fourth only waited for my arrival to get away himself; Lampron, detained by my Lord Bishop and the forest shades, gives no sign of his existence; even Monsieur and Madame Plumet have locked up their flat and taken the train for Barbizon.

Thus it happens that the old clerk Jupille and I have been thrown together. I enjoy his talk. He is a simple-hearted, honorable man, with a philosophy that I am sure can not be in the least German, because I can understand it. I have gradually told him all my secrets. I felt the need of a confidant, for I was stifling, metaphorically as well as literally. Now, when he hands me a deed, instead of saying "All right," as I used to, I say, "Take a chair, Monsieur Jupille"; I shut the door, and we talk. The clerks think we're talking law, but the clerks are mistaken.

Yesterday, for instance, he whispered to me:

"I have come down the Rue de l'Université. They will soon be back."

"How did you learn that?"

"I saw a man carrying coals into the house, and asked for whom they were, that's all."

Again, we had a talk, just now, which shows what progress I have made in the old clerk's heart. He had just submitted a draft to me. I had read it through and grunted my approval, yet M. Jupille did not go.

"Anything further, Monsieur Jupille?"

"Something to ask of you—to do me a kindness, or, rather, an honor."

"Let's hear what it is."

"This weather, Monsieur Mouillard, is very good for fishing, though rather warm."

"*Rather* warm, Monsieur Jupille!"

"It is not too warm. It was much hotter than this in 1844, yet the fish bit, I can tell you! Will you join us next Sunday in a fishing expedition? I say 'us,' because one of your friends is coming, a great amateur of the rod who honors me with his friendship, too."

"Who is he?"

"A secret, Monsieur Mouillard, a little secret. You will be surprised. It is settled then—next Sunday?"

"Where shall I meet you?"

"Hush, the office-boy is listening. That boy is too sharp; I'll tell you some other time."

"As you please, Monsieur Jupille; I accept the invitation unconditionally."

"I am so glad you will come, Monsieur Mouillard.

I only wish we could have a little storm between this and then."

He spoke the truth; his satisfaction was manifest, for I never have seen him rub the tip of his nose with the feathers of his quill pen so often as he did that afternoon, which was with him the sign of exuberant joy, all his gestures having subdued themselves long since to the limits of his desk.

July 20th.

I have seen Lampron once more. He bears his sorrow bravely. We spoke for a few moments of his mother. I spoke some praise of that humble soul for the good she had done me, which led him to enlarge upon her virtues.

"Ah," he said, "if you had only seen more of her! My dear fellow, if I am an honest man; if I have passed without failing through the trials of my life and my profession; if I have placed my ideal beyond worldly success; in a word, if I am worth anything in heart or brain, it is to her I owe it. We never had been parted before; this is our first separation, and it is the final one. I was not prepared for it."

Then he changed the subject brusquely:

"What about your love-affair?"

"Fresher than ever."

"Did it survive half an hour's conversation?"

"It grew the stronger for it."

"Does she still detest you?"

I told him the story of our trip to Desio, and our conversation in the carriage, without omitting a detail.

[181]

He listened in silence. At the end he said:

"My dear Fabien, there must be no delay. She must hear your proposal within a week."

"Within a week! Who is to make it for me?"

"Whoever you like. That's your business. I have been making inquiries while you were away; she seems a suitable match for you. Besides, your present position is ridiculous; you are without a profession; you have quarrelled, for no reason, with your only relative; you must get out of the situation with credit, and marriage will compel you to do so."

CHAPTER XVI

A FISHING-TRIP AND AN OLD FRIEND

July 21st.

 JUPILLE had written to tell me where
I was to meet him on the Sunday,
giving me the most minute directions.
I might take the train to Massy, or to
Bièvres. However, I preferred to take
the train to Sceaux and walk from
there, leaving Chatenay on my left,
striking across the woods of Verrières
toward the line of forts, coming out between Igny and
Amblainvilliers, and finally reaching a spot where the
Bièvre broadens out between two wooded banks into
a pool as clear as a spring and as full of fish as a
nursery-pond.

"Above all things, tell nobody where it is!" begged
Jupille. "It is our secret; I discovered it myself."

When I left Sceaux to meet Jupille, who had started
before daybreak, the sun was already high. There was
not a cloud nor a breath of wind; the sway of summer
lay over all things. But, though the heat was broiling,
the walk was lovely. All about me was alive with voice
or perfume. Clouds of linnets fluttered among the
branches, golden beetles crawled upon the grass, thousands of tiny whirring wings beat the air—flies, gnats,

gadflies, bees—all chorusing the life-giving warmth of
the day and the sunshine that bathed and penetrated all
nature. I halted from time to time in the parched glades
to seek my way, and again pushed onward through the
forest paths overarched with heavy-scented leafage, onward over the slippery moss up toward the heights,
below which the Bièvre stole into view.

There it lay, at my feet, gliding between banks of
verdure which seemed a season younger than the grass
I stood on. I began to descend the slope, knowing that
M. Jupille was awaiting me somewhere in the valley.
I broke into a run. I heard the murmur of water in
the hollows, and caught glimpses of forget-me-not tufts
in low-lying grassy corners. Suddenly a rod outlined
itself against the sky, between two trees. It was he,
the old clerk; he nodded to me and laid down his
line.

"I thought you never were coming."

"That shows you don't know me. Any sport?"

"Not so loud! Yes, capital sport. I'll bait a line for
you."

"And where is your friend, Monsieur Jupille?"

"There he is."

"Where?"

"Staring you in the face; can't you see him?"

Upon my word, I could see nobody, until he directed
my gaze with his fishing-rod, when I perceived, ten
yards away, a large back view of white trousers and
brown, unbuckled waistcoat, a straw hat which seemed
to conceal a head, and a pair of shirt-sleeves hanging
over the water.

This mass was motionless.

"He must have got a bite," said Jupille, "else he would have been here before now. Go and see him."

Not knowing whom I was about to address, I gave a warning cough as I came near him.

The unknown drew a loud breath, like a man who wakes with a start.

"That you, Jupille?" he said, turning a little way; "are you out of bait?"

"No, my dear tutor, it is I."

"Monsieur Mouillard, at last!"

"Monsieur Flamaran! Jupille told the truth when he said I should be surprised. Are you fond of fishing?"

"It's a passion with me. One must keep one or two for one's old age, young man."

"You've been having sport, I hear."

"Well, this morning, between eight and nine, there were a few nibbles; but since then the sport has been very poor. However, I'm very glad to see you again, Mouillard. That essay of yours was extremely good."

The eminent professor had risen, displaying a face still red from his having slept with his head on his chest, but beaming with good-will. He grasped my hand with heartiness and vigor.

"Here's rod and line for you, Monsieur Mouillard, all ready baited," broke in Jupille. "If you'll come with me I'll show you a good place."

"No, no, Jupille, I'm going to keep him," answered M. Flamaran; "I haven't uttered a syllable for three hours. I must let myself out a little. We will fish side by side, and chat."

"As you please, Monsieur Flamaran; but I don't call that fishing."

He handed me the implement, and sadly went his way.

M. Flamaran and I sat down together on the bank, our feet resting on the soft sand strewn with dead branches. Before us spread the little pool I have mentioned, a slight widening of the stream of the Bièvre, once a watering-place for cattle. The sun, now at high noon, massed the trees' shadow close around their trunks. The unbroken surface of the water reflected its rays back in our eyes. The current was barely indicated by the gentle oscillation of a few water-lily leaves. Two big blue dragonflies poised and quivered upon our floats, and not a fish seemed to care to disturb them.

"Well," said M. Flamaran, "so you are still managing clerk to Counsellor Boule?"

"For the time."

"Do you like it?"

"Not particularly."

"What are you waiting for?"

"For something to turn up."

"And carry you back to Italy, I suppose?"

"Then you know I have just been there?"

"I know all about it. Charnot told me of your meeting, and your romantic drive by moonlight. By the way, he's come back with a bad cold; did you know that?"

I assumed an air of sympathy:

"Poor man! When did he get back?"

"The day before yesterday. Of course I was the first

to hear of it, and we spent yesterday evening together.
It may surprise you, Mouillard, and you may think I
exaggerate, but I think Jeanne has come back prettier
than she went."

"Do you really think so?"

"I really do. That southern sun—look out, my dear
Mouillard, your line is half out of water—has brought
back her roses (they're brighter than ever, I declare),
and the good spirits she had lost, too, poor girl. She is
cheerful again now, as she used to be. I was very anxious about her at one time. You know her sad story?"

"Yes."

"The fellow was a scoundrel, my dear Mouillard, a
regular scoundrel! I never was in favor of the match,
myself. Charnot let himself be drawn into it by an old
college friend. I told him over and over again, 'It's
Jeanne's dowry he's after, Charnot—I'm convinced of
it. He'll treat Jeanne badly and make her miserable,
mark my words.' But I wasted my breath; he wouldn't
listen to a word. Anyhow, it's quite off now. But it
was no slight shock, I can tell you; and it gave me
great pain to witness the poor child's sufferings."

"You are so kind-hearted, Monsieur Flamaran!"

"It's not that, Mouillard; but I have known Jeanne
ever since she was born. I watched her grow up, and
I loved her when she was still a little mite; she's as good
as my adoptive daughter. You understand me when I
say adoptive. I do not mean that there exists between
us that legal bond in imitation of nature which is per-
mitted by our codes—*adoptio imitatur naturam;* not
that, but that I love her like a daughter—Sidonie never

having presented me with a daughter, nor with a son either, for that matter."

A cry from Jupille interrupted M. Flamaran:

"Can't you hear it rattle?"

The good man was tearing to us, waving his arms like a madman, the folds of his trousers flapping about his thin legs like banners in the wind.

We leaped to our feet, and my first idea, an absurd one enough, was that a rattlesnake was hurrying through the grass to our attack.

I was very far from the truth. The matter really was a new line, invented by M. Jupille, cast a little further than an ordinary one, and rigged up with a float like a raft, carrying a little clapper. The fish rang their own knell as they took the hook.

"It's rattling like mad!" cried Jupille, "and you don't stir! I couldn't have thought it of you, Monsieur Flamaran."

He ran past us, brandishing a landing-net as a warrior his lance; he might have been a youth of twenty-five. We followed, less keen and also less confident than he. He was right, though; when he drew up his line, the float of which was disappearing in jerks, carrying the bell along with it beneath the water, he brought out a fair-sized jack, which he declared to be a giant.

He let it run for some time, to tire it, and to prolong the pleasure of playing it.

"Gentlemen," he cried, "it is cutting my finger off!"

A stroke from the landing-net laid the monster at our

feet, its strength all spent. It weighed rather under four pounds. Jupille swore to six.

My learned tutor and I sat down again side by side, but the thread of our conversation had been broken past mending. I tried to talk of *her*, but M. Flamaran insisted on talking of me, of Bourges, of his election as professor, and of the radically distinct characteristics by which you can tell the bite of a gudgeon from that of a stickleback.

The latter part of this lecture was, however, purely theoretical, for he got up two hours before sunset without having hooked a fish.

"A good day, all the same," he said. "It's a good place, and the fish were biting this morning. We'll come here again some day, Jupille; with an east wind you ought to catch any quantity of gudgeons." He kept pace beside me on our way home, but wearied, no doubt, with long sitting, with the heat, and the glare from the water, fell into a reverie, from which the incidents of the walk were unable to rouse him.

Jupille trotted before us, carrying his rod in one hand, a luncheon-basket and a fishbag in the other. He turned round and gave us a look at each cross-road, smiled beneath his heavy moustache, and went on faster than before. I felt sure that something out of the way was about to happen, and that the silent quill-driver was tasting a quiet joke.

I had not guessed the whole truth.

At a turn of the road M. Flamaran suddenly pulled up, looked all around him, and drew a deep breath.

RENÉ BAZIN

"Hallo, Jupille! My good sir, where are you taking
us? If I can believe my eyes, this is the Chestnut Knoll,
down yonder is Plessis Piquet, and we are two miles
from the station and the seven o'clock train!"

There was no denying it. A donkey emerged from
the wood, hung with tassels and bells, carrying in its
panniers two little girls, whose parents toiled behind,
goad in hand. The woods had become shrubberies,
through which peeped the thatched roofs of rustic summerhouses, mazes, artificial waterfalls, grottoes, and
ruins; all the dread handiwork of the rustic decorator
burst, superabundant, upon our sight, with shy odors
of beer and cooking. Broken bottles strewed the paths;
the bushes all looked weary, harassed, and overworked;
a confused murmur of voices and crackers floated toward us upon the breeze. I knew full well from these
signs that we were nearing "ROBINSON CRUSOE," the
land of rustic inns. And, sure enough, here they all
were: "THE OLD ROBINSON," "THE NEW ROBIN-
SON," "THE REAL ORIGINAL ROBINSON," "THE
ONLY GENUINE ROBINSON," "ROBINSON'S CHESTNUT
GROVE," "ROBINSON'S PARADISE," each unique and
each authentic. All alike have thatched porches,
sanded paths, transparencies lighted with petroleum
lamps, tinsel stars, summerhouses, arrangements for
open-air illumination and highly colored advertisements, in which are set forth all the component elements
of a "ROBINSON," such as shooting-galleries, bowling-
alleys, swings, private arbors, Munich beer, and dinner
in a tree.

"Jupille!" exclaimed M. Flamaran, "you have

shipwrecked us! This is Crusoe's land; and what the dickens do you mean by it?"

The old clerk, utterly discomfited, and wearing that hangdog look which he always assumed at the slightest rebuke from Counsellor Boule, pulled a face as long as his arm, went up to M. Flamaran and whispered a word in his ear.

"Upon my word! Really, Jupille, what are you thinking of? And I a professor, too! Thirty years ago it would have been excusable, but to-day! Besides, Sidonie expects me home to dinner——"

He stopped for a moment, undecided, looking at his watch.

Jupille, who was eying him intently, saw his distinguished friend gradually relax his frown and burst into a hearty laugh.

"By Jove! it's madness at my age, but I don't care. We'll renew our youth for an hour or so. My dear Mouillard, Jupille has ordered dinner for us here. Had I been consulted I should have chosen any other place. Yet what's to be done? Hunger, friendship, and the fact that I can't catch the train, combine to silence my scruples. What do you say?"

"That we are in for it now."

"So be it, then." And led by Jupille, still carrying his catch, we entered THE ONLY GENUINE ROBINSON.

M. Flamaran, somewhat ill at ease, cast inquiring glances on the clearings in the sgrubberies. I thought I heard stifled laughter behind the trees.

"You have engaged Chestnut Number Three,

gentlemen," said the proprietor. "Up these stairs, please."

We ascended a staircase winding around the trunk. Chestnut Number 3 is a fine old tree, a little bent, its sturdy lower branches supporting a platform surrounded by a balustrade, six rotten wooden pillars, and a thatched roof, shaped like a cocked hat, to shelter the whole. All the neighboring trees contain similar constructions, which look from a little distance like enormous nests. They are greatly in demand at the dinner hour; you dine thirty feet up in the air, and your food is brought up by a rope and pulley.

When M. Flamaran appeared on the platform he took off his hat, and leaned with both hands on the railing to give a look around. The attitude suggested a public speaker. His big gray head was conspicuous in the light of the setting sun.

"He's going to make a speech!" cried a voice. "Bet you he isn't," replied another.

This was the signal. A rustling was heard among the leaves, and numbers of inquisitive faces peeped out from all corners of the garden. A general rattling of glasses announced that whole parties were leaving the tables to see what was up. The waiters stopped to stare at Chestnut Number 3. The whole population of Juan Fernandez was staring up at Flamaran without in the least knowing the reason why.

"Gentlemen," said a voice from an arbor, "Professor Flamaran will now begin his lecture."

A chorus of shouts and laughter rose around our tree.

"Hi, old boy, wait till we're gone!" "Ladies, he will discourse to you on the law of husband and wife!" "No, on the foreclosure of mortgages!" "No, on the payment of debts!" "Oh, you naughty old man! You ought to be shut up!"

M. Flamaran, though somewhat put out of countenance for the moment, was seized with a happy inspiration. He stretched out an arm to show that he was about to speak. He opened his broad mouth with a smile of fatherly humor, and the groves, attentive, heard him thunder forth these words:

"Boys, I promise to give you all white marks if you let me dine in peace!"

The last words were lost in a roar of applause.

"Three cheers for old Flamaran!"

Three cheers were given, followed by clapping of hands from various quarters, then all was silence, and no one took any further notice of our tree.

M. Flamaran left the railing and unfolded his napkin.

"You may be sure of my white marks, young men," he said, as he sat down.

He was delighted at his success as an orator, and laughed gayly. Jupille, on the other hand, was as pale as if he had been in a street riot, and seemed rooted to the spot where he stood.

"It's all right, Jupille; it's all right, man!' A little ready wit is all you need, dash my wig!"

The old clerk gradually regained his composure, and the dinner grew very merry. Flamaran's spirits, raised by this little incident, never flagged. He had a story for every glass of wine, and told them all with a quiet humor of his own.

Toward the end of dinner, by the time the waiter came to offer us "almonds and raisins, pears, peaches, preserves, méringues, brandy cherries," we had got upon the subject of Sidonie, the pearl of Forez. M. Flamaran narrated to us, with dates, how a friend of his one day depicted to him a young girl at Montbrison, of fresh and pleasing appearance, a good housekeeper, and of excellent family; and how he—M. Flamaran—had forthwith started off to find her, had recognized her before she was pointed out to him, fell in love with her at first sight, and was not long in obtaining her affection in return. The marriage had taken place at St. Galmier.

"Yes, my dear Mouillard," he added, as if pointing a moral, "thirty years ago last May I became a happy man; when do you think of following my example?"

At this point, Jupille suddenly found himself one too many, and vanished down the corkscrew stair.

"We once spoke of an heiress at Bourges," M. Flamaran went on. "Apparently that's all off?"

"Quite off."

"You were within your rights; but now, why not a Parisienne?"

"Yes, indeed; why not?"

"Perhaps you are prejudiced in some way against Parisiennes?"

"I? Not the least."

"I used to be, but I've got over it now. They have a charm of their own, a certain style of dressing, walking, and laughing which you don't find outside the fortifications. For a long time I used to think that these qualities stood them in lieu of virtues. That was a slander; there are plenty of Parisiennes endowed with every virtue; I even know a few who are angels."

At this point, M. Flamaran looked me straight in the eyes, and, as I made no reply, he added:

"I know one, at least: Jeanne Charnot. Are you listening?"

"Yes, Monsieur Flamaran."

"Isn't she a paragon?"

"She is."

"As sensible as she is tender-hearted?"

"So I believe."

"And as clever as she is sensible?"

"That is my opinion."

"Well, then, young man, if that's your opinion—excuse my burning my boats, all my boats—if that's your opinion, I don't understand why——Do you suppose she has no money?"

"I know nothing about her means."

"Don't make any mistake; she's a rich woman. Do you think you're too young to marry?"

"No."

"Do you fancy, perhaps, that she is still bound by that unfortunate engagement?"

"I trust she is not."

"I'm quite sure she is not. She is free, I tell you, as free as you. Well, why don't you love her?"

"But I do love her, Monsieur Flamaran!"

"Why, then, I congratulate you, my boy!"

He leaned across the table and gave me a hearty grasp of the hand. He was so agitated that he could not speak—choking with joyful emotion, as if he had been Jeanne's father, or mine.

After a minute or so, he drew himself up in his chair, reached out, put a hand on each of my shoulders and kept it there as if he feared I might fly away.

"So you love her, you love her! Good gracious, what a business I've had to get you to say so! You are quite right to love her, of course, of course—I could not have understood your doing otherwise; but I must say this, my boy, that if you tarry too long, with her attractions, you know what will happen."

"Yes, I ought to ask for her at once."

"To be sure you ought."

"Alas! Monsieur Flamaran, who is there that I can send on such a mission for me? You know that I am an orphan."

"But you have an uncle."

"We have quarrelled."

"You might make it up again, on an occasion like this."

"Out of the question; we quarrelled on her account; my uncle hates Parisiennes."

"Damn it all, then! send a friend—a friend will do under the circumstances."

"There's Lampron."

"The painter?"

"Yes, but he doesn't know Monsieur Charnot. It would only be one stranger pleading for another. My chances would be small. What I want——"

THE INK-STAIN

"Is a friend of both parties, isn't it? Well, what am I?"

"The very man!"

"Very well. I undertake to ask for her hand! I shall ask for the hand of the charming Jeanne for both of us; for you, who will make her happy; and for myself, who will not entirely lose her if she marries one of my pupils, one of my favorite graduates—my friend, Fabien Mouillard. And I won't be refused—no, damme, I won't!"

He brought down his fist upon the table with a tremendous blow which made the glasses ring and the decanters stagger.

"Coming!" cried a waiter from below, thinking he was summoned.

"All right, my good fellow!" shouted M. Flamaran, leaning over the railings. "Don't trouble. I don't want anything."

He turned again toward me, still filled with emotion, but somewhat calmer than he had been.

"Now," said he, "let us talk, and do you tell me all."

And we began a long and altogether delightful talk.

A more genuine, a finer fellow never breathed than this professor let loose from school and giving his heart a holiday—a simple, tender heart, preserved beneath the science of the law like a grape in sawdust. Now he would smile as I sang Jeanne's praises; now he would sit and listen to my objections with a truculent air, tightening his lips till they broke forth in vehement denial. "What! You dare to say! Young man, what are you afraid of?" His overflowing kindness dis-

charged itself in the sincerest and most solemn assev-
erations.

We had left Juan Fernandez far behind us; we were
both far away in that Utopia where mind penetrates
mind, heart understands heart. We heard neither the
squeaking of a swing beneath us, nor the shouts of
laughter along the promenades, nor the sound of a band
tuning up in a neighboring pavilion. Our eyes, raised
to heaven, failed to see the night descending upon us,
vast and silent, piercing the foliage with its first stars.
Now and again a warm breath passed over us, blown
from the woods; I tasted its strangely sweet perfume;
I saw in glimpses the flying vision of a huge dark tulip,
striped with gold, unfolding its petals on the moist bank
of a dyke, and I asked myself whether a mysterious
flower had really opened in the night, or whether it was
but a new feeling, slowly budding, unfolding, blossoming within my heart.

CHAPTER XVII

PLEASURES OF EAVESDROPPING

July 22d.

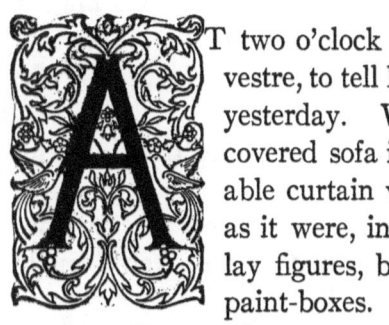T two o'clock to-day I went to see Sylvestre, to tell him all the great events of yesterday. We sat down on the old covered sofa in the shadow of the movable curtain which divides the studio, as it were, into two rooms, among the lay figures, busts, varnish-bottles, and paint-boxes. Lampron likes this chiaroscuro. It rests his eyes.

Some one knocked at the door.

"Stay where you are," said Sylvestre; "it's a customer come for the background of an engraving. I'll be with you in two minutes. Come in!" As he was speaking he drew the curtain in front of me, and through the thin stuff I could see him going toward the door, which had just opened.

"Monsieur Lampron?"

"I am he, Monsieur."

"You don't recognize me, Monsieur?"

"No, Monsieur."

"I'm surprised at that."

"Why so? I have never seen you."

"You have taken my portrait!"

[199]

"Really!"

I was watching Lampron, who was plainly angered at this brusque introduction. He left the chair which he had begun to push forward, let it stand in the middle of the studio, and went and sat down on his engraving-stool in the corner, with a somewhat haughty look, and a defiant smile lurking behind his beard. He rested his elbow on the table and began to drum with his fingers.

"What I have had the honor to inform you is the simple truth, Monsieur. I am Monsieur Charnot of the Institute."

Lampron gave a glance in my direction, and his frown melted away.

"Excuse me, Monsieur; I only know you by your back. Had you shown me that side of you I might perhaps have recognized——"

"I have not come here to listen to jokes, Monsieur; and I should have come sooner to demand an explanation, but that it was only this morning I heard of what I consider a deplorable abuse of your talents. But picture-shows are not in my line. I did not see myself there. My friend Flamaran had to tell me that I was to be seen at the last Salon, together with my daughter, sitting on a tree-trunk in the forest of Saint-Germain. Is it true, Monsieur, that you drew me sitting on a trunk?"

"Quite true."

"That's a trifle too rustic for a man who does not go outside of Paris three times a year. And my daughter you drew in profile—a good likeness, I believe."

"It was as like as I could make it."

"Then you confess that you drew both my daughter and myself?"

"Yes, I do, Monsieur."

"It may not be so easy for you to explain by what right you did so; I await your explanation, Monsieur."

"I might very well give you no explanation whatever," replied Lampron, who was beginning to lose patience. "I might also reply that I no more needed to ask your permission to sketch you than to ask that of the beeches, oaks, elms, and willows. I might tell you that you formed part of the landscape, that every artist who sketches a bit of underwood has the right to stick a figure in——"

"A figure, Monsieur! do you call me a figure?"

"A gentleman, I mean. Artists call it figure. Well, I might give you this reason, which is quite good enough for you, but it is not the real one. I prefer to tell you frankly what passed. You have a very beautiful daughter, Monsieur."

M. Charnot made his customary bow.

"One of my friends is in love with her. He is shy, and dares not tell his love. We met you by chance in the wood, and I was seized with the idea of making a sketch of Mademoiselle Jeanne, so like that she could not mistake it, and then exhibiting it with the certainty of her seeing it and guessing its meaning. I trusted she would recall to her mind, not myself, for my youth is past, but a young friend of mine who is of the age and build of a lover. If this was a crime, Monsieur, I am ready to take the blame for it upon myself, for I alone committed it."

"It certainly was criminal, Monsieur; criminal in
you, at any rate—you who are a man of weight, respected for your talent and your character—to aid and
abet in a frivolous love-affair."

"It was the deepest and most honorable sentiment,
Monsieur."

"A blaze of straw!"

"Nothing of the sort!"

"Don't tell me! Your friend's a mere boy."

"So much the better for him, and for her, too! If
you want a man of middle age for your son-in-law, just
try one and see what they are worth. You may be sorry
that you ever refused this boy, who, it is true, is only
twenty-four, has little money, no decided calling, nor
yet that gift of self-confidence which does instead of
merit for so many people; but who is a brave and noble
soul, whom I can answer for as for myself. Go, Monsieur, you will find your daughter great names, fat
purses, gold lace, long beards, swelling waistbands,
reputations, pretensions, justified or not, everything, in
short, in which he is poor; but him you will never
find again! That is all I have to tell you."

Lampron had become animated and spoke with heat.
There was the slightest flash of anger in his eyes.

I saw M. Charnot get up, approach him, and hold
out his hand.

"I did not wish you to say anything else, Monsieur;
that is enough for me. Flamaran asked my daughter's
hand for your friend only this morning. Flamaran
loses no time when charged with a commission. He,
too, told me much that was good of your friend. I also

questioned Counsellor Boule. But however flattering characters they might give him, I still needed another, that of a man who had lived in complete intimacy with Monsieur Mouillard, and I could find no one but you."

Lampron stared astonished at this little thin-lipped man who had just changed his tone and manner so unexpectedly.

"Well, Monsieur," he answered, "you might have got his character from me with less trouble; there was no need to make a scene."

"Excuse me. You say I should have got his character; that is exactly what I did not want; characters are always good. What I wanted was a cry from the heart of a friend outraged and brought to bay. That is what I got, and it satisfies me. I am much obliged to you, Monsieur, and beg you will excuse my conduct."

"But, since we are talking sense at present, allow me to put you a question in my turn. I am not in the habit of going around the point. Is my friend's proposal likely to be accepted or not?"

"Monsieur Lampron, in these delicate matters I have decided for the future to leave my daughter entirely free. Although my happiness is at stake almost as entirely as hers, I shall not say a word save to advise. In accordance with this resolve I communicated Flamaran's proposal to her."

"Well?"

"I expected she would refuse it."

"But she said 'Yes'?"

"She did not say 'No;' if she had, you can guess that I should not be here."

At this reply I quite lost my head, and was very near tearing aside the curtain, and bursting forth into the studio with a shout of gratitude.

But M. Charnot added:

"Don't be too sure, though. There are certain serious, and, perhaps, insurmountable obstacles. I must speak to my daughter again. I will let your friend know of our final decision as soon as I can. Good-by, Monsieur."

Lampron saw him to the street, and I heard their steps grow distant in the passage. A moment later Sylvestre returned and held out both hands to me, saying:

"Well, are you happy now?"

"Of course I am, to a certain extent."

"'To a certain extent'! Why, she loves you."

"But the obstacles, Sylvestre!"

"Nonsense!"

"Perhaps insurmountable—those were his words."

"Why, obstacles are the salt of all our joys. What a deal you young men want before you can be called happy! You ask Life for certainties, as if she had any to give you!"

And he began to discuss my fears, but could not quite disperse them, for neither of us could guess what the obstacles could be.

August 2d.

After ten days of waiting, during which I have employed Lampron and M. Flamaran to intercede for me, turn and turn about; ten days passed in hovering between mortal anguish and extravagant hopes, during which I have formed, destroyed, taken up again and abandoned more plans than I ever made in all my life before, yesterday, at five o'clock, I got a note from M. Charnot, begging me to call upon him the same evening.

I went there in a state of nervous collapse. He received me in his study, as he had done seven months before, at our first interview, but with a more solemn politeness; and I noticed that the paper-knife, which he had taken up from the table as he resumed his seat, shook between his fingers. I sat in the same chair in which I had felt so ill at ease. To tell the truth, I felt very much the same, yesterday. M. Charnot doubtless noticed it, and wished to reassure me.

"Monsieur," said he, "I receive you as a friend. Whatever may be the result of our interview, you may be assured of my esteem. Therefore do not fear to answer me frankly."

He put several questions to me concerning my family, my tastes, and my acquaintance in Paris. Then he requested me to tell the simple story of my boyhood and my youth, the recollections of my home, of the college at La Châtre, of my holidays at Bourges, and of my student life.

He listened without interruption, playing with the ivory paper-knife. When I reached the date—it was only last December—when I saw Jeanne for the first time:

"That's enough," said he, "I know or guess the rest. Young man, I promised you an answer; this is it——"

For the moment, I ceased to breathe; my very heart seemed to stop beating.

"My daughter," went on M. Charnot, "has at this moment several proposals of marriage to choose from. You see I hide nothing from you. I have left her time to reflect; she has weighed and compared them all, and communicated to me yesterday the result of her reflections. To richer and more brilliant matches she prefers an honest man who loves her for herself, and you, Monsieur, are that honest man."

"Oh, thank you, thank you, Monsieur!" I cried.

"Wait a moment, there are two conditions."

"Were there ten, I would accept them without question!"

"Don't hurry. You will see; one is my daughter's, the other comes from both of us."

"You wish me to have some profession, perhaps?"

"No, that's not it. Clearly my son-in-law will never sit idle. Besides, I have some views on that subject, which I will tell you later if I have the chance. No, the first condition exacted by my daughter, and dictated by a feeling which is very pleasant to me, is that you promise never to leave Paris."

"That I swear to, with all the pleasure in life!"

"Really? I feared you had some ties."

"Not one."

"Or dislike for Paris."

"No, Monsieur; only a preference for Paris, with freedom to indulge it. Your second condition?"

"The second, to which my daughter and I both attach importance, is that you should make your peace with your uncle. Flamaran tells me you have quarrelled."

"That is true."

"I hope it is not a serious difference. A mere cloud, isn't it?"

"Unfortunately not. My uncle is very positive——"

"But at the same time his heart is in the right place, so far as I could judge from what I saw of him—in June, I think it was."

"Yes."

"You don't mind taking the first step?"

"I will take as many as may be needed."

"I was sure you would. You can not remain on bad terms with your father's brother, the only relative you have left. In our eyes this reconciliation is a duty, a necessity. You should desire it as much as, and even more than, we."

"I shall use every effort, Monsieur, I promise you."

"And in that case you will succeed, I feel sure."

M. Charnot, who had grown very pale, held out his hand to me, and tried hard to smile.

"I think, Monsieur Fabien, that we are quite at one, and that the hour has come——"

He did not finish the sentence, but rose and went to open a door between two bookcases at the end of the room.

"Jeanne," he said, "Monsieur Fabien accepts the two conditions, my dear."

And I saw Jeanne come smiling toward me.

And I, who had risen trembling, I, who until then had lost my head at the mere thought of seeing her, I, who had many a time asked myself in terror what I should say on meeting her, if ever she were mine, I felt myself suddenly bold, and the words rushed to my lips to thank her, to express my joy.

My happiness, however, was evident, and I might have spared my words.

For the first half-hour all three of us talked together.

Then M. Charnot pushed back his armchair, and we two were left to ourselves.

He had taken up a newspaper, but I am pretty sure he held it upside down. In any case he must have been reading between the lines, for he did not turn the page the whole evening.

He often cast a glance over the top of the paper, folded in four, to the corner where we were sitting, and from us his eyes travelled to a pretty miniature of Jeanne as a child, which hung over the mantelpiece.

What comparisons, what memories, what regrets, what hopes were struggling in his mind? I know not, but I know he sighed, and had not we been there I believe he would have wept.

To me Jeanne showed herself simple as a child, wise and thoughtful as a woman. A new feeling was growing every instant within me, of perfect rest of heart; the certainty of happiness for all my life to come.

Yes, my happiness travelled beyond the present, as I looked into the future and saw a long series of days passed by her side; and while she spoke to me, tranquil, confident, and happy too, I thought I saw the great wings of my dream closing over and enfolding us.

We spoke in murmurs. The open window let in the warm evening air and the confused roar of the city.

"I am to be your friend and counsellor?" said she.

"Always."

"You promise that you will ask my advice in all things, and that we shall act in concert?"

"I do."

"If this very first evening I ask you for a proof of this, you won't be angry?"

"On the contrary."

"Well, from what you have told me of your uncle, you seem to have accepted the second condition, of making up your quarrel, rather lightly."

"I have only promised to do my best."

"Yes, but my father counts upon your success. How do you intend to act?"

"I haven't yet considered."

"That's just what I foresaw, and I thought it would perhaps be a good thing if we considered it together."

"Mademoiselle, I am listening; compose the plan of campaign, and I will criticise it."

Jeanne clasped her hands over her knees and assumed a thoughtful look.

"Suppose you wrote to him."

"There is every chance that he would not answer."

"Reply paid?"

"Mademoiselle, you are laughing; you are no counsellor any longer."

"Yes, I am. Let us be serious. Suppose you go to see him."

"That's a better idea. He may perhaps receive me."

"In that case you will capture him. If you can only get a man to listen——"

14 [209]

"Not my uncle, Mademoiselle. He will listen, and do you know what his answer will be?"

"What?"

"This, or something like it: 'My worthy nephew, you have come to tell me two things, have you not? First, that you are about to marry a Parisienne; secondly, that you renounce forever the family practice. You merely confirm and aggravate our difference. You have taken a step further backward. It was not worth while your coming out of your way to tell me this, and you may return as soon as you please.'"

"You surprise me. There must be some way of getting at him, if he is really good-hearted, as you say. If I could see your uncle I should soon find out a way."

"If *you* could see him! Yes, that would be the best way of all; it couldn't help succeeding. He imagines you as a flighty Parisienne; he is afraid of you; he is more angry with me for loving you than for refusing to carry on his practice. If he could only see you, he would soon forgive me."

"You think so?"

"I'm sure of it."

"Do you think that if I were to look him in the face, as I now look at you, and to say to him: 'Monsieur Mouillard, will you not consent to my becoming your niece?' do you think that then he would give in?"

"Alas! Mademoiselle, why can not it be tried?"

"It certainly is difficult, but I won't say it can not."

We explained, or rather Jeanne explained, the case to M. Charnot, who is assuredly her earliest and most complete conquest. At first he cried out against the idea. He said it was entirely my business, a family matter in which he had no right to interfere. She insisted. She carried his scruples by storm. She boldly proposed a trip to Bourges, and a visit to M. Mouillard. She overflowed with reasons, some of them rather weak, but all so prettily urged! A trip to Bourges would be delightful—something so novel and refreshing! Had M. Charnot complained on the previous evening, or had he not, of having to stop in Paris in the heat of August? Yes, he had complained, and quite right too, for his colleagues did not hesitate to leave their work and rush off to the country. Then she cited examples: one off to the Vosges, another at Arcachon, yet another at Deauville. And she reminded him, too, that a certain old lady, one of his old friends of the Faubourg St. Germain, lived only a few miles out of Bourges, and had invited him to come and see her, she didn't know how many times, and that he had promised and promised and never kept his word. Now he could take the opportunity of going on from Bourges to her château. Finally, as M. Charnot continued to urge the singularity of such behavior, she replied:

"My dear father! not at all; in visiting Monsieur Mouillard you will be only fulfilling a social duty."

"How so, I should like to know?"

"He paid you a visit, and you will be returning it!"

M. Charnot tossed his head, like a father who, though he may not be convinced, yet admits that he is beaten.

. . . .

As for me, Jeanne, I'm beginning to believe in the fairies again.

CHAPTER XVIII

August 3d.

HAVE made another visit to the Rue de l'Université. They have decided to make the trip. I leave for Bourges tomorrow, a day in advance of M. and Mademoiselle Charnot, who will arrive on the following morning.

I am sent on first to fulfil two duties: to engage comfortable rooms at the hotel—first floor with southern aspect—and then to see my uncle and prepare him for his visitors.

I am to prepare him without ruffling him. Jeanne has sketched my plan of campaign. I am to be the most affectionate of nephews, though he show himself the crustiest of uncles; to prevent him from recurring to the past, to speak soberly of the present, to confess that Mademoiselle Charnot is aware of my feelings for her, and shows herself not entirely insensible to them; but I am to avoid giving details, and must put off a full explanation until later, when we can study the situation together. M. Mouillard can not fail to be appeased by such deference, and to observe a truce while I hint at the possibility of a family council. Then, if these first advances are well received, I am to tell him that M.

THE INK-STAIN

Charnot is actually travelling in the neighborhood, and, without giving it as certain, I may add that if he stops at Bourges he may like to return my uncle's visit.

There my *rôle* ends. Jeanne and M. Charnot will do the rest. It is with Jeanne, by the light of her eyes and her smile, that M. Mouillard is "to study the situation;" he will have to struggle against the redoubtable arguments of her youth and beauty. Poor man!

Jeanne is full of confidence. Her father, who has learned his lesson from her, feels sure that my uncle will give in. Even I, who can not entirely share this optimism, feel that I incline to the side of hope.

When I reached home, the porter handed me two cards from Larivé. On the first I read:

CH. LARIVÉ,

Managing Clerk.

P. P. C.

The second, on glazed cardboard, announced, likewise in initials, another piece of news:

CH. LARIVÉ,

Formerly Managing Clerk.

P. F. P. M.

So the Parisian who swore he could not exist two **days** in the country is leaving Paris. That was fated. **He is**

RENÉ BAZIN

about to be married; I'm sure I don't object. The only consequence to me is that we never shall meet again, and I shall not weep over that.

If you have ever been in Bourges, you may have seen the little Rue Sous-les-Ceps, the Cours du Bât d'Argent and de la Fleur-de-lys, the Rues de la Mère-de-Dieu, des Verts-Galants, Mausecret, du Moulin-le-Roi, the Quai Messire-Jacques, and other streets whose ancient names, preserved by a praiseworthy sentiment or instinctive conservatism, betoken an ancient city still inhabited by old-fashioned people, by which I mean people attached to the soil, strongly marked with the stamp of the provincial in manners as in language; people who understand all that a name is to a street—its honor, its spouse if you will, from which it must not be divorced.

My Uncle Mouillard, most devoted and faithful citizen of Bourges, naturally lives in one of these old streets, the Rue du Four, within the shadow of the cathedral, beneath the swing of its chimes.

Within fifteen minutes after my arrival at Bourges I was pulling the deer's foot which hangs, depilated with long use, beside his door. It was five o'clock, and I knew for certain that he would not be at home. When the courts rise, one of the clerks carries back his papers to the office, while he moves slowly off, his coat-tails flapping in the breeze, either to visit a few friends and clients, respectable dames who were his partners in the dance in the year 1840, or more often to take a "constitutional" along the banks of the Berry Canal, where, in the poplar shade, files of little gray donkeys are towing string after string of big barges.

So I was sure not to meet him.

Madeleine opened the door to me, and started as if shot.

"Monsieur Fabien!"

"Myself, Madeleine. My uncle is not at home?"

"No, Monsieur. Do you really mean to come in, Monsieur?"

"Why not?"

"The master's so changed since his visit to Paris, Monsieur Fabien!"

Madeleine stood still, with one hand holding up her apron, the other hanging, and gazed at me with reproachful anxiety.

"I must come in, Madeleine. I have a secret to tell you."

She made no answer, but turned and walked before me into the house.

It was not thus that I used to be welcomed in days gone by! *Then* Madeleine used to meet me at the station. She used to kiss me, and tell me how well I looked, promising the while a myriad sweet dishes which she had invented for me. Hardly did I set foot in the hall before my uncle, who had given up his evening walk for my sake, would run out of his study, heart and cravat alike out of their usual order at seeing me—*me*, a poor, awkward, gaping schoolboy. To-day that is ancient history. To-day I am afraid to meet my uncle, and Madeleine is afraid to let me in.

She told me not a word of it, but I easily guessed that floods of tears had streamed from her black eyes down her thin cheeks, now pale as wax. Her face is quite transparent, and looks as if a tiny lamp were lighting it from within. There are strong feelings, too, beneath that impassive mask. Madeleine comes from Bayonne, and has Spanish blood in her. I have heard that she was lovely as a girl of twenty. With age her features have grown austere. She looks like a widow who is a widow indeed, and her heart is that of a grandmother.

She glided before me in her slippers to that realm of peace and silence, her kitchen. I followed her in. Two things that never found entrance there are dust and noise. A lonely goldfinch hangs in a wicker cage from the rafters, and utters from time to time a little shrill call. His note and the metallic tick-tick of Madeleine's clock alone enliven the silent flight of time. She sat down in the low chair where she knits after dinner.

"Madeleine, I am about to be married; did you know it?"

She slowly shook her head.

"Yes, in Paris, Monsieur Fabien; that's what makes the master so unhappy."

"You will soon see her whom I have chosen, Madeleine."

"I do not think so, Monsieur Fabien."

"Yes, yes, you will; and you will see that it is my uncle who is in the wrong."

"I have not often known him in the wrong."

"That has nothing to do with it. My marriage is fully decided upon, and all I want is to get my uncle's

consent to it. Do you understand? I want to make
friends with him."

Madeleine shook her head again.

"You won't succeed."

"My dear Madeleine!"

"No, Monsieur Fabien, you won't succeed."

"He must be very much changed, then!"

"So much that you could hardly believe it; so much
that I can hardly keep myself from changing too. He,
who had such a good appetite, now has nothing but
fads. It's no good my cooking him dainties, or buying
him early vegetables; he never notices them, but looks
out of the window as I come in at the door with a surprise for him. In the evening he often forgets to go out
in the garden, and sits at table, his elbows on his rum-
pled napkin, his head between his hands, and what he
thinks of he keeps to himself. If I try to talk of you—
and I have tried, Monsieur Fabien—he gets up in a
rage, and forbids me to open my mouth on the subject.
The house is not cheerful, Monsieur Fabien. Every
one notices how he has changed; Monsieur Lorinet and
his lady never enter the doors; Monsieur Hublette and
Monsieur Horlet come and play dummy, looking all the
time as if they had come for a funeral, thinking it will
please the master. Even the clients say that the master treats them like dogs, and that he ought to sell his
practice."

"Then it isn't sold?"

"Not yet, but I think it will be before long."

"Listen to me, Madeleine; you have always been
good and devoted to me; I am sure you still are fond of

me; do me one last service. You must manage to put me up here without my uncle knowing it."

"Without his knowing it, Monsieur Fabien!"

"Yes, say in the library; he never goes in there. From there I can study him, and watch him, without his seeing me, since he is so irritable and so easily upset, and as soon as you see an opportunity I shall make use of it. A sign from you, and down I come."

"Really, Monsieur Fabien——"

"It must be done, Madeleine; I must manage to speak to him before ten o'clock to-morrow morning, for my bride is coming."

"The Parisienne? She coming here!"

"Yes, with her father, by the train which gets in at six minutes past nine to-morrow."

"Good God! is it possible?"

"To see you, Madeleine; to see my uncle, to make my peace with him. Isn't it kind of her?"

"Kind? Monsieur Fabien! I tremble to think of what will happen. All the same, I shall be glad to have a sight of your young lady, of course."

And so we settled that Madeleine was not to say a word to my uncle about my being in Bourges, within a few feet of him. If she perceived any break in the gloom which enveloped M. Mouillard, she was to let me know; if I were obliged to put off my interview to the morrow, and to pass the night on the sofa-bed in the library, she was to bring me something to eat, a rug, and "the pillow you used in your holidays when you were a boy."

I was installed then in the big library on the first

floor, adjoining the drawing-room, its other door opening on the passage opposite M. Mouillard's door, and
its two large windows on the garden.   What a look
of good antique middle-class comfort there was about
it, from the floor of bees'-waxed oak, with its inequal-
ities of level, to the four bookcases with glass doors,
surmounted by four bronzed busts of Herodotus,
Homer, Socrates, and Marmontel!   Nothing had been
moved; the books were still in the places where I had
known them for twenty years; Voltaire beside Rousseau,
the *Dictionary of Useful Knowledge,* and Rollin's *Ancient History,* the slim, well bound octavos of the
Meditations of St. Ignatius, side by side with an enormous quarto on veterinary surgery.

The savage arrows, said to be poisoned, which always
used to frighten me so much, were still arranged like a
peacock's tail over the mantel-shelf, each end of which
was adorned by the same familiar lumps of white coral.
The musical-box, which I was not allowed to touch till
I was eighteen, still stood in the left-hand corner, and
on the writing-table, near the little blotting-book that
held the note-paper, rose, still majestic, still turning obedient to the touch within its graduated belts, the terrestrial globe "on which are marked the three voyages of
Captain Cook, both outward and homeward."   Ah,
captain, how often have we sailed those voyages together!   What grand headway we made as we scoured
the tropics in the heel of the trade-wind, our ship thread-
ing archipelagoes whose virgin forests stared at us in
wonder, all their strange flowers opening toward us,
seeking to allure us and put us to sleep with their dan-

gerous perfumes. But we always guessed the snare, we saw the points of the assegais gleaming amid the tall grasses; you gave the word in your full, deep voice, and our way lay infinite before us; we followed it, always on the track of new lands, new discoveries, until we reached the fatal isle of Owhyhee, the spot where this terrestrial globe is spotted with a tear—for I wept over you, my captain, at the age when tears unlock themselves and flow easily from a heart filled with enchantment!

Seven o'clock sounded from the cathedral; the garden door slammed to; my uncle was returning.

I saw him coming down the winding path, hat in hand, with bowed head. He did not stop before his graftings; he passed the clump of petunias without giving them that all-embracing glance I know so well, the glance of the rewarded gardener. He gave no word of encouragement to the Chinese duck which waddled down the path in front of him.

Madeleine was right. The time was not ripe for reconciliation; and more, it would need a great deal of sun to ripen it. O Jeanne, if only you were here!

"Any one called while I've been out?"

This, by the way, is the old formula to which my uncle has always been faithful. I heard Madeleine answer, with a quaver in her voice:

"No, nobody for you, sir."

"Some one for you, then? A lover, perhaps, my faithful Madeleine? The world is so foolish nowadays that even you might take it into your head to marry and leave me. Come, serve my dinner quickly, and if the gentleman with the decoration calls—you know whom I mean?"

THE INK-STAIN

"The tall, thin gentleman?"

"Yes. Show him into the drawing-room."

"A gentleman by himself into the drawing-room? No, sir, no. The floor was waxed only yesterday, and the furniture's not yet in order."

"Very well! I'll see him in here."

My uncle went into the dining-room underneath me, and for twenty minutes I heard nothing more of him, save the ring of his wineglass as he struck on it to summon Madeleine.

He had hardly finished dinner when there came a ring at the street door. Some one asked for M. Mouillard, the gentleman with the decoration, I suppose, for Madeleine showed him in, and I could tell by the noise of his chair that my uncle had risen to receive his visitor.

They sat down and entered into conversation. An indistinct murmur reached me through the ceiling. Occasionally a clearer sound struck my ear, and I thought I knew that high, resonant voice. It was no doubt delusion, still it beset me there in the silence of the library, haunting my thoughts as they wandered restlessly in search of occupation. I tried to recollect all the men with fluty voices that I had ever met in Bourges: a corn-factor from the Place St. Jean; Rollet, the sacristan; a fat manufacturer, who used to get my uncle to draw up petitions for him claiming relief from taxation. I hunted feverishly in my memory as the light died away from the windows, and the towers of St. Stephen's gradually lost the glowing aureole conferred on them by the setting sun.

After about an hour the conversation grew heated.

My uncle coughed, the flute became shrill. I caught these fragments of their dialogue.

"No, Monsieur!"

"Yes, Monsieur!"

"But the law?"

"Is as I tell you."

"But this is tyranny!"

"Then our business is at an end."

Apparently it was not, though; for the conversation gradually sank down the scale to a monotonous murmur. A second hour passed, and yet a third. What could this interminable visit portend?

It was near eleven o'clock. A ray from the rising moon shone between the trees in the garden. A big black cat crept across the lawn, shaking its wet paws. In the darkness it looked like a tiger. In my mind's eye I saw Madeleine sitting with her eyes fixed on her dead hearth, telling her beads, her thoughts running with mine: "It is years since Monsieur Mouillard was up at such an hour." Still she waited, for never had any hand but hers shot the bolt of the street door; the house would not be shut if shut by any other than herself.

At last the dining-room door opened. "Let me show you a light; take care of the stairs."

Then followed the "Good-nights" of two weary voices, the squeaking of the big key turning in the lock, a light footstep dying away in the distance, and my uncle's heavy tread as he went up to his bedroom. The business was over.

How slowly my uncle went upstairs! The burden of sorrow was no metaphor in his case. He, who used to be as active as a boy, could now hardly support his own weight.

He crossed the landing and went into his room. I thought of following him; only a few feet lay between us. No doubt it was late, but his excited state might have predisposed him in my favor. Suddenly I heard a sigh—then a sob. He was weeping; I determined to risk all and rush to his assistance.

But just as I was about to leave the library a skirt rustled against the wall, though I had heard no sound of footsteps preceding it. At the same instant a little bit of paper was slipped in under the door—a letter from the silent Madeleine. I unfolded the paper and saw the following words written across from one corner to the other, with a contempt for French spelling, which was thoroughly Spanish:

"Ni allais pat ceux soire."

Very well, Madeleine, since that's your advice, I'll refrain.

I lay down to sleep on the sofa. Yet I was very sorry for the delay. I hated to let the night go by without being reconciled to the poor old man, or without having attempted it at least. He was evidently very wretched to be affected to tears, for I had never known him to weep, even on occasions when my own tears had flowed freely. Yet I followed my old and faithful friend's advice, for I knew that she had the peace of the household as much at heart as I; but I felt that I should seek long and vainly before I could discover what this latest trouble was, and what part I had in it.

CHAPTER XIX

JEANNE THE ENCHANTRESS

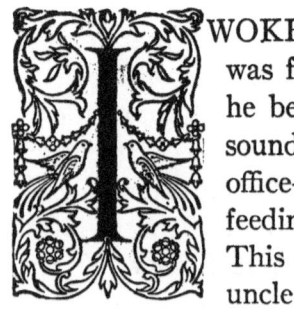WOKE up at seven; my first thought was for M. Mouillard. Where could he be? I listened, but could hear no sound. I went to the window; the office-boy was lying flat on the lawn, feeding the goldfish in the fountain. This proved beyond a doubt that my uncle was not in.

I went downstairs to the kitchen.

"Well, Madeleine, has he gone out?"

"He went at six o'clock, Monsieur Fabien."

"Why didn't you wake me?"

"How could I guess? Never, never does he go out before breakfast. I never have seen him like this before, not even when his wife died."

"What can be the matter with him?"

"I think it's the sale of the practice. He said to me last night, at the foot of the staircase: 'I am a broken-hearted man, Madeleine, a broken-hearted man. I might have got over it, but that monster of ingratitude, that cannibal'—saving your presence, Monsieur Fabien—'would not have it so. If I had him here I don't know what I should do to him.'"

"Didn't he tell you what he would do to the cannibal?"

"No. So I slipped a little note under your door when I went upstairs."

"Yes. I am much obliged to you for it. Is he any calmer this morning?"

"He doesn't look angry any longer, only I noticed that he had been weeping."

"Where is he?"

"I don't know at all. Besides, you might as well try to catch up with a deer as with him."

"That's true. I'd better wait for him. When will he be in?"

"Not before ten. I can tell you that it's not once a year that he goes out like this in the morning."

"But, Madeleine, Jeanne will be here by ten!"

"Oh, is Jeanne her name?"

"Yes. Monsieur Charnot will be here, too. And my uncle, whom I was to have prepared for their visit, will know nothing about it, nor even that I slept last night beneath his roof."

"To tell the truth, Monsieur Fabien, I don't think you've managed well. Still, there is Dame Fortune, who often doesn't put in her word till the last moment."

"Entreat her for me, Madeleine, my dear."

But Dame Fortune was deaf to prayers. My uncle did not return, and I could find no fresh expedient. As I made my way, vexed and unhappy, to the station, I kept asking myself the question that I had been turning over in vain for the last hour:

"I have said nothing to Monsieur Mouillard. Had I better say anything now to Monsieur Charnot?"

My fears redoubled when I saw Jeanne and M. Charnot at the windows of the train, as it swept past me into the station.

A minute later she stepped on to the platform, dressed all in gray, with roses in her cheeks, and a pair of gull's wings in her hat.

M. Charnot shook me by the hand, thoroughly delighted at having escaped from the train and being able to shake himself and tread once more the solid earth. He asked after my uncle, and when I replied that he was in excellent health, he went to get his luggage.

"Well!" said Jeanne. "Is all arranged?"

"On the contrary, nothing is."

"Have you seen him?"

"Not even that. I have been watching for a favorable opportunity without finding one. Yesterday evening he was busy with a visitor; this morning he went out at six. He doesn't even know that I am in Bourges."

"And yet you were in his house?"

"I slept on a sofa in his library."

She gave me a look which was as much as to say, "My poor boy, how very unpractical you are!"

"Go on doing nothing," she said; "that's the best you can do. If my father didn't think he was expected he would beat a retreat at once."

At this instant, M. Charnot came back to us, having seen his two trunks and a hatbox placed on top of the omnibus of the Hôtel de France.

THE INK-STAIN

"That is where you have found rooms for us?"

"Yes, sir."

"It is now twelve minutes past nine; tell Monsieur Mouillard that we shall call upon him at ten o'clock precisely."

I went a few steps with them, and saw them into the omnibus, which was whirled off at a fast trot by its two steeds.

When I had lost them from my sight I cast a look around me, and noticed three people standing in line beneath the awning, and gazing upon me with interest. I recognized Monsieur, Madame, and Mademoiselle Lorinet. They were all smiling with the same look of contemptuous mockery. I bowed. The man alone returned my salute, raising his hat. By some strange freak of fate, Berthe was again wearing a blue dress.

I went back in the direction of the Rue du Four, happy, though at my wits' end, forming projects that were mutually destructive; now expatiating in the seventh heaven, now loading myself with the most appalling curses. I slipped along the streets, concealed beneath my umbrella, for the rain was falling; a great storm-cloud had burst over Bourges, and I blessed the rain which gave me a chance to hide my face.

From the banks of the Voizelle to the old quarter around the cathedral is a rather long walk. When I turned from the Rue Moyenne, the Boulevard des Italiens of Bourges, into the Rue du Four, a blazing sun was drying the rain on the roofs, and the cuckoo clock at M. Festuquet's—a neighbor of my uncle—was striking the hour of meeting.

I had not been three minutes at the garden door, a key to which had been given me by Madeleine, when M. Charnot appeared with Jeanne on his arm.

"To think that I've forgotten my overshoes, which I never fail to take with me to the country!"

"The country, father?" said Jeanne, "why, Bourges is a city!"

"To be sure—to be sure," answered M. Charnot, who feared he had hurt my feelings.

He put on his spectacles and began to study the old houses around him.

"Yes, a city; really quite a city."

I do not remember what commonplace I stammered.

Little did I care for M. Charnot's overshoes or the honor of Bourges at that moment! On the other side of the wall, a few feet off, I felt the presence of M. Mouillard. I reflected that I should have to open the door and launch the Academician, without preface, into the presence of the lawyer, stake my life's happiness, perhaps, on my uncle's first impressions, play at any rate the decisive move in the game which had been so disastrously opened.

Jeanne, though she did her best to hide it, was extremely nervous. I felt her hand tremble in mine as I took it.

"Trust in God!" she whispered, and aloud: "Open the door."

I turned the key in the lock. I had arranged that Madeleine should go at once to M. Mouillard and tell him that there were some strangers waiting in the garden. But either she was not on the lookout, or she did not at once perceive us, and we had to wait a few minutes at the bottom of the lawn before any one came.

I hid myself behind the trees whose leafage concealed the wall.

M. Charnot was evidently pleased with the view before him, and turned from side to side, gently smacking his lips like an epicure. And, in truth, my uncle's garden was perfection; the leaves, washed by the rain, were glistening in the fulness of their verdure, great drops were falling from the trees with a silvery tinkle, the petunias in the beds were opening all their petals and wrapping us in their scent; the birds, who had been mute while the shower lasted, were now fluttering, twittering, and singing beneath the branches. I was like one bewitched, and thought these very birds were discussing us. The greenfinch said:

"Old Mouillard, look! Here's Princess Goldenlocks at your garden gate."

The tomtit said:

"Look out, old man, or she'll outwit you."

The blackbird said:

"I have heard of her from my grandfather, who lived in the Champs Elysées. She was much admired there."

The swallow said:

"Jeanne will have your heart in the time it takes me to fly round the lawn."

The rook, who was a bit of a lawyer, came swooping down from the cathedral tower, crying:

"Caw, caw, caw! Let her show cause—cause!"

And all took up the chorus:

"If you had our eyes, Monsieur Mouillard, you would see her looking at your study; if you had our ears, you would hear her sigh; if you had our wings, you would fly to Jeanne."

No doubt it was this unwonted concert which attracted Madeleine's attention. We saw her making her way, stiffly and slowly, toward the study, which stood in the corner of the garden.

M. Mouillard's tall figure appeared on the threshold, filling up the entire doorway.

"In the garden, did you say? Whatever is your idea in showing clients into the garden? Why did you let them in?"

"I didn't let them in; they came in of themselves."

"Then the door can't have been shut. Nothing is shut here. I'll have them coming in next by the drawing-room chimney. What sort of people are they?"

"There's a gentleman and a young lady whom I don't know."

"A young lady whom you don't know—a judicial separation, I'll warrant—it's indecent, upon my word it is. To think that there are people who come to me about judicial separations and bring their young ladies with them!"

As Madeleine fled before the storm and found shelter in her kitchen, my uncle smoothed back his white hair with both his hands—a surviving touch of personal vanity —and started down the walk around the grass-plot.

I effaced myself behind the trees. M. Charnot, thinking I was just behind him, stepped forward with airy freedom.

THE INK-STAIN

My uncle came down the path with a distracted air, like a man overwhelmed with business, only too pleased to snatch a moment's leisure between the parting and the coming client. He always loved to pass for being overwhelmed with work.

On his way he flipped a rosebud covered with blight, kicked off a snail which was crawling on the path; then, half-way down the path, he suddenly raised his head and gave a look at his disturber.

His bent brows grew smooth, his eyes round with the stress of surprise.

"Is it possible? Monsieur Charnot of the Institute!"

"The same, Monsieur Mouillard."

"And this is Mademoiselle Jeanne?"

"Just so; she has come with me to repay your kind visit."

"Really, that's too good of you, much too good, to come such a way to see me!"

"On the contrary, the most natural thing in the world, considering what the young people are about."

"Oh! is your daughter about to be married?"

"Certainly, that's the idea," said M. Charnot, with a laugh.

"I congratulate you, Mademoiselle!"

"I have brought her here to introduce her to you, Monsieur Mouillard, as is only right."

"Right! Excuse me, no."

"Indeed it is."

"Excuse me, sir. Politeness is all very well in its way, but frankness is better. I went to Paris chiefly to get certain information which you were good enough to give me. But, really, it was not worth your while to come from Paris to Bourges to thank me, and to bring your daughter too."

"Excuse me in my turn! There are limits to modesty, Monsieur Mouillard, and as my daughter is to marry your nephew, and as my daughter was in Bourges, it was only natural that I should introduce her to you."

"Monsieur, I have no longer a nephew."

"He is here."

"And I never asked for your daughter."

"No, but you have received your nephew beneath your roof, and consequently——"

"Never!"

"Monsieur Fabien has been in your house since yesterday; he told you we were coming."

"No, I have not seen him; I never should have received him! I tell you I no longer have a nephew! I am a broken man, a—a—a——"

His speech failed him, his face became purple, he staggered and fell heavily, first in a sitting posture, then on his back, and lay motionless on the sanded path.

I rushed to the rescue.

When I got up to him Jeanne had already returned from the little fountain with her handkerchief dripping, and was bathing his temples with fresh water. She was the only one who kept her wits about her. Madeleine had raised her master's head and was wailing aloud.

"Alas!" she said, "it's that dreadful colic he had ten years ago which has got him again. Dear heart! how ill he was! I remember how it came on, just like this, in the garden."

THE INK-STAIN

I interrupted her lamentations by saying:

"Monsieur Charnot, I think we had better take Monsieur Mouillard up to bed."

"Then why don't you do it?" shouted the numismatist, who had completely lost his temper. "I didn't come here to act at an ambulance; but, since I must, do you take his head."

I took his head, Madeleine walked in front, Jeanne behind. My uncle's vast proportions swayed between M. Charnot and myself. M. Charnot, who had skilfully gathered up the legs, looked like a hired pallbearer.

As we met with some difficulty in getting upstairs, M. Charnot said, with clenched teeth:

"You've managed this trip nicely, Monsieur Fabien; I congratulate you sincerely!"

I saw that he intended to treat me to several variations on this theme.

But there was no time for talk. A moment later my uncle was laid, still unconscious, upon his bed, and Jeanne and Madeleine were preparing a mustard-plaster together, in perfect harmony. M. Charnot and I waited in silence for the doctor whom we had sent the office-boy to fetch. M. Charnot studied alternately my deceased aunt's wreath of orange-blossoms, preserved under a glass in the centre of the chimney-piece, and a painting of fruit and flowers for which it would have been hard to find a buyer at an auction. Our wait for the doctor lasted ten long minutes. We were very anxious, for M. Mouillard showed no sign of returning consciousness. Gradually, however, the remedies began to act upon him. The eyelids fluttered feebly; and just as the doctor opened the door, my uncle opened his eyes.

We rushed to his bedside.

"My old friend," said the doctor, "you have had plenty of people to look after you. Let me feel your pulse—rather weak; your tongue? Say a word or two."

"A shock—rather sudden——" said my uncle.

The doctor, following the direction of the invalid's eyes, which were fixed on Jeanne, upright at the foot of the bed, bowed to the young girl, whom he had not at first noticed; turned to me, who blushed like an idiot; then looked again at my uncle, only to see two big tears running down his cheeks.

"Yes, I understand; a pretty stiff shock, eh? At our age we should only be stirred by our recollections, emotions of bygone days, something we're used to; but our children take care to provide us with fresh ones, eh?"

M. Mouillard's breast heaved.

"Come, my dear fellow," proceeded the doctor; "I give you leave to give your future niece one kiss, and that in my presence, that I may be quite sure you don't abuse the license. After that you must be left quite alone; no more excitement, perfect rest."

Jeanne came forward and raised the invalid's head.

"Will you give me a kiss, uncle?"

She offered him her rosy cheek.

"With all my heart," said my uncle as he kissed her; "good girl—dear girl."

Then he melted into tears, and hid his face in his pillow.

"And now we must be left alone," said the doctor.

He came down himself in a moment, and gave us an encouraging account of the patient.

Hardly had the street door closed behind him when we heard the lawyer's powerful voice thundering down the stairs.

"Charnot!"

The old numismatist flew up the flight of stairs.

"Did you call me, Monsieur?"

"Yes, to invite you to dinner. I couldn't say the words just now, but it was in my mind."

"It is very kind of you, but we leave at nine o'clock."

"I dine at seven; that's plenty of time."

"It will tire you too much."

"Tire me? Why, don't you think I dine every day?"

"I promise to come and inquire after you before leaving."

"I can tell you at once that I am all right again. No, no, it shall never be said that you came all the way from Paris to Bourges only to see me faint. I count upon you and Mademoiselle Jeanne."

"On all three of us?"

"That makes three, with me; yes, sir."

"Excuse me, four."

"I hope the fourth will have the sense to go and dine elsewhere."

"Come, come, Monsieur Mouillard; your nephew, your ward——"

"I ceased to be his guardian four years ago, and his uncle three weeks ago."

"He longs to put an end to this ill feeling——"

"Allow me to rest a little," said M. Mouillard, "in

order that I may be in a better condition to receive my guests."

He lay down again, and showed clearly his intention of saying not another word on the subject.

During the conversation between M. Charnot and my uncle, to which we had listened from the foot of the staircase, Jeanne, who had a moment before been rejoicing over the completeness of the victory which she thought she had achieved, grew quite down-hearted.

"I thought he had forgiven you when he kissed me," she said. "What can we do now? Can't you help us, Madeleine?"

Madeleine, whose heart was beginning to warm to Jeanne, sought vainly for an expedient, and shook her head.

"Ought he to go and see his uncle?" asked Jeanne.

"No," said Madeleine.

"Well, suppose you write to him, Fabien?"

Madeleine nodded approval, and drew from the depths of her cupboard a little glass inkstand, a rusty penholder, and a sheet of paper, at the top of which was a dove with a twig in its beak.

"My cousin at Romorantin died just before last New Year's Day," she explained; "so I had one sheet more than I needed."

I sat down at the kitchen table with Jeanne leaning over me, reading as I wrote. Madeleine stood upright and attentive beside the clock, forgetting all about her kitchen fire as she watched us with her black eyes.

This is what I wrote beneath the dove:

THE INK-STAIN

"MY DEAR UNCLE:

"I left Paris with the intention of putting an end to the misunderstanding between us, which has lasted only too long, and which has given me more pain than you can guess. I had no possible opportunity of speaking to you between five o'clock yesterday afternoon, when I arrived here, and ten o'clock this morning. If I had been able to speak with you, you would not have refused to restore me to your affection, which, I confess, I ought to have respected more than I have. You would have given your consent to my union, on which depends your own happiness, my dear uncle, and that of your nephew,

"FABIEN."

"Rather too formal," said Jeanne. "Now, let me try."

And the enchantress added, with ready pen:

"It is I, Monsieur Mouillard, who am chiefly in need of forgiveness. Mine is the greater fault by far. You forbade Monsieur Fabien to love me, and I took no steps to prevent his doing so. Even yesterday, when he came to your house, it was my doing. I had assured him that your kind heart would not be proof against his loving confession.

"Was I really wrong in that?

"The words that you spoke just now have led me to hope that I was not.

"But if I was wrong, visit your anger on me alone. Forgive your nephew, invite him to dinner instead of us, and let me depart, regretting only that I was not judged worthy of calling you uncle, which would have been so pleasant and easy a name to speak.

"JEANNE."

I read the two letters over aloud. Madeleine broke into sobs as she listened.

A smile flickered about the corners of Jeanne's mouth.

[237]

We left the house, committing to Madeleine the task of choosing a favorable moment to hand M. Mouillard our joint entreaty.

And here I may as well confess that from the instant we got out of the house, all through breakfast at the hotel, and for a quarter of an hour after it, M. Charnot treated me, in his best style, to the very hottest "talking-to" that I had experienced since my earliest youth. He ended with these words: "If you have not made your peace with your uncle by nine o'clock this evening, Monsieur, I withdraw my consent, and we shall return to Paris."

I strove in vain to shake his decision. Jeanne made a little face at me, which warned me I was on the wrong track.

"Very well," I said to her, "I leave the matter in your hands."

"And I leave it in the hands of God," she answered. "Be a man. If trouble awaits us, hope will at any rate steal us a happy hour or two."

We were just then in front of the gardens of the Archbishop's palace, so M. Charnot walked in. The current of his reflections was soon changed by the freshness of the air, the groups of children playing around their mothers—whom he studied ethnologically and with reference to the racial divisions of ancient Gaul —by the beauty of the landscape—its foreground of flowers, the Place St. Michel beyond, and further yet, above the barrack-roofs, the line of poplars lining the Auron. He ceased to be a father-in-law, and became a tourist again.

THE INK-STAIN

Jeanne stepped with airy grace among the groups of strollers, and the murmurs which followed her path, though often envious, sounded none the less sweetly in my ears for that. I hoped to meet Mademoiselle Lorinet.

After we had seen the gardens, we had to visit the Place Séraucourt, the Cours Chanzy, the cathedral, Saint-Pierre-le-Guillard, and the house of Jacques-Cœur. It was six o'clock by the time we got back to the Hôtel de France.

A letter was waiting for us in the small and badly furnished entrance-hall. It was addressed to Mademoiselle Jeanne Charnot.

I recognized at once the ornate hand of M. Mouillard, and grew as white as the envelope.

M. Charnot cried, excitedly:

"Read it, Jeanne. Read it, can't you!"

Jeanne alone of us three kept a brave face.

She read:

"MY DEAR CHILD:

"I treated you perhaps with undue familiarity this morning, at a moment when I was not quite myself. Nevertheless, now that I have regained my senses, I do not withdraw the expressions of which I made use—I love you with all my heart; you are a dear girl.

"You will not get an old stager like me to give up his prejudices against the capital. Let it suffice that I have surrendered to a Parisienne. My niece, I forgive him for your sake.

"Come this evening, all three of you.

"I have several things to tell you, and several questions to ask you. My news is not all good. But I trust that all regrets will be overwhelmed in the gladness you will bring to my old heart.

"BRUTUS MOUILLARD."

RENÉ BAZIN

When we rang at M. Mouillard's door, it was opened to us by Baptiste, the office-boy, who waits at table on grand occasions.

My uncle received us in the large drawing-room, in full dress, with his whitest cravat and his most camphorous frock-coat: "not a moth in ten years," is Madeleine's boast concerning this garment.

He saluted us all solemnly, without his usual effusiveness; bearing himself with simple and touching dignity. Strong emotion, which excites most natures, only served to restrain his. He said not a word of the past, nor of our marriage. This, the decisive engagement, opened with polite formalities.

I have often noticed this phenomenon; people meeting to "have it out" usually begin by saying nothing at all.

M. Mouillard offered his arm to Jeanne, to escort her to the dining-room. Jeanne was in high spirits. She asked him question after question about Bourges, its dances, fashions, manufactures, even about the procedure of its courts.

"I am sure you know that well, uncle," she said.

"Uncle" smiled at each question, his face illumined with a glow like that upon a chimney-piece when someone is blowing the fire. He answered her questions, but presently fell into a state of dejection, which even his desire to do honor to his guests could not entirely conceal. His thoughts betrayed themselves in the looks he kept casting upon me, no longer of anger, but of suffering, almost pleading, affection.

M. Charnot, who was rather tired, and also absorbed

in Madeleine's feats of cookery, cast disjointed remarks and ejaculations into the gaps in the conversation.

I knew my uncle well enough to feel sure that the end of the dinner would be quite unlike the beginning.

I was right. During dessert, just as the Academician was singing the praises of a native delicacy, *la jorestine*, my uncle, who had been revolving a few drops of some notable growth of Médoc in his glass for the last minute or two, stopped suddenly, and put down his glass on the table.

"My dear Monsieur Charnot," said he, "I have a painful confession to make to you."

"Eh? What? My dear friend, if it's painful to you, don't make it."

"Fabien," my uncle went on, "has behaved badly to me on certain occasions. But I say no more of it. His faults are forgotten. But I have not behaved to him altogether as I should."

"You, uncle?"

"Alas! It is so, my dear child. My practice, the family practice, which I faithfully promised your father to keep for you——"

"You have sold it?"

My uncle buried his face in his hands.

"Last night, my poor child, only last night!"

"I thought so."

"I was weak; I listened to the prompting of anger; I have compromised your future. Fabien, forgive me in your turn."

He rose from the table, and came and put a trembling hand on my shoulder.

"No, uncle, you've not compromised anything, and I've nothing to forgive you."

"You wouldn't take the practice if I could still offer it to you?"

"No, uncle."

"Upon your word?"

"Upon my word!"

M. Mouillard drew himself up, beaming:

"Ah! Thank you for that speech, Fabien; you have relieved me of a great weight."

With one corner of his napkin he wiped away two tears, which, having arisen in time of war, continued to flow in time of peace.

"If Mademoiselle Jeanne, in addition to all her other perfections, brings you fortune, Fabien, if your future is assured——"

"My dear Monsieur Mouillard," broke in the Academician with ill-concealed satisfaction. "My colleagues call me rich. They slander me. Works on numismatics do not make a man rich. Monsieur Fabien, who made some investigations into the subject, can prove it to you. No; I possess no more than an honorable competence, which does not give me everything, but lets me lack nothing."

"*Aurea mediocritas*," exclaimed my uncle, delighted with his quotation. "Oh, that Horace! What a fellow he was!"

"He was indeed. Well, as I was saying, our daily bread is assured; but that's no reason why my son-in-law should vegetate in idleness which I do not consider my due, even at my age."

THE INK-STAIN

"Quite right."

"So he must work."

"But what is he to work at?"

"There are other professions besides the law, Monsieur Mouillard. I have studied Fabien. His temperament is somewhat wayward. With special training he might have become an artist. Lacking that early moulding into shape, he never will be anything more than a dreamer."

"I should not have expressed it so well, but I have often thought the same."

"With a temperament like your nephew's," continued M. Charnot, "the best he can do is to enter upon a career in which the ideal has some part; not a predominant, but a sufficient part, something between prose and poetry."

"Let him be a notary, then."

"No, that's wholly prose; he shall be a librarian."

"A librarian?"

"Yes, Monsieur Mouillard; there are a few little libraries in Paris, which are as quiet as groves, and in which places are to be got that are as snug as nests. I have some influence in official circles, and that can do no harm, you know."

"Quite so."

"We will put our Fabien into one of those nests, where he will be protected against idleness by the little he will do, and against revolutions by the little he will be. It's a charming profession; the very smell of books is improving; merely by breathing it you live an intellectual life."

"An intellectual life!" exclaimed my uncle with enthusiasm. "Yes, an intellectual life!"

"And cataloguing books, Monsieur Mouillard, looking through them, preserving them as far as possible from worms and readers. Don't you think that's an enviable lot?"

"Yes, more so than mine has been, or my successor's will be."

"By the way, uncle, you haven't told us who your successor is to be."

"Haven't I, really? Why, you know him; it's your friend Larivé."

"Oh! That explains a great deal."

"He is a young man who takes life seriously."

"Very seriously, uncle. Isn't he about to be married?"

"Why, yes; to a rich wife."

"To whom?"

"My dear boy, he is picking up all your leavings; he is going to marry Mademoiselle Lorinet."

"He was always enterprising! But, uncle, it wasn't with him you were engaged yesterday evening?"

"Why not, pray?"

"You told Madeleine to admit a gentleman with a decoration."

"He has one."

"Good heavens! What is it?"

"The Nicham Iftikar,* if it please you."

"It doesn't displease me, uncle, and surprises me

* A Tunisian order, which can be obtained for a very moderate sum.

still less. Larivé will die with his breast more thickly plastered with decorations than an Odd Fellow's; he will be a member of all the learned societies in the department, respected and respectable, the more thoroughly provincial for having been outrageously Parisian. Mothers will confide their anxieties to him, and fathers their interests; but when his old acquaintances pass this way they will take the liberty of smiling in his face."

"What, jealous? Are you jealous of his bit of ribbon?"

"No, uncle, I regret nothing; not even Larivé's good fortune."

M. Mouillard fixed his eyes on the cloth, and began again, after a moment's silence:

"I, Fabien, do regret some things. It will be mournful at times, growing old alone here. Yet, after all, it will be some consolation to me to think that you others are satisfied with life, to welcome you here for your holidays."

"You can do better than that," said M. Charnot. "Come and grow old among us. Your years will be the lighter to bear, Monsieur Mouillard. Doubtless we must always bear them, and they weigh upon us and bend our backs. But youth, which carries its own burden so lightly, can always give us a little help in bearing ours."

I looked to hear my uncle break out with loud objections.

"It is a fine night," he said, simply; "let us go into the garden, and do you decide whether I can leave roses like mine."

[245]

M. Mouillard took us into the garden, pleased with himself, with me, with Jeanne, with everybody, and with the weather.

It was too dark to see the roses, but we could smell them as we passed. I had taken Jeanne's arm in mine, and we went on in front, in the cool dusk, choosing all the little winding paths.

The birds were all asleep. But the grasshoppers, crickets, and all manner of creeping things hidden in the grass, or in the moss on the trees, were singing and chattering in their stead.

Behind us, at some distance—in fact, as far off as we could manage—the gravel crackled beneath the equal tread of the two elders, and in a murmur we could catch occasional scraps of sentences:

"A granddaughter like Jeanne, Monsieur Charnot. . . ."

"A grandson like Fabien, Monsieur Mouillard. . . ."

CHAPTER XX

PARIS, September 18th.

E are married. We are just back from the church. We have said good-by to all our friends, not without a quick touch or two of sadness, as quickly swallowed up in the joy which for the first time in the history of my heart is surging there at full tide, and widening to a limitless horizon. In the two hours I have to spare before starting for Italy, I am writing the last words in this brown diary, which I do not intend to take with me.

Jeanne, my own Jeanne, is leaning upon me and reading over my shoulder, which distracts the flow of my recollections.

There were crowds at the church. The papers had put us down among the fashionable marriages of the week. The Institute, the army, men of letters, public officials, had come out of respect for M. Charnot; lawyers of Bourges and Paris had come out of respect for my uncle. But the happiest, the most radiant, next to ourselves, were the people who came only for Jeanne's sake and mine; Sylvestre Lampron, painter-in-ordinary to Mademoiselle Charnot, bringing his pretty sketch as a wedding-present; M. Flamaran and Sidonie; Jupille, who wept as he used to "thirty years ago;" and M. and Madame Plumet, who took it in turns to carry their white-robed infant.

Jeanne and I certainly shook hands with a good many persons, but not with nearly as many as M. Mouillard. Clean-shaven, his cravat tied with exquisite care, he spun round in the crowd like a top, always dragging with him some one who was to introduce him to some one else. "One should make acquaintances immediately on arrival," he kept saying.

Yes, Uncle Mouillard has just arrived in Paris; he has settled down near us on the Quai Malaquais, in a pretty set of rooms which Jeanne chose for him. He thinks them perfect because she thought they would do. The tastes and interests of old student days have suddenly reawakened within him, and will not be put to sleep again. He already knows the omnibus and tramway lines better than I; he talks of Bourges as if it were twenty years since he left it: "When I used to live in the country, Fabien——"

My father-in-law has found in him a whole-hearted admirer, perhaps even a future pupil in numismatics. Their friendship makes me think of that——

· ["You don't mind, Jeanne?"

"Of course not, my dear; the brown diary is for our two selves alone."]

——of that of the town mouse and the country mouse. Just now, on their way back to the house, they had a conversation, by turns pathetic and jovial, in which their different temperaments met in the same feeling, but at opposite ends of the scale of its shades.

I caught this fragment of their talk:

"My dear Charnot, can you guess what I'm thinking about?"

"No, I haven't the least idea."

"I think it is very queer."

"What is queer?"

"To see a librarian begin his career with a blot of ink. For you can not deny that Fabien's marriage and situation, and my return to the capital, are all due to that. It must have been sympathetic ink—eh?"

"*Felix culpa*, as you say, Monsieur Mouillard. There are some blunders that are lucky; but you can't tell which they are, and that's never any excuse for committing them."

I could hardly get hold of Lampron for a moment in the crowd he so dislikes. He was more uncouth and more devoted than ever.

"Well, are you happy?" he said.

"Quite."

"When you're less happy, come and see me."

"We shall always be just as happy as we are now," said Jeanne.

And I think she is right.

Lampron smiled.

"Yes, I am quite happy, Sylvestre, and I owe my happiness to you, to her, and to others. I have done nothing myself to deserve happiness beyond letting myself drift on the current of life. Whenever I tried to row a stroke the boat nearly upset. Everything that others tried to do for me succeeded. I can't get over it. Just think of it yourself. I owed my introduction to Jeanne to Monsieur Flamaran, who drove me to call on her father, his friend; you courted her for me by painting her portrait; Madame Plumet told her you had done so, and also removed the obstacle in my path. I met her in Italy, thanks entirely to you; and you clinched the proposal which had been begun by Flamaran. To crown all, the very situation I desired has been obtained for me by my father-in-law. What have I had to do? I have loved, sorrowed, and suffered, nothing more; and now I tremble at the thought that I owe my happiness to every one I know except myself."

"Cease to tremble, my friend; don't be surprised at it, and don't alter your system in the least. Your happiness is your due; what matter how God chooses to grant it? Suppose it is an income for life paid to you by your relatives, your friends, the world in general, and the natural order of things? Well, draw your dividends, and don't bother about where they come from."

Since Lampron said so, and he is a philosopher, I think I had better follow his advice. If you don't mind, Jeanne, I will cherish no ambition beyond your love, and refrain from running after any increase in wealth or reputation which might prove a decrease in happiness. If you agree, Jeanne, we shall see little of society, and much of our friends; we shall not open our windows wide enough for Love, who is winged, to fly out of them. If such is your pleasure, Jeanne, you shall direct the household of your own sweet will—I should say, of your sweet wisdom; you shall be queen in all matters of domestic economy, you shall rule our goings-out and our comings-in, our visits, our travels. I shall leave you to guide me, as a child, along the joyous path in which I follow your footsteps.

I am looking up at Jeanne.

She has not said "No."

THE
MAN THAT BROUGHT THE RIVER

THE

MAN THAT BROUGHT THE RIVER

HIS, my children, happened in Spain, long ago.

Imagine a large plain enclosed by mountains, from which one could see no outlet toward the east or the west, the north or the south. The circle of jagged peaks which enveloped it lost but rarely, and then only in spots, that blue haze with which distant places, though sombre, are beautified. At dawn and at evening, a few brief rays of the sun showed them in their savage nakedness; pyramids of rocks, frowning cliffs, and whirling spirals of sand, which clouds and winds dissolved. But nowhere could be seen any traces of forest or the slightest spot of green—everywhere was desolation in twisted and broken lines, and the glaring reflection of barren earth. Hardly any one had ever climbed up there. Hunters told of having almost died of thirst in those mountains, and said that no creatures were to be seen there save eagles, swept thither in the swirl of sudden storms, and hastening to return to less inhospitable regions.

The plain was equally desolate. Here and there flocks of sheep browsed the short grass, which had hardly time to pierce the surface of the soil and to grow green ere it was seized and withered by the blazing sun. A humid heat settled all summer long upon this shut-in valley, and mirages were frequent in it. Wheat hardly pushed its stalk more than a hand's-breadth above the earth, which was cracked in all directions. There was no softening shade, for water itself was lacking, and the small quantity that could be gathered in cisterns during the winter rains barely sufficed to water man and beast.

A hard country! But the heart of man is such that those who inhabited that valley loved it, and were jealous of one another for its sake, each person toiling, enduring, struggling to increase his own plot of earth, from which the harvest was but a hope often betrayed. They had very little communication with the rest of the world. Their methods of cultivation remained primitive, their manners violent. Their dwellings of stone and dried mud, sparsely scattered across the plain, had witnessed bloody dramas, caused frequently by the conflicting claims of two families to the use of the same well, from which arose lasting rivalries, rancor, and vengeances, for old scores of twenty years' standing. A young girl who had a cistern as a marriage-portion might pass for rich and marry readily; the same was true of a young man.

Probably this peculiar condition of affairs had contributed to render stranger and more solitary than his neighbors Agaré, son of Munoz, sixth child of the richest proprietor in the valley. The father had said: "I have five cisterns. I shall leave one each to my first five sons.

THE MAN THAT BROUGHT THE RIVER

But Agaré shall have the right, for the use of his house and his herds, to each of the five cisterns. He shall have the windlass in common with the master of the water, as well as the hollowed stone from which the cattle drink. He shall have right of way over the lands of his brothers. He shall respect their oats and wheat in passing. His elder brothers shall respect his train of mules laden with leathern bottles. Thus shall peace be established."

Alas! Already a sullen warfare had shown itself among the brothers. Under the very eye of their father they twitted the youth Agaré, assuring him that they would keep him strictly within his rights and would deprive him of them when the seasons were hard.

"Agaré," they said, "heir of lands without water and of herds without cisterns, you would do well not to come too close to our supplies when summer begins. The girls will laugh to see you for begging from one to another and driving your mules with their water-bottles to the brink of our wells. But we, the men, shall be there also, and we have knives to cut the girths of the harness and the tanned goat-skins where the water is kept." And they touched significantly the long, slender blades of the daggers within their leather belts.

Agaré said nothing. But more and more he shunned his brothers and followed his roving fancy. He was a little fellow, and had given signs of a dreamy and passionate nature. He left his goats to set traps for bustards, giant birds, fleet of foot, which abounded in the plain. He forgot to return at stated hours. More than once they had sought him anxiously, and had found him seated on a stone, playing to himself, by starlight, tunes upon a boxwood pipe. He was almost the only person that knew the mountains well, and now that he had reached manhood he passed part of his life among them. What did he do there? No one knew. Laborers, sheep-shearers, and wandering swineherds made way for him as he returned, taking him for a species of sorcerer and a being of ill-omen. He, however, young and supple, happy when men were not by, roamed the plain day and night. At his belt, beside his knife, hung his pipe. From his excursions, which lasted sometimes half a week, he brought back nothing of more consequence than pebbles of various colors, which he ranged along the walls of his room, and plants that no one ever had seen, the names of which were unknown.

"What is the use of all your trips to the mountains?" said his brothers, "You don't bring back any game or any useful plants. You'll be poor all your life, and since you don't want to earn your bread you'll get none from us."

One day, after Agaré had travelled over half of the vast amphitheatre of heights which enclosed the plain, he was returning home at twilight, when the noise of the farms is stilled and the animals are gathered to the fold. On his way home he had run across the carcasses of sheep and goats, dead of hunger and thirst. He had heard the lamentations of the shepherds and the furious cries of peasants whose beasts were perishing. For it was the end of May, and since the beginning of February not a cloud had passed over the valley, not a shower of rain had fallen from the rocky summits that held them fast. Misery reigned, and still deeper misery was in prospect. The water became stagnant in the almost empty cisterns. The half-ripe ears of corn drooped their heads low. The countryside had taken on the color of ashes, and the wind drove along whirls of dust formed of withered flowers, leaves, and crumbled grains of wheat and oats.

In the room that Agaré entered, the five brothers were seated around their father, near a rude hearth where a fire of turf and dried dung was burning. The smoke rose freely, blackening the vault and escaping by a gaping hole in the roof. The faces of the men were tired and hard, and they had been quarrelling because of the numerous losses of mules and sheep that had occurred during the week, the responsibility for which they bandied about from one to another. A young girl, with a dark veil on her head, and eyes that shone in the firelight, sat on a chest placed against the wall, her feet dangling from its edge. She was a relative of the Munoz family, and had come to get some fresh water from them. Two full jars were at her feet. She was resting before setting out for her own home.

"Listen, Juanita!" said the father, whose hair was covered with a handkerchief, and who wore a semicircle of white beard around his face. "Make your people understand distinctly that these are the last jars of water I shall give you. That is all the water we have."

Agaré, standing near the door that he had just opened, with his arm extended toward the young girl who sat in the shadow, cried:

"Juanita! soon there will be plenty of water for everybody!"

RENÉ BAZIN

"Ah, tramp! vagabond! idler! it is you, is it?" cried the sons of old Munoz. "What have you been doing all these days, while we have been struggling to water our bean-fields and our last beds of maize that are fast dying? We hadn't hands enough to do the work; we searched for you, and, as usual, you were wasting your time somewhere else. Curses upon you!"

"Don't curse him," said the father, "but let me talk to him fittingly. Agaré, you are useless on the farm. I can no longer feed a child that refuses to aid me. You must swear to leave no more your duties at home, or I shall drive you away, and your share of the heritage will go to your brothers."

"Well said!" responded the ringing voices of the men.

"What do you say?" demanded the father. "Are you resolved to stay with us?"

Agaré glanced around the assembly that judged him, and the faces were so hard and menacing that he finally withdrew his gaze and let it rest upon the young girl with the two water-jars, who listened, motionless, under her blue veil, in the shadow. And half as if addressing her, and half as if he prophesied, he said:

"I shall return to the mountains; but I shall come back, and I shall be accompanied by a living joy of which you know not. My long toil shall be rewarded. Look at my torn clothes, my bloody feet, my hands knotty like the boxwood of my pipe. But I tell you that I have found the salvation of all the men and of all the flocks. When I descend the people of the valley shall run before me. My name shall be blessed above the

names of my elder brothers. All shall sing the glory of
the conquest that I shall bring back."

"He is mad!" was the answering chorus. "The
winds of the barren mountains have turned his head!"

The brothers reviled him, but the father's heart went
out to his youngest son. But Agaré had already slipped
outside and was hastening away in the tranquil night.
His sandals made no noise save in stepping upon dry
and crackling stalks.

"Take my bread for your sustenance," murmured a
voice near him.

He turned. Little Juanita had followed him.

"Take my bread and drink the water in my jar. It
still belongs to your father, who gave it to me."

She carried the two earthen pitchers upon her shoulders. She bent one of them forward, lowering the arm
which held it by the top handle, and the young man
drank his fill, looking into Juanita's face, which wore a
smile of compassion and regret. They stood in a path
that ran through the dead wheat. Around them rose
the sound of grasshoppers and the croak of frogs seeking
for dew upon the parched earth.

"Poor lad!" continued Juanita, "I am sorry to see
you driven away; you have no refuge anywhere now. If
I knew your hiding-place, though the way was never so
hard, I would go every night to carry you half my
bread."

Agaré wiped his lips, took half the bread that she held
in her folded apron, and said:

"I thank you, my sweet one! You have a true
woman's heart, and some day you will be good to your

children. So I will tell you: When you hear the sound of my pipe, raise your pretty eyes from the ground where you are working; and when you see me, run to meet me, so that you may share in the triumph of Agaré."

She did not understand. With a doubtful air she shook her head beneath her veil, while Agaré passed deep into the transparent shadow of that starry night, which made the great bare plain gleam like the half of a pearl shell. His form diminished along the pathway. It became still smaller and less distinct in outline than the occasional tamarisks that here and there swayed in the night wind. Juanita gazed still, her arms raised and clasped behind her head, until Agaré was far away, beyond the cultivated fields where the crop was losing, from hour to hour, the last drops of its sap.

Agaré walked all night. A little before dawn he arrived at the top of a defile formed of rocks and fallen masses of earth, dominated by two peaks of black granite. These ramparts opened out as they inclined toward the plain, appearing against the sky like towers and turrets of prodigious height. The country people called this place "The Iron Castle." Agaré let himself down into a hole that he had already dug at the foot of one of these great walls. He felt the bottom of it with his hand. The stones were as wet as if it had rained.

"Good!" said he. "The dampness continues. If I have only the courage to keep on digging, the spring will burst forth."

He went down upon his knees and with his sinewy fingers he tore up the stones, one by one, and threw them on the bank. In spite of the cold, sharp wind of the heights, the sweat ran down his forehead. He took off his jacket and threw it among the rubbish.

"Work, Agaré!" said he. "To-day is the great day!"

A fever of courage and hope had seized him. Leaning over, he felt the freshness of water, living and near. The sky grew lighter above him.

At last, just as the sun threw a rosy hue over the crests of the mountains, Agaré heard a rumbling as of thunder. He uttered a cry. A turbulent jet of water, larger than a man's body, burst from the bottom of the hole.

"The river! The river! Behold the river!"

Pale with joy and weariness, Agaré climbed up the slope of the trench that he had spent a hundred days in digging. He stood on its extreme edge and turned toward the plain, his eyes filled with tears, for he saw his father's house in the valley, a tiny spot in the distance.

"House of my father," said he, "I shall return to you, with the salvation of my country behind me. I have discovered the water-source! I have driven thirst from the valley! O ye whose villages and farms I perceive! you shall no longer be forced to husband the water in your cisterns. You shall no longer fear the length of the summer. Your cattle shall drink from the running blue river, and your fields, unto the borders of the plain, shall feel the nearness of living water. The smallest roots shall quiver and grow. Soon trees shall grow in ground that never knew them. I see the shade mounting with new branches from the depths of the soil. I see the tall grass, the glad flowers, the harvests become like those of favored lands, and my name blessed for generations. Listen to the voice of the river newly born. It is about to escape from the cradle I have made for it. It is about to dash toward you, and its two banks shall be called Joy and Wealth."

He turned. The great hole that he had dug was full of water, cold and pure, across which swept eddies of bubbles, like comets' tails, attesting the vigor of the fount soon to overflow. Agaré was exalted, intoxicated with his triumph. Stooping over to pick up his jacket he heard, or thought he heard, though he knew not whence it came, a voice which said:

"Take thy pipe, Agaré, and lead the river! It will obey thee as a serpent charmed by the flute. Thou shalt lead thy betrothed, descending from the mountains. She shall go only where thou wilt. But take care that thou cease not playing; for she will roll upon thee her waters, and nothing shall restrain them!"

The young man drew his pipe from his belt, carried it to his lips, and, jumping from rock to rock, descended the slope. Behind him, in sheaves of spray, overflowing the dry rocks, splashing the granite walls, rushed the river. Above it, in the mist that rose from it to the very summit of the mount, a rainbow trembled.

The descent lasted two hours.

In the mean time, the men on the plain, starting for the day's work, noticed the long trail of silver which striped the mountain. Some paid no heed to it. Others said: "It is a cloud, a morning fog that the wind has blown against the slopes."

THE MAN THAT BROUGHT THE RIVER

But when all the inhabitants were scattered over the plain, and the sun struck a reflection along the whole length of the torrent, they began to grow uneasy. A shiver of cold air ran across the fields. The aureole of the rainbow, like an arch of ruby and emerald, rested upon the towers of the "Iron Castle." Soon the shrill sound of a pipe reached their ears. They saw at the end of the valley a man running, and behind him rolled a wave which advanced without breaking, round, shining, quivering at its edge, ready to crush whomsoever should withstand it.

Then they came together, and running in front of Agaré, they brandished their spades and shovels with furious cries.

"Wretch! What are you about? You will flood our houses and our property. Get away with you! This is my field! That's mine, too! Go somewhere else! Get out of here!"

Laborers and keepers rushed in groups from all sides to meet Agaré, and threatened him with drawn knives. When they had closed upon him he stopped playing upon his pipe for a moment, and the wave, breaking over the two banks of the channel it had cut for itself, put the aggressors to flight. But they followed him, and their clamor attracted new crowds. The young man, affrighted, dashed to right and left to avoid the stones they cast at him.

"Let me alone!" he cried. "I am bringing you wealth. It means salvation for all."

Threats of death multiplied about him. Mounted keepers galloped ahead of the river and, savage, clothed in the skins of beasts, tried to reach Agaré with the ends of their iron-tipped staffs. A stone wounded him on the right arm. He seized his pipe in his left hand, and, covered with dust and blood, pale at the fierce clamor he had awakened, he continued his way. The torrent spread out behind him in a long, tumultuous streak. From one bank to the other the men, separated by the waves, cursed and challenged one another because of their property now swallowed up. The herds fled away among the oats and wheat. An immense cloud of dust, like a whirlwind, blackened a quarter of the valley.

Agaré walked slowly now. He felt upon his heels the chill of the water searching its prey. The sound of his pipe grew feebler. Stones, better aimed now, struck his head and chest, already bloody. But he, no longer answering back, raised his eyes toward the paternal farm. He was approaching the village. "If I can only reach it," he thought, "my father and brothers will save me." And, at the extremity of a large field of corn upon which he had entered, and which belonged to his father, he saw a party of men who worked hurriedly. "Our servants," said he, "and my brothers."

The little flute took up its refrain in the midst of the din of the crowds and the ever-following waters. A man on horseback passed in front of Agaré and, bending over, struck him with his fist, crying: "Brother of misfortune! My father sends me to tell you to return whence you came. Take care!"

"I have only strength enough left to go straight ahead," said Agaré.

At this moment the crowds that followed the torrent

gave vent to a louder outcry, for they saw their man was about to fall. Rushing forward, they ranged themselves in front of him as in line of battle, to oppose themselves to him who was bringing the river. Their faces were dark with rage, and they yelled like a pack of hounds.

Agaré advanced toward them. In the first rank he recognized his father and his five brothers; Juanita · also. He began to hope. But, as far away as he could make himself heard, the father cried: "Turn away the scourge! We have dug a ditch that will carry off the water if you don't stop it. Accursed son! do not set foot upon my bean-field, for it bears the whole of my earnings for a year!"

The poor lad could hardly see any longer when he came upon the ditch. A hail of stones and sticks broke upon him. At the same time a voice, high and clear, rose above the tumult:

"Agaré! Agaré! Stretch out your hand to me, and I will help you over."

Juanita rushed forward, and stood alone, ten paces in advance of the others. Agaré extended the arm that held the pipe. But he could touch only the hand of the young girl bending toward him. The river broke into foam, with a roar louder than the cries of the crowd; and the body of Agaré rolled under the wave let loose, into the trench that his brothers had dug.

The waters had separated the crowds of people, the flocks and herds, and the clusters of houses. They rushed forward, without guide, at will, in their reckless course. In a few minutes the valley was crossed with a line of living water, which grew larger, ever widening its banks, and, encountering the mountain at its opposite extremity, it turned into a defile, where it was engulfed, and finally disappeared.

For three days there was an indescribable confusion over the whole plain. Men and women of the same family sought one another, calling from bank to bank, and were not able to come together. Corpses of animals, seized and drowned by the current, drifted by. At times the stream would suddenly break from its bed to hollow out new channels or pools which glistened in the midst of the devastated land. Fleeing goats strayed along the blue cliffs.

Then the current of the river abated. The men found a ford. At length they built a bridge. Grass sprouted in the ooze of the drenched lands and traces of meadows began to frame with bands of green the now calmly flowing river. The herds forgot the way to the cisterns and drank at watering-places along the banks among the reeds. In the springtime, flowers, never before seen, and trees, that never had grown in the valley, sprang up here and there. A delicate verdure outlined the spots where orchards and woods were later to grow.

Then they remembered Agaré, who had brought them the river.

But his name was no longer spoken with wrath. The women commiserated the sad fate of the youngest son of Munoz. They pointed out, as a reflection to his glory, the young girl that had loved him. The men thought: "He has been the honor and wealth of the country. He who never handled a spade nor held a plow has transformed the land. Long may his memory live among us!" They erected a column on which was graven the name of Agaré.

Little Juanita, sad and proud—yes, proud above all —said:

"He touched the end of this little finger of mine!"

THE BLUE MARE

THE BLUE MARE

ON'T forget your cloak, little one; you might catch cold."

"I have it on my arm."

"Take your *sabots* with you."

"They are hanging around my neck."

"Take your stick with you, for fear of hungry wolves."

"It is fastened to my wrist, mother, and it is as tough as one of my fingers."

"Good-night, my dear!"

"Good-night, mother!"

Every night, when Jean-Marie Bénic, of the "coast country"* set out with his mares, his mother never failed thus to caution him. She was a widow with five sons, of whom he was the youngest, a lad nearing his eighteenth year. The farm, sheltered by the wind-beaten girdle of woods, was separated by them, on that side, from the beach, where the waves foamed, roared, and leaped during three quarters of the year. It was called "La Grénetière"†—badly named, in truth, for grain grew but poorly in the salty soil, and it was only

---

*In Brittany, comprising the present department of Cotes-du-Nord, etc.

†Literally, "The Seedswoman."

of buckwheat that good crops were to be seen, raising thickly its red stalks, with its flowers, like summer clouds in color, among which the bees love to gather their honey. Elsewhere there were stretches of broom and furze, marshes and waste lands, sown by the wind, where the frosts of winter reaped all sorts of useless weeds. But the wide meadows were superb; rich and fertile, they yielded hay in abundance, with second and third crops after the first mowing, without counting five months of pasturage. They were damp meadows, of course, winding between low hills along the banks of a brook, no broader than the back of your hand during the dry season, but spreading out into a lake after the autumn rains.

In these meadows, from the end of June to the middle of November, foraged at large the six mares which were alike the pride and the wealth of La Grénetière. None finer were to be seen in the coast country, noted for its horses. A tall man hardly reached to their withers. They could trot as fast as many horses could gallop. As for their color, though varying somewhat, it approached a slate tint, and there was one three-year-old colt, the favorite of Jean-Marie Bénic, whose coat was actually blue, with a star in the middle of her forehead. The dealers all said:

"Will you sell us your colt, Mistress Bénic?"

"No, no, my good sirs, you shall not have her."

"Then the Emperor will take her."

"He is too far away."

"The Emperor is never far away, Mistress Bénic. He needs men. He knows at Paris the age of your mare, and her name, and all about her coat. Believe us, and sell her."

She refused, because she was sure that no one would take away from her "La Nielle," her beautiful blue colt, which had already begun to draw the plow, and could trot three hours at a stretch without tiring. Assuredly she knew that the Emperor was raising men and sending them to the war; one of her sons was on the Rhine, another on the Spanish frontier. She heard continually of battles won, of cities taken, of cannon captured, of *Te Deums*, of massacres and spoils; at the bottom of her heart she wished for the end of these victories, which cost many poor mothers like her their sons, leaving the happiest of them without support, with fields too large and harvests that spoiled for lack of hands to gather them; but she did not believe that the Emperor knew of the beauty of La Nielle, nor of her speed, nor of her blue coat and the white star on her forehead.

"Good-night, my boy," said she, "be careful, and beware of wolves."

And Jean-Marie, mounted on the oldest of the mares, would set out, whistling, to spend the night in the meadows. He loved the work. He had built for himself a cabin of branches on a slope backed by the woods, whence he could see the whole meadow, and there, covered by an old cloak, his dog "Fine-Ear" at his feet, he would drop into a sleep that the slightest sound would break. The night covered him with shadow and mist, but he knew where his horses were browsing by their snorts and the slow rhythm of their tread. When the wind was cold he drove them into a thicket of willows, whose foliage never stirred save in stormy weather; and always he would make three rounds before sunrise to keep his horses from lying on their flanks in the grass soaked with rain or dew. A neigh would waken him, or the scream of a bird, or the stamping of the animals crowding together at the approach of danger. Then he would run out of the cabin, cracking his whip in a certain manner that frightened the wolves away and reassured the horses. They would run to him as soon as they saw him, and he would stroke them. The blue mare would sometimes lean her head against the lad's shoulder, and he would caress her, saying:

"Never fear, La Nielle, you shall always remain at La Grénetière. You are too pretty to go to the war."

He was mistaken. The time for that separation soon came. An order was published ordaining that all four-year-olds, horses and mares, be taken to the city for examination by a commission of officers. La Nielle had reached her fourth year a few weeks before. The closing days of March, rainy, swept by storms of snow and hail, had rendered the roads almost impassable. Desolation reigned for a whole week at the home of the widow of La Grénetière. Her three sons surrounded her during the evening, discussing by candlelight what was to be done. The two elder, whose hair was already turning gray, were for hiding La Nielle in the deep, impenetrable thickets that surrounded the farm. Jean-Marie said nothing. On the evening before the day fixed for the conscription of the horses, however, the mother said to him:

"My son, you say nothing; but you must have an idea."

"I have one, indeed, but it isn't like that of my brothers."

"Let us hear it, my boy."

"I am afraid that it will make you weep."

"Poor dear!" said the mother, embracing him, "it is not those that weep who are the most unhappy, but those that have no love for one another."

"Well, mother dear, I don't think that we could hide La Nielle very long in the woods; she would be found, and perhaps my eldest brother would be taken to prison. It would be better to give her to the Emperor, who needs her, and, since my turn to go to the war must come soon, my opinion is that both of us, La Nielle and I, should go together. I will look out for her and take care of her."

"You are out of your senses, my boy! A common soldier never would be allowed to mount the blue mare. She will be given to an officer, and I shall lose you both, my son and my Nielle."

"Let me go, mother. I have thought it all over at night while watching my horses. Some day you will see La Nielle bringing back Jean-Marie Bénic with lace on his sleeves. I was born for a soldier, and I can tell you that La Nielle is brave too, for I have led her against the wolves."

He spoke in a manner so firm and decided that the widow, without the courage to say "Yes," thought it would not be wise to say "No." She wept, as Jean-Marie had foreseen, and remained seated for a long time on the seat in the great hall of La Grénetière, giving council to her son, repeating it over and over, but more fondly and more tearfully each time. As for the brothers, good-hearted, in spite of their hard faces, they watched for more than half an hour their mother and their youngest brother without saying a word, and went to bed, leaving untouched on the table their mugs full of cider.

The next day, before dawn, Jean-Marie Bénic went into the stable, and, unfastening La Nielle, jumped upon the back of the pretty mare, pressed her sides with his heels and rode her once more to the meadow.

"I want you to have one more feed of the grass of Grénetière," said he, "and I, too, wish to see once more and to say good-by to the place where I have so often watched over you."

No one was up, even on that farm where the cock was usually not the first to stir. The low-lying country was white with fog, and the woods at the two ends of the meadow appeared as if seen through a fine veil. Jean-Marie, who had placed on his horse neither bridle nor halter, rode her along the brook, beside which grew mint and clover, knee-high, and, letting her browse, he looked with emotion on the beautiful stretches of meadow where he should not mow the grass nor toss the hay for years to come; and those dark woods, like clouds of smoke in the fog, would have grown taller and larger before his return. Behind them he saw, in memory, the whole farm where he had always lived, the fields where the oats that he had sown himself, already higher than the sides of the drills, were tossing in the sea breezes, the fallow lands, the moors, the clump of pines on the dunes, the paths around the fields, solitary and hung with spiders' webs. "Eat your fill, La Nielle," said he, "because you will get no mint or clover in the Emperor's army."

That was an excuse for not leaving quite yet. He thought that he was staying for the sake of his horse, but in truth his heart failed him.

As the morning broke, and the tops of the oaks became red on the crests of the hills, Jean-Marie Bénic stood up on La Nielle's back, so that he might see still farther; then he drank a little water from the brook to recall its taste, and when the first ray of sunlight touched the grass of the meadow the young man, with a wild cry as if he had been wounded, put the mare into a gallop and dashed toward the village.

At two o'clock he presented himself before the purchasing-commission under the trees of the public promenade. Hundreds of peasants were there, holding their horses by the bridle, deploring the war while they counted their money. Several said:

"Look, there's the mare of La Grénetière—the Emperor hasn't any prettier. She'll be shot. Oh, this sad war! She'll be killed by the cannon-balls. Look at her—isn't she a proud one!"

La Nielle, her head tossing, was neighing, and pawing the ground. The officer in charge of the remounts watched her coming in the midst of the clamor, and admired also the swaggering air of Jean-Marie Bénic.

"That's an officer's mount," said he, "a colonel's mount, at least. I'll give you the highest price allowed by the tariff, my boy. Does that suit you?"

"No."

"What do you want?"

"To be enlisted in the same regiment with La Nielle. I don't want to leave her."

The officer, who had fierce white moustaches, and a good-natured expression, began to laugh, then all of a sudden a tear came unbidden to his eye and he said, extending his hand to Jean-Marie:

"You're a brave lad—I'll give you my word on it."

"We'll do our best, La Nielle and I," said the boy.

Four days later they were in the same regiment, far from the coast country, far from the Breton farm where they had grown up. And a good soldier and a good war-horse they made.

La Nielle fell to the colonel of the regiment, a young man that the Emperor had always in his train. What fine travels he had had for ten years! He had seen all Europe except the islands; he knew the colors of all flags; he had received in his hand the keys of several cities; he had returned unwounded from twenty charges at the head of his lancers, and regularly each time he had been promoted by the order of him who knew everything and forgot nobody: corporal, quartermaster-sergeant, sergeant-major, sublieutenant, lieutenant, captain, major, colonel. He had carried every stripe, whether of worsted or silver, at the point of the lance: he was awaiting the twenty-first charge to win his generalcy. Ten horses had been killed under him. La Nielle carried him proudly, as if she understood. From time to time the Colonel, during the silent marches, bending over her neck, stroked the white star on her forehead.

THE BLUE MARE

Jean-Marie, bearded, bronzed, broad of shoulder, and trim as the best, had matured rapidly outside of France, and had taken on the appearance of an old soldier. He loved war, and La Nielle above all. For her he had more than once cut grass or oats with his sword in the face of the enemy's camp, with the bullets whistling among the crops. He twined flowers in her forelock on the days when they were about to enter a conquered city, and when it was a capital he adorned her with a big bouquet. She knew his voice. She would paw with joy when passing near him on review days, when the visors of the helmets shone above the lances, and when, as before battle, there were shouts of command, trumpet blasts, and flashing of steel passing and repassing on the plain.

The Emperor commanded his lancers to attack a kingdom. The lancers, who were in Italy, crossed the mountains. To see them coming down the slopes one would have said that the woods were on the march; but God knows, the whiteness of their points did not come from the dew nor from the snows! The country people in the hollows of the valleys gazed upward and were afraid. "May the Emperor's wrath depart from us!" said they.

The Emperor's wrath was only passing through. At night, on the sides of the opposite mountains, could be seen the rising shadow of the regiments.

La Nielle went forward, never tired, always in advance. When the hour of battle arrived the Emperor was there. Nobody knew how he came.

My children, I never have seen a battle, and I can't

tell you the name of this one, but I have heard from my
dead uncle, who was there, that it was terrible. The
fields were full of dead, and you couldn't count the
wounded. Among the latter, Jean-Marie Bénic had
fallen upon a furrow in a field of ripe corn, with a ball
in his shoulder. The blue mare had carried the Colonel
clear across the plain amid the smoke of the cannon.

The poor lad thought of La Grénetière. The sun
was so hot that it baked the blood of his wound; and
through weariness and sadness, Jean-Marie Bénic, of
the coast company, was beginning to be blind to everything around him, when he perceived a blue speck coming nearer. It was like a cannon-ball with two puffs of
fire to right and left. Soon he made out ears, feet, a
mane, a rider; he recognized La Nielle, in flight, with
the Colonel half off her back, but clinging to her, the
reins escaped from his hands. She jumped a ditch,
entered the corn-field, and passed at full speed; but the
wounded lad had time to shout: "La Nielle!"

Then, like a great winter raven, sweeping a circle
before alighting, the beautiful war-horse galloped
around the field, and returning toward her wounded
master stopped behind him, stretching out her neck.

"Bénic," cried the Colonel, "are your two legs left?"

"Yes, sir."

"Have you any arms?"

"I have only one that's any good."

"My hands are crushed. Get up behind me and let
us charge. Quick! My lancers have given way—look
at them scattering!"

"Yes, sir."

THE BLUE MARE

"Ah! Bénic, if only I had my two hands!"

"I have one for both of us and that's enough. Charge the enemy, my blue Nielle!"

The lancers, in fact, were flying, believing that the Colonel was fleeing himself. But on the road, going the wrong way, when they heard the voice of their commander, when they saw La Nielle galloping in the dust with two men on her back they turned about, seized their lances again, and charged also.

Jean-Marie Bénic and La Nielle won the battle. The Emperor was satisfied. Making the round of the bivouac that night, he ran across Jean-Marie Bénic seated on the ground weeping, holding the bridle of the blue mare with his unwounded arm. Surprised, he approached.

"A lancer of my guard! You are weeping on the day of a great victory! Are you wounded?"

"Yes, your Majesty; but that is not what grieves me."

"What is the matter?"

"My Colonel is dead."

"I know it. I regret it more than you. I saw you charge. What else is the matter?"

"My mare, which I raised in the coast country——"

He could say no more. He wept. The Emperor, by the light of the fires burning on all sides saw that La Nielle had been struck by a piece of a shell on the rump. He crossed his hands behind his back under the skirts of his long coat and said:

"Go and get cured, both of you; it is my wish. When you are well go back to the coast country. You have served me well. Only, I reserve her first colt for my guard, and twenty years hence you shall send me your son: I will make an officer of him."

"Yes, your Majesty."

That day made Jean-Marie proud for life. He saw again La Grénetière, the woods, the meadows, the brooks, where the mint drinks in the fog, and the mother who had prayed and waited for him. He had only one arm, and La Nielle had only three hoofs; but with that one arm he could direct a plow, drive his cattle, and hold a glass. The men of his own age saluted his broken shoulder when he passed along the road. On market-days, when a big peasant, blank of countenance, came to town, mounted on a mare that limped badly, parents pointed them out, saying:

"There goes Jean-Marie Bénic, and there's the blue Nielle—the two cripples of the Emperor!"

THE POST-BOX

THE POST-BOX

THE peace that enveloped this country presbytery was indescribable. The parish was small, middling honest, easy-going, accustomed to the priest that had directed it for thirty years. The village ended at the presbytery, which stood on the border of the meadows sloping toward the river, from which mounted, during the hot season, the varied song of the fields mingled with the perfume of the grasses. Behind the rambling old house, a vegetable-garden encroached upon the meadow. It caught the first ray of sunshine, and held the last. Cherries might be seen there in May, and gooseberries even earlier, and usually a week before Assumption one could not pass within a hundred yards of the garden without inhaling between the hedges the heavy perfume of ripening melons.

But my readers must not think that the parish priest of St. Philemon was a high liver. He was at the age when the appetite is but a memory; his back was bent, his face wrinkled, and he could no longer see out of one of his little gray eyes. He wore large round spectacles, and he was so hard of hearing in one ear, that one had to go around and change sides in case one came upon him from that direction. No! No! The good priest did not eat all the fruit in his orchard! The boys stole their share of it, and also the birds—the blackbirds which lived there comfortably all the season, and sang at the tops of their voices on their return; the gold-finches, pretty travellers, assisted them during the weeks of great abundance. Then there were sparrows, linnets of all kinds, and tomtits, a noisy, swarming lot, little tufts of feathers no bigger than your thumb, hanging from branches, turning, climbing, pecking at a grape-seed, scratching a pear, genuine birds of plunder in short, whose only thanks was a sharp little cry like the rasp of a saw. But even toward them, old age had rendered the good father indulgent. "You can't correct animals," he would say; "if I held anything against them for not changing their ways, I should have to bear grudges against many of my parishioners." And he contented himself with clapping his hands in warning as he entered his orchard, in order not to be a witness of too flagrant depredations.

Then followed a rush of wings, as if all the flowers, gone mad and blown by a gale, had started to fly: gray, white, yellow, mottled; a little flight, a rustling of leaves, and then quiet, for five minutes. The most profound stillness! You must know that there was not a workshop in the village, not a loom nor a sledge-hammer, and the sounds made by men and their horses and cattle, spread over the fields, solitary and unseen, melted and died in the shimmering air that rose all day from the heated earth. Mills were unknown, the roads were little frequented, and railroads far away. If the repentance of these garden robbers had lasted, the Abbé would have gone to sleep over his breviary for the stillness.

But the return was prompt; a sparrow would set the example; a jay would follow; then the whole flock was at work again. And the Abbé might pass and repass, open or shut his book, murmuring: "They won't leave me a seed this year!" but not a bird would leave his spoils any more than if only a thick-leaved, cone-shaped pear-tree were swaying to and fro on the sandy walk.

Birds understand that those who bark never bite. Every spring they built their nests around the presbytery of St. Philemon in greater numbers than anywhere else. The best places were quickly taken up: the hollows in the trees, holes in the walls, the three-forked crotches of the apple-trees or of the yoke-elms; and brown bills, like sword-points, might be seen peeping out of a handful of coarse hay between the rafters of the roof. One year a thrifty tomtit observed the evenly cut slot, protected by a shelf, sunk in the thick, rough stones on the right of the main entrance to the presbytery; she slipped inside, then returned, satisfied by the exploration, and soon brought thither the where-withal to build a nest, neglecting nothing that might serve to keep it warm, neither feathers, horsehair, wool, nor scales of lichen plucked from the trunks of trees.

One morning Philomena, the maidservant, came out, with a furious air, to meet the Abbé in the laurel arbor at the end of the garden. In her hand she held a sheet of paper.

"Look here, your reverence! here's a paper belonging to you, and dirty besides. If they don't beat all!"

"Whom do you mean, Philomena?"

"Those precious birds of yours—all the birds that you have around here. They'll be making nests in your soup-tureens next!"

"I've only one, my good Philomena!"

"They have gone and laid eggs in your letter-box, your reverence! I opened it because the postman rang, which doesn't happen every day. And I'm blessed if the box wasn't full! There was hay, horsehair, spiders' webs, and feathers enough to stuff a pillow, and in the middle of the whole mess was a creature the like of which I never have seen before, hissing like a viper!"

The good priest began to laugh, like a grandfather hearing of the pranks of a youngster.

"It must be a coal tomtit," said he. "You can't beat them for tricks like that. But don't touch it, whatever you do, Philomena."

"No danger, your reverence! There's no fear of my touching the thing!"

The Abbé hastened across the garden, through the house and the court, planted with asparagus, to the wall of the enclosure that separated the house from the highway; and there, with a cautious movement of the hand, he opened slightly the monumental letter-box which could easily have contained the entire annual correspondence of the village.

He was not deceived. The form of the nest, shaped like a pine-cone, its color, the composition of the warp and woof, and of the lining showing through, delighted him. He listened to the hissing of the unseen sitter, and said:

"Never mind, little one! I know you. Twenty-one days for hatching; three weeks to raise your family. Is that what you want? Well, you shall have it: I'll take away the key with me."

And carry away the key he did; and when he had performed his morning's duties—visits to his parishioners in sorrow or in trouble; directions to the messenger going to the city to choose seeds for him; a climb up to the belfry, where a storm had loosened some stones—he bethought himself of the tomtit, and reflected that she might be disturbed by the arrival of a letter falling upon her in the midst of her sitting.

The possibility was not very likely. St. Philemon received no more letters than it sent out. The postman was hardly more than a passing visitor, taking supper with one family, drinking a glass with another, and handing at rare intervals some conscript's letter or a tax notice to some out-of-the-way farm. However, as St. Robert's day was approaching, which, as every one knows, falls on the twenty-ninth day of April, the Abbé thought it prudent to write to the only three friends worthy of the name that death had left him, one layman, and two clergymen, thus: "Dear Friend: Don't send me any remembrances of my birthday this year, I beg. It would be inconvenient for me to receive a letter just now. Later I will explain, and you will understand my reasons."

They thought that his sight was failing, and did not write.

The good old priest was delighted thereby. For three weeks he never passed his doorstep without thinking of the pink-speckled eggs that lay within the box, and when the twenty-second day had arrived, he stooped over and listened, with his ear close to the opening of the box. Then he rose, radiant: "They're chirping Philomena, they're chirping! And they owe their lives to me, too! I'll wager that they don't regret what I have done. No more do I."

He had within him, old as he was, a child's soul that never had grown old.

Now, at this same time, in the green drawing-room of the Bishop's palace, in the capital of the department, the Bishop deliberated over the nominations in hand, with his regular counselors: his two vicars-general, the dean of the chapter, the secretary-general of the bishopric, and the director of the large seminary. Having provided for several vicarages and parishes, he expressed himself thus:

"Gentlemen of the council: I have a candidate, excellent in all points for the parish of X——; but it seems to me only proper to offer first, at least, this charge and this honor to one of our oldest priests, the Abbé of St. Philemon. He will not accept, of course, his modesty, not less than his age, will prevent him; but we shall have rendered homage, as far as we can, to his virtue."

The five counsellors approved unanimously, and that very evening a letter left the episcopal palace, signed by the Bishop, and bearing this postscript: "Reply immediately, my dear Abbé, or, rather, come to see me, because I shall be obliged to submit my nominations to the government three days hence."

The letter arrived at St. Philemon the very day of the hatching of the tomtits. The postman squeezed it with difficulty into the opening of the box; it disappeared, and dropped to the bottom of the nest, like a white plate at the bottom of a *camera obscura*.

After a time the blue quills, stemlike on the wings of the little tomtits, became garnished with down. Fourteen little ones, squalling, trembling on their soft feet, their mouths wide open, never ceased from dawn till dark to call for food, to eat it, to digest it, and to demand more. This was during the first period, when the nestlings have no spirit. This lasts but a short time among birds. Soon quarrels broke out in the nest, which gave way under strokes of the wings; then there were tumbles overboard, trips along the wall of the box, pauses near the entry of the cavern, through which entered the air of the outer world. At last they ventured outside.

The old priest, from a neighboring meadow, was a delighted spectator of this garden-party. Watching the little ones appear from under the shelf of the letter-box, in twos and threes, taking wing, returning, leaving again, like bees at the entrance of a hive, he said: "Their babyhood is over, and it is a good thing; they are fully fledged now."

The next day, during the rest hour following dinner, he went to the box, key in hand. Tap, tap! No response. "I thought so," he murmured. Then he opened the box, and, mingled with the rubbish of the nest, a letter fell into his hand.

"Heaven bless me!" said he, recognizing the writing, "a letter from his lordship. And look at it! How long has it been here?" He turned pale as he read it.

"Philomena, harness Robin, and be quick about it!" he called.

The maid came to find out what was the matter before obeying.

"What's wrong now, your reverence?"

"The Bishop has been waiting for me for three weeks!"

"You can't make up for all that loss of time," said the old woman.

The Abbé was away until the evening of the next day. When he returned home he wore a peaceful air; but peace is not always attained without effort, and often we have to struggle to maintain it. When he had helped to unharness Robin, had given him some oats, changed his cassock, and emptied the box in which he had brought back a score of little packages bought during the trip to the city, it was about the time when the birds in the branches gossip together of the doings of the day. A shower had fallen, and drops of water still fell from the leaves shaken by these gipsy pairs seeking shelter for the night.

Recognizing their master and friend coming down the sandy walk, they dropped down, fluttered about, making a great racket, and the tomtits of the letter-box nest, the whole fourteen, still half-feathered, attempted their first spiral flight around the pear-trees, and trilled their first notes in the open air.

The priest regarded them with a paternal eye, but with a melancholy tenderness, as we look on those who have cost us dear.

"Very well, my dears," said he, "but for me you wouldn't be here, and but for you I should have a cantonal pastorate. I don't regret anything, of course, but don't be too insistent; your gratitude is too noisy." He clapped his hands, provoked.

Never had he had any ambition, and he was quite truthful then in what he said. The next morning, however, after a night broken by sleeplessness, speaking to Philomena, he said:

"Next year, Philomena, if the tomtits come back, you must tell me about it. It is decidedly inconvenient to have them there!"

But the tomtits did not return, nor did any imposing letter bearing the arms of the Bishop!

TWO SORROWS

TWO SORROWS

T first sight, one took her for a *grande dame;* a second glance gave one above all an impression of goodness, which was the right one.

The house where she lived was at the corner of the street, and through one of its eleven windows—the one at the corner—was a marvellous view of a long avenue planted with trees and shrubbery—so long that late in the afternoons, when the foliage was dark with shadows, its entrance might have been taken for the opening to a forest, were it not for the multitude of pedestrians and passing vehicles. There, behind the window, the old woman sat almost all day long, reading, sewing, even knitting: she would have spun, as did her forebears, had it still been possible to buy a spinning-wheel anywhere outside of the remote villages of Brittany, Flanders, or Lorraine. And, whatever she might be doing, she had but one thought, which seemed to have written itself on her countenance. One had only to see her, erect, pale, and wasted of visage, wearing upon her face the undeniable trace of rare beauty and of sorrow that had faded her before her time, to say: "Here is a mother!" One needed further only to encounter her glance to add: "She is a mother who has lost her child."

Not that she complained. She spoke of her grief, that is to say, of herself, so discreetly, that no one was reluctant to see her. The world, although it seeks joy, does not shun resignation, and it met her kindly. Before the high-backed armchair, which faced the angle of the window, passed and repassed, at long intervals, it is true—the friends of Madame Le Minquier. Some were of her own age, others were younger. There were even a few men, attracted by the gentle spirit of the woman and by the former renown of her house.

One hot afternoon in June all the people were out of doors. Throngs walked in the sunshine; bursts of laughter mounted up to the windows. Parasols, like huge soap-bubbles, struck back flashes of sunlight from their tightly stretched changeable silk. The solitude of Madame Le Minquier's great sitting-room seemed more profound than usual. No one had called as yet. Madame Le Minquier took up a photograph of a very young girl, framed in black, which always stood near her, and thought: "It is not she: photographs deceive us; lenses do not see as we do. Where is the grace of the glance with which she used to look upon me? Where is the gentle oval of that face wrought of softened light? All is forced, darkened, disfigured. The more I look at it, the more different it seems from the image I cherish at the bottom of my heart. What would I not give for a picture that would render her as I hold her in memory! But who could make it? No one!"

TWO SORROWS

By stress of mental contemplation of the image of her departed child, the mother came to feel within her so vividly the presence of that dear image that one day she took an old box of pastels and a sheet of white paper, and tried to fix thereon a distinct representation of the vision of her affection. She never had known how to draw very well, but heedless of that, she began her work hurriedly in the fever of desire that had seized her, without consulting the bad portrait, now thrown aside upon the table. First she drew the hair, which the young girl had worn in the manner seen in pictures of the Virgin, but which waved and made a transparent shadow at the edges of the flat bandeaux. The hair appeared under the caress of that hand which had loved it, coiled, fastened, and uncoiled it so often; then the neck, faultless in line; the wide lips, pale rose, where the smile of a young soul had clung even in death; then the eyes, the lids showing their natural curve, a little raised at the corners, shadowed by golden lashes through which the charming soul was about to bloom and live.

The mother, bent over the table, did not fully realize the miracle of tenderness that she was achieving at that moment; she only felt, with anguish, that something was still lacking in the half-traced drawing, and an eagerness to finish before the sketch should become effaced in the weariness of unaccustomed work. She longed to draw, with the same crayon that had run so lightly till now, the iris, to give expression to the whole face. She felt herself obliged to reflect, and became conscious, after several ineffectual touches, that she no longer knew the color of those dear eyes—that perhaps she had never known it.

She stopped, the tears blinding her. "Oh!" she thought, "is it possible that a mother can forget the color of the eyes that still gaze upon her every minute of the day and night?" Rarely had she suffered so cruelly. It seemed to her that this was a proof of forgetfulness and the beginning of the fatal falling away of memory that causes the most sacred and the oftenest evoked of our recollections to grow faint, to become altered, as if a haze covered also the soul's distances.

At this moment the door at the end of the room opened. Madame Le Minquier hastily concealed the drawing between the leaves of a writing-pad, pressed her handkerchief to her eyes, and tried to regain her footing in the present, from which for several hours she had been absent. The man who entered was young. He had not been to see her for a long time—in fact, she had seen him but once since her great sorrow. With an effort, like one awakening from a dream, she smiled and said:

"How good of you, Monsieur, to remember an old woman, who no longer receives nor appears in society, and whose name recalls only wrinkles to your generation. See how inconsiderate I am of my time! On recognizing you, I imagined that I should have the good fortune to be of service to you."

"Of what service?"

"Whatever you might ask."

"No, Madame."

"You have come just to see me?"

TWO SORROWS

"Just to see you."

"You are a little fatigued—admit it!"

"I have just driven up here."

"You had nothing better to do, then?"

"I can not tell you exactly why I came, Madame. I was passing, and I entered, obedient to an impulse of which I shall tell you. You know the passion children have for building hiding-places, where they store old toys, knickknacks, little nothings that possess for them a mysterious value. I have remained a child in this weakness, at least. And so I make certain pilgrimages, you see."

Madame Le Minquier regarded her visitor attentively, and saw in his smile and in the depths of his eyes the traces of real emotion. Becoming very grave, she said:

"You met my daughter here several times?"

"Four times. The last time was at a ball, on a Thursday, the twenty-second day of April; she wore white satin slippers, embroidered with daisies."

"I have them still," said the mother. "And you remember her?"

"Do I remember! I do not believe that in all Paris that night was a complexion of such rare and transparent freshness as was hers. I do not wish to revive——"

"On the contrary, do, do, Monsieur!"

"I do not know why a certain comparison came to me on seeing her, which often returns to me now. You know, when you strip the petals from a rose, there is in each a spot where the light hardly penetrates, and which it reaches only after passing through a protected zone. So delicate of tint is it that it seems a pink that is almost white. Her complexion was like that."

Madame Le Minquier reflected an instant; her voice, less assured, seemed to crave forgiveness for a maternal weakness and for the necessity of making a painful disclosure.

"Would you believe it, Monsieur, I can no longer recall the color of my daughter's eyes! Her dear gaze is continually upon me, her expression, and that joy that was all my own; but the rest, no. I have come to think that those who love with a mother's love see nothing but the soul in the look."

"I am sure of the contrary, Madame. Familiarity is a cause of disregard and forgetfulness."

"What were her eyes like? If you know, tell me. The doubt is so cruel to me. Do you understand?"

The visitor had bowed his head. He appeared to be attentively following the curves of the twisted column which supported the table, while he replied:

"They were pale blue, with tinges of violet. When she was serious, the violet was dominant; when she laughed, the blue seemed to expand. And always in their depths was a little moving flame, now here, now there."

The mother with an abrupt gesture opened the blotter, took up the drawing, laid it flat upon the table, and, with the manner of those who tear away the secret veil from their grief and demand that it be known, exclaimed, imperiously:

"There! I have only this, and it lacks reality."

TWO SORROWS

The man had arisen. For a moment he considered the portrait. His features changed a little.

"Give me the crayon," said he.

She hesitated. She became pale as her hands when she saw that the young man held the bit of colored crayon in the tips of his fingers, that he was about to change the precious work, retouch the picture, to spoil it forever perhaps. She turned half around. He bent over the table, made a few strokes, and lo! the eyes became transparent; a few more touches and the flash of life awakened in the blue orbs!

The portrait was finished. The mother had only sketched it in—another had completed it.

Madame Le Minquier felt a cry arising from the bottom of her heart: "You loved her, then?" Whether it sprang from jealousy, or from something else, she did not disclose.

The visitor stood silent, took his leave almost immediately, and never returned.

THE WOLF'S WIDOW

THE WOLF'S WIDOW

ITTLE ELISE, what is there in the pond of Agubeil?"

"There are flags which no one dares gather, and fish which no one dares catch."

"And what else?"

"A kingfisher, some dragon-flies with green wings, and frogs that croak, and there are salamanders that cry sorrowfully, and crows which fly and never stop."

"Is that all?"

"No. There is the shadow of the Wolf's Widow, who goes and comes but is never far away."

"Don't ever go there, little Elise, for evil would come to you on the banks of the Agubeil pond."

The child promised, and her grandfather, who was a pedler by occupation, was very careful himself to turn out of his way to avoid even the outskirt of this wild place, where a peril only too real lay in wait for him and his race.

The Agubeil pond was very old, and was formed by water that drained a narrow tortuous, and uninhabited valley, which, for more than a league, gave a pictur-esque view of a stretch of meadow locked between wooded hills. The hill that stood at the end of the valley was of slaty formation, abrupt and serried, full of deep holes and excavations, where snakes had their nests, and where roots of wild broom were hidden. Not another shrub had been able to grow upon this rocky knoll; but here it attained to magnificent height, and reigned supreme; here, during five months of the year, the brightness of its yellow blooms shone among the green foliage of the oaks bordering the pond. Faded petals often fell upon the water, and were wafted like fairy sails by the wind to the edges of the pond, so that the peasants said: "Even when all the broom on the earth has disappeared, you will still find its seed in Agubeil." Nevertheless, they did not like to approach the banks; they watched the light on the water while plowing their fields on the uplands. A few venturesome souls would risk casting a line to the bottom of the pond, or a net in haymaking time; but none cared to remain in the neighborhood of the Wolf's Widow, whose domain this was.

Alas! That phrase takes one back to a far-away and sorrowful time! I had not known the Wolf's Widow until she had grown very old and was universally detested. The townsfolk turned out of her way in order not to admit by any sign that they knew her. Tradesmen refused to sell her flour, salt, or potatoes, which she needed in order to live, and she was often forced to go to the peasants and merchants of far distant towns. She was tall, dry, imperious, and hard of face, and the children were frightened at her approach. Her hair, her shoulders, her whole body were hidden in the folds of

THE WOLF'S WIDOW

a black cloak, such as peasant women used to wear on
Sundays, which she always wore when she quitted her
house. Was it worn to hide her poverty, or was it rather
a sign of mourning? Who could tell? She was altogether mysterious. No one offered a hand to this
woman, no one spoke to her, no one would have thought
of going to her house even to find out whether she were
alive, when for weeks and weeks she was not seen.
Mothers would say to their children: "If you aren't
good, I'll tell the Wolf's Widow," and the little ones
would be still and hide themselves in their mother's arms.

Nevertheless, this strange woman had been very
beautiful, and perhaps good, once upon a time. She
had loved and married a miller, whose mill, now
ruined, had once whirled its wooden wheel beside the
pond, on the same spot where, with the fragments of
its stones and beams, she had rebuilt the hut in which
she still lived. The times were still troublous, as I have
said, and the men were fighting, sometimes with the
last remaining bands of *Chouans*,* who held the country for the king, and others in the armies of the repub-
lic. A day came when, through weariness of the war,
peace was made, and the volunteers came home. The
guerillas quitted the woods and the clumps of furze.
The voices of children were heard again on the little
farms, and the women, with their spinning-wheels,
were seen sitting quietly on the thresholds of their
dwellings.

The grandfather of little Elise, and the village miller,
belonged to the two hostile parties. Young and ardent

* Royalist guerillas.

then, antagonized, and holding against each other old village grudges, no one knew exactly from what cause, they returned the same day from the two armies. After seeking each other in vain a dozen times during the battles, now, in the road which came out of the wood and bordered the edge of the rocky knoll, they met, one evening in May. The miller wore his grenadier uniform, high gaiters, and the tricolored cockade in his big felt hat. The *Chouan* had a sprig of hawthorn in the buttonhole of his red corduroy jacket. No sooner did they catch sight of each other than they cocked their muskets.

"Jean-François," cried the miller, "you've got to salute me, for I am the winner!"

"There's no question of a winner," said Jean-François, pulling his hat down over his ears. "You take the right and I'll take the left. The war's over."

"Not with me. You've spoken wrong of my wife! You laughed at the burning of my mill! You have fired on my comrades!"

"And you on mine! I was fighting in war."

"You haven't lost anything, and you're beaten; I've lost everything, and I come home a beggar. Take off your hat!"

"Never to you!"

They raised their muskets. At that moment the miller's wife appeared on the knoll. She uttered a cry. Below her, in the road, green with the springtime foliage, two men stood on the slope, forty paces apart, levelling their muskets at each other.

"Jean-François!" she screamed.

THE WOLF'S WIDOW

But the cry was lost in the noise of the two reports. A cloud of smoke arose from the hollow road. The grenadier was down on his back, his heart pierced by a bullet. Jean-François jumped over a hedge and made his escape into the country.

Oh, the horrible vision! Forty years had passed, and she was still there, filling with horror that cursed place, where the last shot of the great war of the peasantry had resounded. The miller's wife, become almost insane, had rebuilt with her own hands the ruins of her home, and rendered fierce and savage by suffering and misery, she had lost everything, even her former name. For the peasants, seeing her live in such a way, and remembering the violent character of her husband, no longer called her anything but "the Wolf's Widow." She pillaged the fields for potatoes, and the woods for her fuel; she poached like a man, and especially she fished with lines and nets in the pond of Agubeil. As rarely as possible, and only when she was out of provisions, or had something worth selling, did she go to the town. The people believed her capable of doing anything terrible, because she spoke of only one thing. She said continually: "The miller is dead; Jean-François shall die. He shall fall where the other fell. I have a bullet ready for him. When he shall pass Agubeil pond, there shall he stay. I shall not go elsewhere to kill him; but I will kill him there—him, or those who are born to him."

And for forty years she waited for her vengeance. For this reason the pedler avoided the hills that enclosed the pond, and he forbade his only granddaugh-

ter, Elise—all that remained of his family, alas!—to
venture upon the road where he had encountered his
enemy. As he was now advanced in years, he re-
proached himself, as for a sin, for having defended himself that day, and every year he caused a mass to be
said for the republican grenadier. He was silent and
sad. Sometimes when he returned at dusk, with his
bale of merchandise over his shoulder, and descried
suddenly over the bank of the sunken roads, a bunch
of blood-red wild poppies, he would prefer to make a
détour of half a league rather than pass by it. His
whole joy, as well as his constant anxiety, was in watching the growth of Elise.

The little one reached her tenth year, and it was a
charming celebration when, dressed in white, pale and
slender, among her more robust companions, but
more graceful, and a greater favorite than the others,
she took her first communion. It was at the beginning
of June, and the town was decorated with green gar-
lands. In the church that day the mothers were all in
their places, behind their little ones, and all were weeping. Jean-François, among them, wept also, and, even
though his eyes never quitted Elise, he could hardly see
her for the tears which would come in spite of him. He
had reason enough to weep. So many sorrows in the
past, so much deep emotion in the present, and a fear,
in spite of himself, for the future! That morning Elise
had said:

"Grandfather, shall I say a prayer for the Wolf's
Widow?" and he had replied: "I have been praying
for her for forty years."

THE WOLF'S WIDOW

After the ceremony, weary with the unusual exertion,
he had confided his little girl to the care of two women
whose route lay past his house, which was at the farther end of the village. He entered a tavern and seated
himself:

"Give me a corked bottle of old wine, that I may see
whether I am still young."

The wine dried his tears, cheered his heart, and
made him forget Elise.

The child soon found herself alone in the house.
She was well used to solitude, but that day she found it
hard to have no one about her. The house had one
door giving on the road, and another opening into the
fields, and through the former she could hear the passing groups of mothers and children. Their voices were
more restrained and harmonious than usual. She took
to playing with the pieces of holy bread she had brought
from the church. They were star-shaped. She thought
they were like the gilt paper stars that glittered on the
church banners.

"One for grandfather," she said to herself, "and one
for Aunt Gothon, and to whom shall I give the other
one?"

She reflected, there being no one to trouble her
dream, and suddenly she felt her heart become so large,
so pure, and so content, that she was afraid of nothing,
as she answered herself:

"To the Wolf's Widow!"

Poor little ten-year-old girl! She knew no evil, because she was so good herself, and she was braver than
a man because she was so happy! So, without think-

ing any more about it, she took the piece of bread and
went out by the back door, through a field of wheat,
her little shoes white in the tall grain, walking sedately,
without fear, and without turning her head. Her veil
caught on the heads of wheat, and she withdrew it,
gathering it across her breast. She looked like a spirit
gliding through the field. The country now appeared
deserted; it was wooded and wild, and she could no
longer hear the hum of voices in the town.

The grandfather still sat at the table in the tavern.
Elise approached the pond of Agubeil. She did not
think of the many times she had been forbidden to go
there. Was not this a day different from all other
days? And who should go, if not she, to take the holy
bread to the Wolf's Widow? No one had thought of
this woman, who had neither children, nor kin, nor
friends to care for her—none but the little girl who was
now climbing up among the broom, on the broken and
moss-covered rocks.

She reached the top, and went down the slope on the
other side to the stone cabin covered with branches, and
up to the half-open door. How poor everything was at
the Wolf's Widow's! It was no better than a pigsty.
The glimmer of the water that filled the neighboring
hollow showed between the knolls. If one leaned over,
hanging to the branches of broom, one could see himself away down there in the water. The child's heart
began to beat faster. She stepped over the threshold
saying:

"Good-day, Madame Wolf's Widow!"

But no one was there. The soup-kettle, some packages of herbs, a gun in one corner, an old hat with a cockade, a chair, a blackened slate hearthstone—that was all she saw. The branches of the broom crackled in the hot June sun, and the crickets chirped distractingly.

"I should like to have her to know that I came," said Elise. So she took her knife, and with its point scratched the five letters of her name on the star-shaped holy bread. Then, after placing it on the hearth, she suddenly became afraid, and, running out of the cabin, she did not stop till she reached home.

"Grandfather, grandfather, I've taken a cake to the Wolf's Widow!" she cried.

When the old man, who was just entering his house, heard that, he became as white as the hawthorn he used to wear in his buttonhole, in the time of the great war.

Four months had passed, and the little Elise was very ill. Every one in the neighborhood thought she was about to die. She was so weak that she was delirious. The village youths, as soon as they caught sight of the roof of her house, would rein up their horses, and stop shouting at the animals they were driving to the fields. Jean-François laughed no more, nor drank any more with his friends. He never left the brick-floored room where the minutes were counted by the uneven breathing of the child, who seemed as if she would exhaust her slender stock of vitality with each quick gasp. If but the faintest whisper came from the bed, Jean-François could hear it above all the sounds of the town, keeping him awake whole nights. Oh, if he could only see ahead! If the fever would only abate! If only Elise would open her eyes, which she kept so obstinately closed! She had not spoken a word for a week. The grandfather had seen all the children of her own age pass before the bed, and as they went out, he could read the same word in all their faces: "Good-by, little Elise!" They had all gone. No one dared enter now, for the end was too near. The doctor had said he would call again, but he had not come. Jean-François sat in a big stuffed armchair, lent him by the rich lady of the town. He had no more tears to weep. He looked at the white bed veiled in shadow, the pale face, from which the only sign of life came in tiny breaths from the parted lips. Night came, and now the village was wrapped in silence.

Toward midnight a ray of moonlight stole through the window, and at the same moment Elise lifted her eyelids. The old man was bent over so that the child could not see him, and he saw neither the moonbeam, nor the smile of little Elise, his only joy; but he heard a half sleepy voice saying:

"Grandfather, where are you?"

"Here, little one, here! Don't you see me?"

She continued:

"I should like one of the fish that swim in the Agubeil pond. He swims close to the edge, and he has two red fins; he goes among the bulrushes. Go and get him. I shall be well if I can eat some fish from Agubeil."

Then she closed her eyes. She had not understood what Jean-François had replied, but smiled one of those child-smiles which ask and thank at once.

THE WOLF'S WIDOW

The old man did not hesitate long. He aroused a neighbor, and, while she watched by the bedside, he climbed to the garret where hung a linen fish-net with a hazel-wood frame. Then he went out by the garden gate, the net over his shoulder. The moonlight shone blue-white on the country roads, and showed the paths where roving animals had left streaks on the wet grass. Poor Jean-François! you know what vengeance lies in wait for you down there. You know that your enemy sleeps lightly; that at the sound of a net falling in the pond of Agubeil, she will glide through the broom, and that the whim of little Elise may cost you your life.

But the old man was one of those who love with their whole being. Not for a moment did he slacken his pace. Only, instead of approaching the pond by the road, he turned through the woods, and when he had descended the slope and left the shadow of the trees, coming out into the moonlight, on a border of meadow that touched the still sheet of water, he trembled a little, and crossed his forehead and his heart.

He extended the hazel pole, and sought the silver fish. He could descry nothing but confused and shadowy gleams roving near the surface, now fading and now moving so quickly that he could not follow them. Where was a good place? He lifted the net and ventured a cast between two branches of reeds. The reflected stars trembled in the shuddering water.

The Wolf's Widow was not asleep. She had heard a noise of crackling branches among the trees, and she had seen him whom she had awaited so many years— the slayer of her husband—coming out of the wood, the enemy whom some inconceivable folly had brought back to the place of his unexpiated crime. She felt a savage elation. Through the window of her house she watched Jean-François standing on the margin of the pond.

"I've got you!" she said, in a low voice, and she laughed. She took down the rusty musket, with which she had so often brought down the swans and ducks on the pond of Agubeil. The broom was so high that Jean-François could not see the black, crouching form approaching the edge of the mound. The barrel of the musket passed between the sprays of verdure, pointing toward the near bank, searching for the right spot on the man's breast. The angels of God winging through the night beheld a horrible sight—the Wolf's Widow taking aim at her enemy!

But, at the moment her finger was about to press the trigger, the woman saw the dancing stars on the surface of the pond, covering the water with their living flames. They surrounded the clod of earth on which the man was poised, and each looked like the star-shaped holy bread which the little Elise had left in her cabin.

"Go away, you stars! Go away!" she muttered.

But the stars still twinkled. Three times the Wolf's Widow lifted her musket, and lowered it again. The third time Jean-François caught a fish in the bottom of his net, seized it, and ran away, leaving the net among the weeds.

The wood crackled as if a hunted stag were charging through it.

Then, uttering a loud cry of rage, for having allowed

her prey to escape, the Wolf's Widow stood erect on the extreme edge of the rock, and threw far out the weapon that had been in the great war. The musket turned, fell, and disappeared among the shimmering stars, and the water closed over it forever.

Jean-François was already out of the wood, running along the paths, with the silver fish which was to save his little Elise.

The next day the Wolf's Widow left the pond of Agubeil, and started for the town. Arriving at the door of the Old People's Home of Refuge, she said:

"I am the Wolf's Widow, who for forty years has lived for her vengeance. The man came to the marked spot. I saw him at the end of my musket. But the stars looked too much like the little one's holy bread which she brought to me. My heart failed me. I am no longer good for anything: take me in."

They thought she was a little mad, so they took her. It was there that I knew her, and that is where she died.

THE WILLOW TAPER

THE WILLOW TAPER

NCE upon a time, in Provence, lived a little boy. This is a true story, and the little boy is still alive, only he is now grown up.

He was the thirteenth of fourteen children. His father had a place which furnished bread for his numerous family, and God added good health, gayety, and courage to the bread, so that if the father, the mother, and the fourteen children had not the richest portion in the world, they perhaps had the best.

Pierre showed a keen taste for music when he was quite young. He would forget all about school, and would listen at a street-corner to the tunes of the Spanish guitar-players, or to the Italian harpists, that wandered begging through the town. He was an adept upon all the instruments that cost nothing, from the primitive viol, made of a gourd, to the jew's-harp, which he could play like an old Basque priest.

By good fortune, he had an elder brother, the only one of the family who had been educated, who was a professor at the college. This elder brother played the violin, rather badly, to be sure, but he had the sense to see that his younger brother might some day play it better than he. He perceived the artist's soul in Pierre, and taught him the notes and scales, and the little he knew of harmony; and out of his slender savings, one day, inspired with liberality, he bought a violin for the boy.

How the little fellow loved that violin! Night and morning, in the house and out of it, he practised to make it speak. It was enchantment to him. This child of the suburbs created all by himself melodies which more accomplished musicians might have envied him. For there are men, you know, who are born with a nightingale in their hearts, and however poor the cage may be, the bird must sing.

To tell the truth, Pierre loved nothing but music, and his father began to grow uneasy about it.

"My son," said he, "fiddlers and flute-players never get rich; besides, playing the violin or the flute is not work. Get a situation. Learn to be a barber, my boy; you will then have some time to yourself, and in the evening, or on Sundays, nothing need prevent you, since it is your taste, from making the young folks dance on the green."

The child obeyed. He became apprenticed to a barber. There, all day long, he shaved, clipped, combed, and twisted curlpapers. But when evening came he ran home, and, with his meagre supper in one hand and his violin in the other, he would go off to play at some farm on the outskirts of the town.

At holiday times the countryside held a festival. The girls and boys of Villeneuve, Roquemaure, Château-Renard, or Aramon, in gala dress, would wait impatiently for him in front of the grange or on the barn-floor. He would mount upon a cask, and, with a flourish, begin the prelude to the dance, playing with such precision, such gayety and power, that all feet began to shuffle at the first notes of the *jarandole*. His music is still remembered, and many preferred it to the playing of much greater performers. He never was tired, and never asked to rest. A glass of red wine during the ball, and a fist full of big coppers at the end, and the little fellow was content. For his joy lay not so much in earning a little money as in playing his violin.

While returning home, over the deserted roads, he stopped more than once in the open country, to play to himself in the peaceful night, under the stars. He never was so happy as in these moments. It was not *jarandoles* that sprang then from the chords of his instrument, but sweet melodies, short, like the inspiration of youth, but of singular power, and followed by sudden bursts of gayety, by a scattering of triumphant notes thrown to the wind; a sort of sad and joyous reverie, which came to him whence he knew not, and to which his bow gave voice without effort.

But alas! time flies quickly; his mother would be waiting for him down there in the little house, to lock the door, and the child would trot along the road, absorbed in his thoughts, enviously dreaming of those who could play the violin at any time without being scolded for it.

Before long they resolved to let him take his first

communion, for he was a good boy and well up in his catechism.

One morning, two days before the communion, while reciting his catechism, without making a single mistake, to one of his older sisters, who helped his mother in the care of the house, he heard his parents talking in low tones.

"How well he knows his lesson!" said his mother, pausing in her work of sorting the silk cocoons heaped near her in a basket.

"If nothing but the lesson were to be considered," replied the father, sadly, "nothing would be lacking."

"There will be nothing lacking, anyway, my dear; he will have everything he needs: Marguerite's massbook, a fine linen shirt, which the tailor's wife has lent me, a suit, which isn't new, to be sure, but without stains or patches, and a pair of new shoes from La Toussaint—what more do you want?"

"Eh! my poor girl, and where will you find a white waxen taper?"

"Lord! sure enough!" said the mother, clasping her hands. "I never thought of that!"

"Well, I thought of it, and that's what is bothering me. The times are bad, there isn't any money in the house, and I don't want to buy on credit."

"Especially from Roufelligues, the chandler, who doesn't like anything but hard cash!" said the mother, sadly; "and the sacristan, Guidolet, is the same. But I think, my dear, that we might sell something. My black velvet neckerchief or the betrothal brooch you gave me—do you remember?—at the Beaucaire fair!"

THE WILLOW TAPER

"Not that," said the father, roughly. "Even if we happen to be a little hard up there is no reason why we should sell the relics of our past joys and better days. No, since we can do no better, he shall have for his first communion the same taper I had for mine."

The same taper! The mother did not dare ask him where it was, for the man did not like to be questioned; but she could not help feeling curious. She searched in her mind every corner of the house, took an inventory of two closets and a coffer, wherein, among the slender wardrobe of the family, were stowed away a few relics of twenty years: the wedding bouquet, a garnet brooch, and her little satin shoes with buckles, which she never had put on since. But in spite of all her efforts of memory, the good housewife could not recall ever having seen in her married life of twenty years her husband's communion taper.

On the morrow at daybreak, the father awoke the child.

"Pierre," said he, "come with me."

"Where are we going so early, father?"

"To get your taper for to-morrow."

"Oh, joy!" cried the child; "say, father, will it have a silver-paper holder like Raymond's, or a gold one like Renaud's? Father, the Viscount Raoul's son is even going to have a white silk one a foot long on his, with a fringe on it!"

"Be quiet!" replied the father, "get up quickly and come along!"

They left the house as the sun was rising.

At the end of the street the child was surprised not

to turn to the right; that was the way to the chandler's, but he thought they must be going to Guidolet's.

They approached the church, where the old sacristan reigned under the name of the curé, and where, in a closet, once richly ornamented, but which had been changed from its original use, Guidolet kept, out of the dust, tapers of all sorts: smooth, figured, serrated; straight tapers and spiral tapers, of which the ends were wrapped in paper, silk, or velvet.

The father did not stop there either. Pierre followed him, wondering, for beyond the church there was no shop where one could buy a taper, and the most one could do would be to find a few pounds of candles in some cheap suburban grocery.

The houses were now fewer, and but one story high. Bits of hedge broke the monotonous line of house-fronts and garden-walls. The country was not far off, and in a few minutes they arrived there.

The sky was pleasant, and everything seemed in good humor that morning—the rustling leaves, and even the grasshoppers chirping among the grain.

They walked a long time in the white dust of the road. The child ran ahead, throwing stones at the skylarks that flew up out of the hay-fields, while the father travelled on at a regular pace, in the shadow of the tamarind hedges. But the good man was taller than the tamarinds, and the rays of the sun, already hot, touched from time to time his bowed gray head.

At length, at the foot of a hill, they entered a little vale full of thick green grass, in the midst of which ran a brook bordered with willows.

THE WILLOW TAPER

"There it is," said the father.

The child looked, but saw nothing resembling a taper.

Without giving any explanation, as was his wont, the father took his knife, and choosing a fine, straight, smooth, and sappy wand of willow, that overhung the water, he cut it off, and threw it to his son.

"Strip it," said he, "and take it home. I am going to work. To-morrow morning we will make the taper."

Pierre, all abashed, returned through the streets of the town, to his mother.

"What have you got there?" asked his eldest sister.

"It's my taper," replied the little fellow, wiping away a tear.

The next day, when Pierre awoke, he saw his father sitting by the window, peeling the willow wand, the bark coming away in long strips, and the tender wood showing whiter than wax. The base was carefully cut and wrapped in figured paper. Then the father drove in a little nail at the top to look like a wick. From a distance one might be easily deceived. The little boy was quite consoled.

They set out, a half dozen brothers and sisters of unequal sizes making up the procession. On arriving at the church, Pierre went to take his place on the benches reserved for the communicants. The nave and chancel soon filled, the organ began to play, and the sacristan, Guidolet, entered, lighter in hand, to light the tapers.

When he arrived at Pierre's, he tried in vain to ignite

the wick, which stood up very straight and stiff on its foundation. Once, twice, three times he tried.

"What is the matter?" he murmured, and he passed his hand over his eyes with a gesture of impatience; for ordinarily, he had a sure hand for poising his lighter just on the edge of a taper and holding it there, motionless.

During this time, Pierre, trembling a little, watched the picture of Jesus lying in the cradle, and thought that, according to the word of God, there was no shame whatever in being poor, and that, if a taper had been needed in the stable of Bethlehem, St. Joseph could have found nothing better than a stripped stick or a palm pith.

Guidolet had to give it up, and, red with anger, he said, in a low voice:

"That came from Roufelligues, I'll wager, that taper there! That'll teach you, sonny, not to buy them from him; his wicks don't light."

And, with a quick gesture, he carried his stick to the next wick, which took light immediately.

The storm had passed. The ceremony continued. The child received the sacrament, and in the joy he felt he forgot for a while his wooden taper, Guidolet, and even his violin. But, upon his return from the mass, he threw his branch into the fire, where it crackled, smouldered, and finally threw out a beautiful white flame.

"Ha! that's the way, Master Guidolet," he cried, "to light that kind of taper!"

And the child thought no more about it.

THE WILLOW TAPER

No, the child thought of it no more, but, after long years, the man recalled it. He lives in Paris now, far from his native place. From the village fiddler, he has become a great artist, loved by the public, decorated by monarchs, and ranked among the masters. Nevertheless, in the midst of his triumphs, he often thinks of the poverty of other days, with a little regret, perhaps, certainly with joy. He remembers the time when, barefooted, he ran along the roads to play the *farandole* for the dancers on the Provençal greens, and the time when, on the hillside, he played serenades to the stars; the time when he took to the parish church a poor taper of white willow, which the sacristan Guidolet could not light.

That which made him weep then, makes him smile to-day.

For poverty, you see, is like a bitter almond that you throw by the roadside, where it falls and is forgotten, but grows. And when, twenty years after, you pass by the same place, you find a blossoming tree.